The Reuniting of America

Major Concepts in Politics and Political Theory

Garrett Ward Sheldon
General Editor

Vol. 11

PETER LANG
New York • Washington, D.C./Baltimore
Bern • Frankfurt am Main • Berlin • Vienna • Paris

Donald H. Roy

The Reuniting of America

Eleven Multicultural Dialogues

PETER LANG
New York • Washington, D.C./Baltimore
Bern • Frankfurt am Main • Berlin • Vienna • Paris

Library of Congress Cataloging-in-Publication Data

Roy, Donald H.
The reuniting of America: eleven multicultural dialogues/ Donald H. Roy.
p. cm. — (Major concepts in politics and political theory; vol. 11)
Includes bibliographical references and index.
1. Pluralism (Social sciences)—United States. 2. Multiculturalism—United
States. 3. Minorities—United States. 4. United States—Race relations.
5. United States—Ethnic relations. I. Title. II. Series.
E184.A1R74   305.8'00973—dc20   95-50418
ISBN 0-8204-3118-4
ISSN 1059-3535

Die Deutsche Bibliothek-CIP-Einheitsaufnahme

Roy, Donald H.:
The reuniting of America: eleven multicultural dialogues/ Donald H. Roy. –
New York; Washington, D.C./Baltimore; Bern; Frankfurt am Main;
Berlin; Vienna; Paris: Lang.
(Major concepts in politics and political theory; Vol. 11)
ISBN 0-8204-3118-4
NE: GT

Cover design by James F. Brisson.

The paper in this book meets the guidelines for permanence and durability
of the Committee on Production Guidelines for Book Longevity
of the Council of Library Resources.

∞

Printed in the United States of America.

"We are a world, not a nation."
    Herman Melville

". . .the shapes of doors giving many exits and entrances and shapes of democracy. . .ever projecting other shapes."
    Walt Whitman

"A people should neither be too united nor too divided if its culture is to flourish."
    T.S. Eliot

TABLE OF CONTENTS

x

PROLOGUE

A MULTICULTURAL ORGANIZING SCHEMA

Multiculturalism is the burning topic of the day. Multiculturalism, culture wars (*Kulturkampf*), political correctness (PC), group rights, hate/abuse speech codes and laws, race-ethnicity-gender criteria—what in the world is sweeping our educational and political environment and institutions? Is America disuniting in the post-cold war period, as we turn inward and take a closer, more intensive look at ourselves and our unresolved domestic problems? Or is it that we are now coming of mature age, finally facing squarely our diversity, our mixed identity, and our tensional inner being as a people? Has there been some breakdown in the kind of pragmatic consensus that previously allowed us more harmoniously to work together politically and socially in a common civic culture?

This stage-setting prologue and the following dialogues seek to provide some guidance and perspective for those struggling through the issues and conflicts surrounding multiculturalism. Already, Arthur Schlesinger, Jr., in his book *The Disuniting of America*, has forcefully addressed the educational and political consequences of multiculturalism that he finds more threatening than auspicious or reassuring. The tone of Professor Schlesinger's book is fairly negative, if not alarmist.

The major problem, however, is not to issue warnings, albeit such a style certainly provokes discussion. Instead, we need to provide sufficient analytical clarity in order for educable persons to determine for themselves where they stand and what is best for our country regarding the arguable reality of our diversity which is today generally called multiculturalism. With this in mind I offer in this prologue a fourfold, multiculturalism schema that will allow us to define ourselves and others. In particular, I take Professor Schlesinger to task for being too slippery and indefinite in light of this analytical schema. The polemics of Schlesinger's book, or if you prefer, the polemics generated by Schlesinger's book, are more likely to drive people to intolerable extremes.

In contrast, I argue that cultural diversity in America is an empirical given. We have never been a very homogeneous country, if only because of our openness to immigrant peoples, our on-and-off commitment to progressive change, and our tenuous belief in a "new order of the ages." Today we certainly are quite heterogeneous culturally, and many sociologists have correctly discerned (contra Schlesinger) an increased awareness and concern about our ethnic identities.

Nevertheless, more than ever in the history of this country we have to wonder about what unity we had in the past, what unity we have today, and whether we need to reconstruct a new basis for unity in the near future. A common unity seems to be the precondition for a people to achieve betterment in their ways of life. Schlesinger correctly has a strong overriding commitment to the importance of unity. Yet so much of the literature on ethnicity and multiculturalism (including Schlesinger, Fuchs, Ravitch, et alii) does not convincingly identify what it is that holds us together. Our unity suffers from a political and philosophical latency more than likely rooted in an all-too-American tendency to be pragmatic in order to just make it through the task at hand. Far better to consider the larger, philosophic dimensions of precarious human existence. Consequently, the multiculturalist debate for the most part rages within modern, secular liberalism far more dedicated to procedural rights than to any substantive outcomes such as ethnic community, religious community, or national community. The recent formation of a communitarian movement questioning modern, individualistic, secularistic liberalism is one sign that something is deficient both practically and theoretically in the house of modern liberalism.

The practical problem is the building and/or reinforcement of national community while acknowledging the positive contributions that diverse ethnic communities make. We need to listen to and understand the voices of diverse representatives of various ethnic communities to be able to advance to a reuniting of America. After this opening prologue, a set of twelve dialogues are tendered. Dialogues (as opposed to treatises with their monological, authoritative voice) are the proper starting point to go from practical, here-and-now experiences of diversity to the greater task of national community.

The first three dialogues involve prominent public policy issues very much before Americans for political resolution: immigration, affirmative action, and political redistricting. All these issues face court decisions as well as campaign debate if not referenda. The next three dialogues cover the volatile categories of race (IQ testing), sex (feminism), and disability (a handicapper culture?). The seventh dialogue brings together an Asian-American, a WASP, a Hispanic-American, a Jewish-American, a Native American, and an African-American to debate their concerns and their recommendations for our civil society. Since there is such diversity within each one of these ethnic communities, this dialogue cannot claim to represent all ethnic voices and variations. Yet it is a start. The next four dialogues involve public communication and education: hate/abuse speech and codes, Native-American logos and the Confederate flag, English as our official language, and the introduction of multiculturalism in our textbooks. The last dialogue, the Epilogue, enjoins the overall argument between the proponents of unity and diversity. Dialogues offer first and foremost some clarity of understanding serving as an indispensable prolegomenon for achieving some broad consensus.

The political problem today is to avoid the degeneration of liberalism and conservatism into statism and libertarianism, respectively. These hard-core, ideological extremes make it more difficult to find some common ground of agreement. Can overbearing governmental providers or liberated, experimenting individuals address the social nature of human beings and help the formation of communities? Those agencies and persons that mediate between the coercive state and the acquisitive individual supply the longing for ties and bonds that a rugged individualistic society lacks and that an impersonal, bureaucratic state cannot provide. The problem with modern, Enlightenment liberalism is that its vision of community, especially a public community, is nonreligious and nonethnic, which is to say antitraditional. Enlightenment liberals counter that religion begets intolerance and ethnicity foments racism. (Such a remarkable change in tone from social science objectivity to pointed, judgmental rhetoric can be found in Mary Waters' book, *Ethnic Options*. Thus, Professor Waters believes Michael Novak "fans the flames of racism" by welcoming the white ethnic revival.) It would appear that any strong ethnic or religious commitment is inherently threatening and divisive to deracinated, liberal intellectuals. So much for the "rainbow coalition." But does not the watering down of mainline political persuasions and religions only encourage the enthusiastic revival of political and religious extremes? Can Enlightenment liberals ignore the aspirations for cultural/ethnic recognition that most people have?

A sort of abstracted, above-it-all, cosmopolitanism exploding the myths of ordinary people and their political manipulators, a belief in the followed a quickly written book, *The Disuniting of America*, drawing on the plentiful resources of an advocacy historian. Perhaps a more disinterested, interpretive historian would have stood farther back from the fray to develop some perspective that had as its primary objective not controversy but understanding.

No matter how strongly I assert to students in my classes that Schlesinger could not possibly be a separatist because the major thrust of his book is against such forces of diversity driving us into hostile separate camps, there always are a few students who claim Schlesinger is a separatist. Almost always these students have turned upside down the statements in Schlesinger's book. Yet there possibly is a perverse logic to these students' mental upheaval: Schlesinger's attack on multiculturalism and Afrocentrism is so divisive and separatistic, compared to a different approach which leads us to locate some middle ground between extremes, that these students find Schlesinger to be the separatist!

How much better Schlesinger's book would have been (and for that matter the whole raging debate about multiculturalism) if the four possible schematic alternatives regarding multiculturalism were analytically clarified, understood, and elaborated as follows:

POSITION I. ASSIMILATIONISM   "The melting pot"
Americanization is the process whereby the dominant White Anglo-Saxon Protestant (WASP) culture amalgamates and homogenizes all other cultures, as the price for realizing the American Dream.

POSITION II. UNITY OVER DIVERSITY   "The tossed salad"
The bowl, which holds us all together in the form of a legal and political framework, takes precedence over the contents; tolerance and respect is accorded diversity, albeit its secondary status.

POSITION III. DIVERSITY OVER UNITY   "The tossed salad"
The diverse, multicultural salad contents are more important than the bowl; unity (a bowl in the process of being formed in agreement with its contents on a potter's wheel) is something to be fashioned in due course since it is not an already-achieved outcome and will vary over time according to its diverse content.

POSITION IV. SEPARATISM "The TV dinner"
   Each ethnic group remains in its own separate compartment;
   ethnic self-determination and fulfillment require autonomous,
   sovereign enclaves.

This schema exhausts the logical possibilities of choice. Furthermore, there is real choice here as opposed to the restrictive and dualistic, either/or polarization of opposites. There is room to maneuver; it is even warrantable that a person could vary his/her position between the middle ground positions, II (unity over diversity) and III (diversity over unity), depending on circumstances and cultural desirabilities. But, most important of all, position I (assimilationism) and position IV (separatism) can not talk very amicably with one another. The extremes tend to be mutually exclusive and divisive. Both positions I and IV become too demanding and ethnocentric. Position IV definitely puts everyone's particular ethnicity above all else, while position I presumes to be ethnically neutral and above it all.

   On the other hand, positions II (unity over diversity) and III (diversity over unity) are not so far apart, unless they respectively degenerate into the extreme positions of I (assimilationism) and IV (separatism). Certainly, position II understands and can deal with position I. Likewise position III understands and appreciates where position IV is coming from. Position II is closer to I than III and position III is closer to IV than II. Yet in a democracy we should be willing and confident enough to venture outside our own political camps. To go "campish" is to become ideological and inflexible, and to move toward the extremes. Positions I and III and positions II and IV are not going to be on the best of terms with each other. Therefore, the only reasonable hope for mutually progressive dialogue, discursively probing the *relative* (not absolute) merits of unity and diversity lies with the middle-ground positions of II and III. The mean between the extremes reminds us of an Aristotelian political science that saw the dangers of both extremes, oppressive unity and anarchic diversity (see Arlene Saxonhouse's *Fear of Diversity*).

   In a democracy, liberty and rights (emphasized by position III) as well as law and constitutional order (emphasized by position II), are essential. Liberty and rights result in diversity; such is the nature of humans when freely allowed to develop their own faculties (James Madison in *Federalist* #10). Law and constitutional order provide for unity and community either in the sense of agreed-upon working rules of collaboration or in the sense of some set of substantive beliefs communally and patriotically affirmed. Perhaps the distinction between form and content is relevant here. Position II stresses a common, basic, legal and institutional form, while position III stresses the diverse content and substance of a multiethnic republic. Horace Kallen's cultural pluralism seems to reflect this form/content distinction. [Note that Schlesinger (36-38) finds Kallen too much of a dissenter from the melting pot, assimilation model.]

With positions II and III, both conservative and liberal dimensions of a body politic are represented. Neither are enemies of democracy unless pushed to their intolerant extremes, namely, anarchy (the tendency of position IV) and tyranny (the tendency of position I). There really is no rational choice between anarchy and tyranny because they feed off one another: anarchy leads people frequently to long for the tyrant (Stalin or Hitler) to return life to "normality," and as for tyranny, once it runs its course, people usually are left unprepared to live in communal harmony (e.g., the former Yugoslavia and parts of the former USSR).

It is difficult to believe that most Americans within or without ethnic groups would find themselves at the extreme positions I (assimilationism) and IV (separatism). Nevertheless, the dynamics of debate and the fears of loss (be it the loss of America or the loss of one's precious ethnic identity) cause movement toward the extremes. There are two common forms of fanaticism: the chauvinism of nation and the parochialism of ethnicity or race. What is it that psychologically draws us in these directions? Position II (unity over diversity) has the responsibility to draw disputants from position IV to position III (diversity over unity). Likewise position III can help rescue position II from resorting to position I. Participants in public/political discourse (and especially those in the teaching profession) should not be so oriented to political stand-taking that they drive their opponents to ideological madness.

Why would one side or the other want to deny diversity or to deny unity? Those mostly (if not entirely) on the side of unity, such as Schlesinger, have read American history and its successes in their own favor. In the past immigrant groups from all over the world have succeeded in "making it in the U.S.A." by assimilating to the dominant WASP culture. Granted the process was difficult, being unfairly obstructionist to some (Chinese), and a trial of nativism, prejudice, deportations (Mexicans), internment (Japanese), brutally destructive and ostracizing (African-American slavery and segregation, and Native-American reservations), and racist/ethnocentric. Not only have many succeeded but most of those who have not succeeded still cherish the American Dream of upward mobility through hard work. Why cannot we all be united as Americans under the banner of equality of opportunity and justice for all? No country is anywhere near perfect (as utopians would demand); does not the U.S.A. come closer than all others to offering an "open field of endeavor" (Lincoln) and a fair shake?

Those mostly on the side of diversity, such as Professor Ronald Takaki, read American history very differently and somewhat negatively. While assimilation occurred, it was at such a heavy price that some later generations (especially since the 1960s) have sought to revive their own ethnic roots. Accordingly, diversity is a healthy and rich experience deserving public recognition and celebration. A heterogeneous people is more likely to explore and fathom political and social reality from a diversity of perspectives. No one cultural perspective has any superior claim on the truth, and apparently there is no position that is not rooted in some culture. America needs to acknowledge its ethnically pluralistic past and present, and avoid attempts at compelling some unity—which unavoidably is one particular culture's unity (hegemony)—at the expense of other cultures. America's success has not been in fashioning and demanding conformity. Only an open, dynamic, and pluralistic environment propels us into a better future. Multiculturalism is the answer. Recognition and respect for varying ethnic ties is the plea.

My own fourfold schema is open to attack from multiculturalists such as Professors Takaki and Stanley Fish. The schema is fundamentally "logocentric" and abstract, as if a rationalistic, logical framework could possibly be neutral. Such a schema is a revelation of my WASP heritage. Furthermore, my schema presumes a center versus margins at the extremes. (Revealingly, Schlesinger wrote a book at the height of McCarthyism called *The Vital Center*.) Consequently, my schema is "marginalizing" voices I prefer not to hear. Images are important. Takaki prefers the image of intersecting streams conjoining and diverging where there is no center nor any margins. All-inclusiveness would be the prominent property of this image. Other multiculturalist images come to mind, such as the mosaic and the orchestra (Kallen). Do orchestras not need conductors and do mosaics not require artists?

My rejoinder is that my schema prepares the way for dialogues as it satisfies the fundamental prior condition for dialogues: a basis for reasonable discussion. Participants in a dialogue are going to have to be clustered around the middle. The extremes do not much care for interactive speaking. Indeed I am assuming that people are fundamentally rational, such that they can resolve or at least understand their differences by way of interchanges. My schema is logical and analytical but, more importantly, it is not static, abstract, or a mere intellectual construction. The problem of the one and the many, unity and diversity is an age-old, transcultural, philosophical dilemma.

There are certain questions that nevertheless remain, such as what is it that brings people together and holds them together since presumably this is not only necessary but also desirable for most human endeavors? What makes our common humanity and what breaks our common humanity? It seems unavoidable that we refer to some "universal" such as humanity that connects and binds us. And is there not something positive as well as negative that we can learn from centuries of human history? Can we inquire, pursue, and know without some logical and rational (i.e., discursive) process? Will not there always be people who refuse to work together to establish the conditions of human discourse? Don't they marginalize themselves? Has the empirical reality of over-abundant liberty and a variety of fanaticisms caused us to lose contact with a central ground?

Both perspectives, unity and diversity, have their merits, but can either one stand alone not just as an adequate and fair interpretation of American history, but also as a practical requirement for a well-functioning civil society? Do not individual liberty and rights, namely, the common basis for the society we share, promote more diversity than unity? Can the "unitarian" who still believes in liberty and rights logically oppose an outcome of great diversity? On the other hand, would a "diversitarian" so much believe in the liberty of a pluralistic outcome that Balkanization and anarchy occur, destroying the basis for any common beliefs and purposes?

The merits of my fourfold schema are the analytical clarity as to the logical possibilities we have before us to choose and the virtue of establishing two middle-ground positions that promise more harmonious discussion and relative, moderate disagreement. Too often our democratic politics has been reduced by political scientists, political commentators, and average folk to the matter of who has the power to do whatever to whom (Harold Lasswell's definitional legacy). Vibrant democratic politics instead rests on rational deliberation and persuasion taking its bearings from both abiding principles and changing circumstances. To forsake this rational deliberation and rely on prevailing configurations of forces and powers means that the better *argument* may not win out over the stronger argument. Strength and weakness will be the nonrational consequence of power arrangements related to numbers, status position, manipulative skills, technology, and money. It is not so much the *force* of arguments, but the *weight* of arguments that should sway us. Diverse ethnicities challenge our judgmental abilities of rational deliberation to achieve a working consensus.

Another characteristic of the extreme positions I (assimilationism) and IV (separatism) should cause us to hesitate and be apprehensive. Both these positions could easily be charged with ethnocentrism, which is to say, pushing their own ethnicity or supposed lack of any ethnicity, to the exclusion of any other ethnicity. Of course, those in position IV would be quick to tell us that you cannot draw meaningful similarities between a dominant oppressive culture (WASP) and those subordinate, oppressed, minority cultures. The dominant culture wants to erase via assimilation all other culture traits, whereas minority cultures simply want to be left alone in their own voluntarily chosen enclaves. The separatist (position IV) argues that superiority and inferiority are the oppressive terms of the assimilationists (position I). Separatists are the true egalitarians, so it would seem.

But can there really be an equality of "otherness" as opposed to an equality of "togetherness"? True, people can be equally separate or equally together. But have we given up so soon the joy of hands joined across our bodies in solidarity? The experiences of mixed-race students on our college campuses reveal considerable pressures on them (hardly voluntary) to choose the black or the white camp. Crossing over from one camp to the other camp can result in fractures among one's "other" students. When people occupy the same campus they will unavoidably have cross-cultural interactions. Are not cross-cultural interactions a healthy and rich part of one's education? There seems to be no way to escape dealing with both unity as well as diversity, rather than skewing oneself to one or the other extremes.

Are not there occasions when position I (assimilationism) and position IV (separatism) are quite understandable and justifiable? During a war or national emergency, the unity of a people (position I) will be necessary for their very survival. Let us pray that peace is the norm as opposed to war. In another circumstance, such as extreme oppression, how could anyone expect any collaboration? Position IV, separatism, is the basis for the very survival of a distinct people (maybe Jews, Kurds, or Armenians). Let us pray that oppression does not exist in our democracy such that the only resort left is separatism.

What should unite and rally positions II (unity over diversity) and III (diversity over unity) is the common objective of *integration*. American history needs to be judged on the basis of integration, i.e., whether it has been inclusive regarding its many ethnic groups. Has integration failed such that multiculturalism has many proponents today (see Glazer)? However, for Schlesinger, integration and assimilation are indistinguishable following the old and dated model of Americanism. Recognition and retention of diversity is what multiculturalism means, and this belief appears ascendent among many Americans today. No wonder Schlesinger is not consistently assimilationist. Cultural pluralism and the recognition of diverse ethnic perspectives in the writing of our American history are essential to the task of a good American historian. Schlesinger (136-137) favors including the histories of as many American ethnic groups as is reasonable and possible, although there are limits to how much can be done in a public educational environment. Nevertheless, for the most part Schlesinger's language betrays an assimilationist bias. Melt, dissolve, submerge, mold, indoctrinate, fit into, forge, and bind and bond, are the definitive terms most often found in Schlesinger's text.

The most Schlesinger can do is quote Fuchs and Ravitch that somehow American unity is its diversity: "our common culture is multicultural" (Ravitch) and "diversity itself was made a source of national identity and unity" (Schlesinger 131, 135). These quotes could place Schlesinger in position II (unity over diversity, yet respectful of diversity) if only these peculiarly paradoxical phrases were explained. How does one make a unity from plurality, *e pluribus unum*? Does such a unity mean the virtual disappearance and loss of a plurality of differences?   What degree or kind of plurality is permissible, not endangering unity?

Perhaps Schlesinger would benefit from a distinction such that pluralism and diversity are the means, never the end, while unity is our common goal as a country. Unity is an essence and pluralism is an accident, a contingency (see Quade). Our country's motto, *e pluribus unum*—from the many, one—suggests that diversity is our means on the way to unity. This scholastic language of essence and accident will be quite unwelcome to those holding to positions III (diversity over unity) and IV (separatism) because this language suggests hierarchy and subordination inherent in any logocentric bias. For example, what particular culture seeking recognition and respect wants to be seen as a "means" rather than an "end in itself"? Kant implores us to treat all individuals at all times as ends not means. Do not cultures deserve the same? Nevertheless, position II (unity over diversity) would gain from such scholastic language a strong argumentative basis for giving priority to unity over diversity without succumbing to the unitarian impulse of position I (assimilationism) that would annihilate diversity.

Schlesinger (138) rightly acknowledges that the different mix of peoples affects their eventual unity, but in what way? What are the particular contributions of different ethnic groups that give a unique flavor and composition to the American unity? The United States may be a multiethnic society, but is it a multiracial society? It may very well be true that positions II (unity over diversity) and III (diversity over unity) have different senses of unity since they clearly establish different priorities for unity. Schlesinger's book can be read in the light of positions I (assimilationism) and II (unity over diversity), although his fears of disunity cause him to more often use the language of position I.

As for integration, position III (diversity over unity) has just as much a claim to advocating integration on the basis of common respect and recognition for ethnic diversity. This diversity establishes new and changing forms of unity over time. Position III contends that there is no prior, dominant model of unity (the WASP way) that other ethnic groups must accommodate themselves to, since this would be violating the integrity of certain ethnic groups. Instead of investigating this claim of "differences," Schlesinger chooses to lambaste and ridicule extreme Afrocentrists. Once again, Schlesinger invites us to go to the extremes. On the other hand, position III only asks that dominant and prevailing legal and linguistic forms undergo adjustment, rather than ethnic peoples being forced to adjust to such *a priori* givens. Just what this means specifically will depend on the give-and-take between positions II and III. (See the dialogues below regarding political redistricting and bilingualism.)

Position II (unity over diversity) counters that the individual, not the individual's ethnic and group status, comes first. Imagine living in a country (such as the former Soviet Union) where everyone has an "internal passport" and an ethnic identity on such a passport indelibly fixed for one's life. In contradistinction, American individualism is based on an individual's efforts and achievements irrespective of ethnic identity. An individual's rights and an individual's achievements are what define us and in some way unite us. Ethnicity, race, and gender are what one is born with, not a matter of choice and freedom. It will be individuals in all their diversity (beyond ethnicity, race, and gender diversities) that will define our American community. This sense of unity and assimilation appears to be what Schlesinger has in mind.

But persons in positions III (diversity over unity) and IV (separatism) have trouble with the hollowness of individual identity alone compared to the richness and unavoidableness of ethnic, racial, and gender identity. Ethnicity includes a whole cultural history, and consequently is a stronger basis for association with others. Of course, in America one can take or leave in varying degrees one's ethnicity (positions II and III would agree, but not IV). In fact, we can consult a whole book, *Ethnic Options* by Mary Waters, that explains how many Americans tend to see ethnicity as a matter of choice, which is to say, something they can choose to emphasize and even vary or ignore depending on circumstances. But how does just being an individual create bonds of association? Besides the crucial question of "who am I?" there is the question of "what am I?" vis-a-vis others. Must we posit some "invisible hand" (such as the market, the Party, the movement, or the State) in order to be able to unite disparate, self-defining individuals?

To conclude, each of the four positions can make a justification for itself. Assimilationists (position I) hearken to the historical achievements and successes of the United States amalgamating such a diversity of different peoples. They contend that only this model of assimilation offers real hope of upward mobility for other unassimilated peoples. Separatists (position IV) claim the assimilationist model not only has failed them (Native Americans, Hispanic-Americans, and African-Americans), but that it has a heavy, oppressive, WASPish price that is unacceptable because it means forsaking non-WASPish ethnic identities in order to succeed.

Neither position I nor position IV discerns any middle-ground resolution; thus the cultural war rages. To the rescue come position II and position III, both of which acknowledge the respective significances of unity and diversity. Position II judges that centrifugal forces most threaten the United States politically and socially today, and therefore there is need for giving priority to unity (community) without denying the value of ethnic diversity. Position III counters that ethnic diversity has the greater priority because of ongoing failures to give value and status to non-WASP ethnicities. Without cultivating ethnicities allowing them to flourish, the unity of Americans will not be true to what ethnic-Americans hold most dearly. Positions II and III represent differences in *degree* and differences in the *means* of constituting our society. Positions I (assimilationism) and IV (separatism) represent unbridgeable differences in *kind* and differences in the *ends*, the very constitution, of our society. A battle over ends, not just means, forewarns of a civil war (a *Kulturkampf*), precisely what Schlesinger is understandably so exercised about.

If this fourfold schema is put to the test, then perhaps we can evaluate it in light of the best essay yet on multiculturalism, "The Politics of Recognition" by Charles Taylor. In terms of the fourfold schema, Taylor positions himself between the extremes of assimilationism and separatism, and goes back and forth between positions II (unity over diversity) and III (diversity over unity). Taylor takes seriously the human need for cultural recognition and identity, and he affirms the equality of individual rights for all in a well-functioning liberal democracy. Further proof that Taylor is somewhere in the middle positions is the moderate criticism of him by a diversity-prone feminist (Susan Wolf) and a unity-prone religionist (Steven Rockefeller).

Both the crudeness of canon supporters and the value subjectivism and power reductionism of extreme multiculturalists are rejected by Taylor. These extremes are equally ethnocentric in their own different ways. The two liberalisms that Michael Walzer identifies to summarize Taylor's position (Taylor 99) conform respectively to positions II and III. Liberalism 1 is committed to individual rights for all and a rigorously culturally-neutral state, i.e., the commonality of all citizens' security, welfare, and safety over their ethnic diversities. Liberalism 2 allows the state to make commitments to the survival and flourishing of cultures and religions as long as the basic rights of all citizens are protected, i.e., the recognition of particularistic diversity over unity.

Significant questions still remain: How far should the state go in recognizing and supporting different cultures and religions? Should not there be some demarcation between the public and the private? Perhaps diversity will flourish more harmoniously at the decentralized, local community and neighborhood level, while only a few, generalized, state-centralized norms and standards need to be guaranteed for all equally? What remains to integrate such a cultural diversity of peoples? Amy Gutmann (Taylor 22-23) suggests a common moral vocabulary and publicly shared standards of evidence. Yet her position founders, for the arguments she uses against racism could just as equally be applied to anti-abortionists even though Gutmann states she respects the anti-abortionist position but certainly not the racists' arguments. It is indeed difficult to draw boundary lines for rational discourse. The much broader issue of a viable public philosophy (see the Epilogue) for a diversity of Americans in a liberal democracy must be substantively engaged.

In the end, I would argue that Taylor adopts a stance closer to a position III (diversity over unity) than to position II (unity over diversity) stance in order to accommodate the "cultural survival" of the Quebecois in Canada. While critical standards of evaluation according to universal, equal rights in a liberal democracy have to be applied to any provisions for diversity, the human condition is dialogical, not monological (Taylor 32-37, 92). At this point one wishes Taylor were more critical of certain multiculturalists who complain of Eurocentric logocentrism, when they should be complaining of monologism as opposed to dialogism. Dialogues permit a full range of oratorical styles. Through a dialogic interaction of diverse cultures, there is first of all the shared basis of reciprocal recognition and respect. After a while a "fusion of horizons" (Taylor 67) may occur, continually transforming our standards of evaluation. In other words, we are always "working out" and revising what holds us together, our unity, in response to our encounters with diversity. A fixed and constant norm of unity goes contrary to the strong belief in change and progress held by liberal democrats, and it also subordinates and alienates our differences and otherness.

For Taylor, every ethnic culture has the presumption of value, albeit in the end not all cultures will be found equal in worth. Equality means an open mind giving the same recognition for all cultures, but diversity of judgment results in different evaluations. Procedural sameness does not disallow substantive distinctions. All cultures have something important to say and to add to the human condition, but not all cultures are equally democratic, liberal, and progressive. Remember that the United States is the "nation of nationalities" (Taylor 101) as opposed to a dominant national culture accepting and rejecting the influences of other cultures.

Once again we are at the crux of the practical matter—what is integration all about and how do we integrate? The crux of the philosophical matter which the philosopher Charles Taylor slights, being so pragmatically Anglo-American, is how do here-and-now particulars (culture, ethnicity) participate in transcendent universals (truth, beauty, justice, goodness)? While it is true that these universals have different meanings to different people, it does not follow that difference and disagreement mean we can not go forward to act on the basis of these universals and principles. For example, a tax system may have a mix of principles of justice: redistribution, fairness, broadness, avoidance of taxing necessities, targeting use or consumption, etc. Certainly some cultures may be more predisposed by tradition and/or circumstances to one or another principle of justice. Furthermore, many people have yet to clarify their sense of justice vis-a-vis others. Different principles of justice can contend with each other as well as coexist in application. Of utmost importance is the grounding of justice in *both* experience (culture, ethnicity) and reason (principle, norm). A particular kind of dialectical conversation going back and forth between experience and reason can constitute the progression in clarity, insight, and rational choice for which we so resolutely strive.

PRACTICAL GUIDE FOR THE READER

To make the most of dialogic learning, all the following dialogues can be analyzed in a way to evaluate the strength and weight of their arguments. (See the worksheet, pages 20-21, that readers can use to understand better what is at stake in any of these dialogues.) First of all, in all dialogues there will be points of convergence (agreement and consensus) and also points of divergence (a parting of the ways). Do the points of convergence make it propitious for compromises, since politics is the art of fashioning compromises? Or are the points of convergence minimal and not fundamental? How do both sides deal with each other's "evidence," which you would expect to be not so disputable? As for points of divergence, are they about just the means to an end, or are they about ends, fundamental matters? Differences over means are less divisive. Do the divergences so set the sides apart that the reaching of a working political consensus is impossible?

There are at least four types of arguments as originally delineated by Professor Richard Weaver in his book *The Ethics of Rhetoric*. Identifying these types in the dialogues will help the reader determine which arguments have more impact in terms of their strength and weight. First of all, there is the argument from principle or definition. Frequently, people will resort to some overriding principle (e.g., humanity, equality, justice, free speech, pluralism) to justify the basis for their argument. Of course, equally good and high principles can conflict with one another. Explaining why you are drawn to one principle or another is decisive. For some people this argument from principle or definition is the most important factor in argumentation since principles are guiding norms that make for the highest quality of life.

Second, there is the argument from cause to effect or simply the argument as to consequences. This type of argument is most prominent in politics, and many choose it as the most important argument because it includes a pragmatic test of any person's standpoint or decision. Frequently, this argument takes the shape of "if we do x, then y will follow." Yet we are never so sure of consequences in human affairs, and different people forewarn of radically different consequences. Human affairs is not always a matter amenable to laboratory experiment. And even if we permit one side to have its way so we can evaluate the actual consequences, there is always the problem of interpreting or explaining away certain consequences. Certainly the American people are quite practical, and politics in general is a practical matter. But can we abide by a position that states that only practical consequences count, no matter how (irrespective of any principle) we achieve such consequences? Does the end justify any means?

Third, there are forceful, compelling analogies that people use in argumentation to connect with other people and to achieve a kind of emotional identification. The use of anecdotes, metaphors, and colorful images give life and substance to arguments. However, the problem always remains whether the analogy being made is really a likeness, a fair representation, and the best image to generalize from. The persuasiveness of an analogy needs to be tempered by its appropriateness and relevance.

Fourth, there is the argument from authority. In the past, scripture and great personages were relied-upon authorities. Today, facts, statistics, research studies, and polls take on an authoritative role. Can authorities be challenged? Beyond the problem of conflicting authorities, should we just let quoted authorities stand without further argumentation and justification? Is it not the *argument* of the authority, rather than just the authority, that we should be paying heed to in our deliberative process? The objective in the end is the constitution of a rational, deliberative community where we listen and weigh arguments presented by all the varying sides.

WORKSHEET FOR ANALYZING THE DIALOGUES

List Points of Convergence in the Dialogue:

List Points of Divergence in the Dialogue:

Identify Types of Arguments, and find two examples for each in the dialogue you are reading.

A. Argument from Principle/Definition:

B. Argument from Cause to Effect:

C. Argument from Analogy:

D. Argument from Authority:

What pivotal argument or set of arguments led you to be on one side or the other? (If you could not decide, then what offsetting arguments do you think stalemated you?)

Can you state what further evidence, argumentation, research, or analysis (if any) needs to be done in order to determine whether one side or the other in dispute is better public policy?

Devise a set of questions covering the prominent issues and arguments in a dialogue to be used to poll your friends, classmates, and dorm residents. How informed are your cohorts regarding these issues?

In the dialogue that you read, find examples of arguments that fit the fourfold schema for multiculturalism.

I. Assimilationism, or the melting pot; oneness and conformity:

II. Unity over Diversity; unity is more important but diversity is respected:

III. Diversity over Unity; diversity is more important and unity is something yet to be fashioned after dealing with diversity:

IV. Separatism, no fruitful coming together.

BIBLIOGRAPHY

Barber, Benjamin. *The Conquest of Politics*. Princeton: Princeton University Press, 1988.

Beer, Samuel. *To Make a Nation*. Cambridge: Harvard University Press, 1993.

Fish, Stanley. *There's No Such Thing as Free Speech, And It's a Good Thing Too*. New York: Oxford University Press, 1994.

Fuchs, Lawrence. *American Kaleidoscope*. Hanover: University Press of New England, 1990.

Glazer, Nathan. *Ethnic Dilemmas*. Cambridge: Harvard University Press, 1983.

Kallen, Horace. "Democracy versus the Melting Pot." *Nation* (February 18, 24, 1915): 190-194, 209-212.

Lind, Michael. *The Next American Nation*. New York: Free Press, 1995.

Novak, Michael. *The Rise of the Unmeltable Ethnics*. New York: Macmillan, 1973.

Quade, Quentin. "Pluralism versus Diversity." *Freedom Review* 11 (1992): 16-19.

Ravitch, Diane. *American Reader*. New York: Harper/Collins, 1990.

Roy, Donald. *Dialogues in American Politics*. Dubuque: Kendall/Hunt, 1992.

_____. *Public Policy Dialogues*. Lanham: University Press of America, 1993.

Saxonhouse, Arlene. *Fear of Diversity: The Birth of Political Science in Ancient Political Thought*. Chicago: University of Chicago Press, 1992.

Schlesinger, Arthur. *The Disuniting of America*. New York: Norton, 1991.

Takaki, Ronald. *A Different Mirror: A History of Multicultural America*. Boston: Little Brown, 1993.

Taylor, Charles. *Multiculturalism and the Politics of Recognition*. Princeton: Princeton University Press, 1993.

Walzer, Michael. *The Politics of Ethnicity*. Cambridge: Harvard University Press, 1980.

Waters, Mary. *Ethnic Options*. Berkeley: University of California Press, 1990.

Weaver, Richard. *The Ethics of Rhetoric*. Chicago: Regnery, 1953.

ONE

IMMIGRATION POLICY:

BOUNDARIES AND RIGHTS

Today the immigration issue is an international phenomenon, with some Western liberal democracies far ahead of the United States in their degree of negative reaction and harshness. France, for example, long a shining beacon for asylum seeking, has amended its constitution so that the precious right of asylum now is the prerogative of the state. Thomas Jefferson would flinch in pain. Thus, France turns away asylum seekers who would be accepted elsewhere in the European Economic Community. Foreign residents who could automatically become citizens now must declare their allegiance to the French republic. The justifiable effort to control illegal immigration threatens to spill over and impose burdens on or threats to legal immigrants. And, of course, neofascists in France, Germany, Italy, and England have found in the issue of immigration a ready-made scapegoat, highly efficacious during an economic downturn or in the context of perceived domestic, social/community breakdown.

Oddly enough, the United States is still somewhat innocent and generous compared to European countries, which have some specific ethnic/religious/racial/linguistic/cultural identity to preserve. At least some Americans feel, believe, or say (and they strike fairly responsive chords of memory) that we are a nation of all nations, a universal nation. "My forebears were immigrants. Can I deny others without denying myself?" American identity is precisely unfixed, uprooted, and ambiguously open to definition and redefinition. Yet there are limits to the capacities of any vessel regarding inflow. Do the public costs of immigration outweigh the public benefits? Is it humane to offer a promise or dream of great opportunities to others that cannot be fulfilled for many who are already residing and struggling here?

Immigration policy generates a considerable amount of fervor regarding what kind of country we intend to be. On one side are the "restrictionists" who contend that we can only assimilate so many "new people" demographically, economically, and culturally speaking. George Washington, Benjamin Franklin, and James Madison questioned whether we could be all things to all kinds and numbers of people. Yet, another American tradition, which we could call "welcomist," harkens back to Jefferson's "all men are created equal" and our religious traditions acknowledging the brotherhood and sisterhood of humankind. The Statue of Liberty with its "Give me your tired, your poor, Your huddled masses yearning to breathe free" remains a powerful, emotional symbol of our country. We should greet all kinds and numbers of immigrants with open arms. We are the "golden door" for the world; we are a nation of immigrants, where anyone can find new opportunities and get a new start. Is there not a basic human right called the freedom of movement? Should we deny those, who are simply exercising their natural right to better themselves, their "pursuit of happiness"? Within this context of conflicting attitudes and traditions, the restrictionist and the welcomist conduct their debate.

THE DIALOGUE

RESTRICTIONIST: No recent American public opinion poll has ever found a majority of Americans favoring increasing immigration levels. A 1993 Gallup Poll found 65% of Americans believing immigration should be decreased. No more than 6% of Americans polled, including recent immigrants, believe there should be an increase. All others polled thought immigration levels should remain the same. Also 56% of Americans believe immigration costs taxpayers too much, and 55% think the cultural diversity of immigrants threatens American culture.

In the 1980s and now the 1990s, immigration numbers have exceeded 1,000,000 persons a year, including the estimated illegal immigrants. There is an all-time high of 20 million first-generation immigrants in the United States today. These numbers exceed the greatest period of immigration in our history, 1900–1914. Until recently, 1907 was the largest single year of immigration when 1,285,349 immigrants entered the United States. In 1989, we had 1,090,024 legal immigrants. In addition, an estimated 300,000 to 500,000 illegal immigrants enter the United States every year. The flood of immigration today, exceeding the 700,000 immigrants plus 130,000 refugees that the 1986 Immigration Reform and Control Act (IRCA) was supposed to control, only proves that we have a federal government management failure.

The American people are not even demanding zero immigration. Why cannot we enforce our existing laws and regulations? Do not we have to write new laws to lower total immigration to 300,000 as the Federation for American Immigration Reform (FAIR) recommends so that we establish control over our own borders?

WELCOMIST: Public opinion polls are not as negative as you make them out to be. For example, 78% of Americans polled by *Newsweek* believe that immigrants work hard and take jobs Americans do not want. Americans are far more worried about "undocumented" immigrants (what you call "illegal immigrants") because we have not been able to control our borders. As for the level and numbers of immigrants, most Americans are charitable, knowing full well that almost all of us were originally immigrants (non-natives). The right of freedom of movement is cherished as essential to the American spirit of progress (so remarked on by Alexis de Tocqueville in the 1830s). We never need fear any people seeking to better themselves. In effect, their ambitions make the rest of us better off.

A practical test or measure of immigration is needed. As immigrants come to our shores, will they have existing opportunities to succeed, or will they make their own opportunities to succeed? Some economic and social understanding of *viability* for immigrants in the United States would appeal to our American sense of fairness. If we are to remain a progressive people, we should not adopt an "enclave attitude" such that we erect high walls to insulate ourselves from change and development. No one should want to live in fear of "the other"; there is nothing to fear.

Your historical comparison to 1900–1914 is somewhat misleading and only generates fears that huge numbers of immigrants are flooding our shores and cannot be accommodated. As a percentage of population, immigration levels are low today and much lower than the 1900–1914 period. We are not experiencing an invasion, and there is no reason to believe we cannot handle and benefit from an injection of new, energetic people stimulating our growing economy and diverse ways of life.

RESTRICTIONIST: The kinds of immigrants coming to the United States today are largely different from those who came in the past. Even when they are not different, our labor market differences today make it quite difficult to contend that we will succeed in accommodating and assimilating so many new people into our economy and society. About 80% of our recent immigrants are from Latin America and Asia. They bring language problems and a much poorer background that makes them underprepared for the United States compared to previous immigrants. There is a strong correlation between middle-class background elsewhere and taking advantage of opportunities as immigrants in this country.

Furthermore, we have undergone significant *structural* economic change in the United States. In other words, our economy has shifted from a blue collar, manufacturing economy to a more sophisticated high tech, special services economy. Consequently, today there are serious economic barriers to the integration and assimilation of low-income immigrants that did not exist in the past.

Many Americans are struggling to find employment in this new economy because the number of low-level entry jobs has declined tremendously in our urban areas. How can we afford to welcome masses of immigrants unless we impose sharp limitations and only accept those with sophisticated skills that we need because of certified labor shortages?

It is not unreasonable for a people now in charge (first come, first served) to determine who belongs, i.e., the rights and responsibilities of property and ownership. We owe it first and foremost to our children and their children to lay the foundation for the best environment they can have.

It is not true that immigrants take jobs Americans will not take. Immigrants displace American workers, and many of these Americans move to other areas where immigrants are not highly concentrated. Consequently, these unemployed Americans are not counted in the statistics for their original, local area of residence. In effect, we do not get a true measure of how much immigrants displace struggling, low-income American workers. The failure to develop a black middle class in some areas of the United States is related to the influx of immigrants. The high concentration of immigrants in certain areas depresses wages and prevents improvements in working conditions that otherwise would occur if employers did not have an abundant supply of compliant, immigrant labor. No wonder labor organizations fear new immigration threatening the standard of living of their workers. Also, immigrants who are highly concentrated in specific living areas are less likely to integrate and assimilate with other Americans. Not only is our economic growth and national income lowered by low-skilled immigrant workers, but our competitive advantage with other countries is weakened as well.

WELCOMIST: Your remarks are culturally prejudiced regarding Latinos and Asians. Your language is very similar to the virulent nativists who made the same claims about "aliens" back in the 1840s when the Irish began to arrive in the United States. Not only the Irish, but the Germans, Slavs, Chinese, and Mexicans were all considered unfit and unassimilable. But we know better today. All kinds of nationalities blend to become full-fledged, productive Americans. We are not overrun with foreign-born persons in the United States. As a percentage of population the foreign born are fewer in the United States than in the United Kingdom, France, Canada, Germany, and Australia.

Furthermore, many immigrants are willing to take jobs and have higher labor participation rates than native-born Americans. Immigrants tend to provoke native-born workers to seek higher-level jobs. It would seem that such immigrants function more in agreement with our American Dream—work hard at whatever job you have, and you and your children will move upward and have the things in life we all want. Immigrants are an economic transfusion of healthy, ambitious, energetic laborers. Our population is aging and not replenishing itself with younger workers. Do not we need more younger workers to provide more Social Security/Medicare financial support for our growing elderly population? In sum, immigrants provide an economic stimulus and an economic benefit.

As for our government immigration policy, skilled laborers should be a more significant part of the mix of immigrants (so-called "designer immigration"). But we also have two superseding humanitarian criteria—families reuniting and refugees fleeing political persecution. Most of our immigration today is family-based (so-called "chain migration"), and this enables people to maintain their most essential human ties. Immigrants with families are more likely to have a responsible stake in their new life here. Not only is it a human right to ensure our family bonds, but also it is a fulfillment of our social nature to nourish extended family relations. The family is a building block of communities, and with communities we have people working together and being productive citizens. Immigrants are known to revitalize some ghetto areas of our cities. As for refugees, they not only need a home because they literally cannot go back to their native land, but they also resemble the suffering many early settlers experienced before coming to this country to escape persecution. We have an honored tradition of ensuring the right of asylum. The world is not a fair and just place, and some people need a haven where they can reconstitute themselves.

RESTRICTIONIST: The Immigration Reform and Control Act of 1986 (IRCA) set immigration at a cap of 700,000 a year: 480,000 family immigrants, 70,000 skilled workers, and 150,000 refugees. The flexibility of the cap for family member immigrants has raised the numbers closer to the 1 million mark. Not only are the caps not being maintained, about 70% of all immigrants end up in five states: Florida, New York, California, Texas, and Illinois. This concentration of immigrants creates severe socioeconomic problems for these particular states. Obviously, the failure of IRCA clearly demonstrates that immigration must become a top priority, national security issue. U.S. immigration policy needs to be radically overhauled. We need to exert our national sovereignty rights to control our borders.

With public opinion on our side in favor of restrictions, we could establish a three-to-five year moratorium of zero immigration. Some Hispanic groups such as the National Hispanic Alliance favor such a moratorium because they feel the pressure on them from Anglos concerned about high concentrations of immigrants and the attendant socioeconomic problems that characterize recent immigrants. Also, their own life chances are diminished by greater numbers competing for the same, limited economic opportunities. In the past we did this (in the 1920s) to provide a "breathing space," and it enabled us to digest all the new immigrants recently allowed in. We especially need a moratorium to devise means to control our borders regarding illegal immigrants. We have no choice but to manufacture a counterfeit-proof, holographic, national identity card required for employment for any and all persons. Employers should be subject to stiff, enforceable penalties for hiring illegal aliens.

While we have a 2,000-mile border with Mexico, only about 200 miles of that border are immigrant flowpoints. Let us light up the border and beef up the Border Patrol, perhaps even using American army and marine forces as part of their training missions. Charging a $2 border crossing fee can help cover the costs of this increased law enforcement effort. We also need to reinstitute a policy of returning Mexicans to places deep within Mexico so that they do not immediately try additional border crossings. The problem of illegal aliens is not unsolvable. If we exercise the will to control our borders, we can then develop more generous policies toward those immigrants who want to stay in the United States, work, and become American citizens.

One proposal, offered by Barry Chiswick, to diminish the illegal immigration problem would be to reinstate the *bracero* program that we had from 1942 to 1964. The advantage of such a "guest worker" program is that we satisfy the need for farm laborers that fruit and vegetables employers have, and we avoid the inflow of costly dependents. This program is more enforceable and prevents the permanent settlement of immigrants.

If we do not go with a moratorium, the least we can do is establish a 300,000 person maximum for immigration. 150,000 would be admitted on the basis of labor skills alone where it is certified that we have shortages and deficiencies in our labor market. In the 1980s less than 4% of all immigrants were *certified* as a labor need. 100,000 would be admitted for family relations, restricted to the *immediate* family—husband, wife, and children. And 50,000 political refugees. At the present time there is a backlog of 364,000 refugees waiting for asylum, and it is growing at a rate of 10,000 a month. FAIR also estimates that there are

20 million persons waiting to immigrate to the United States under the extended family criterion. A very real numerical threat of invasion exists. One New York City immigrant brought in 64 relatives under the family criterion provision.

It is surprising that you are so supportive of the family criterion for immigration because it simply supports a severely biased "national origins" system as well as "nepotism." Obviously, those countries that already have many immigrants in the United States will be overly favored by the family criterion. Yet in 1965 we scrapped the highly prejudicial "national origins" system established in 1921 because it discriminated against non-Western European countries. We should put an end to the so-called fifth preference, which allows brothers and sisters to get immigration favors. The immediate nuclear family relationships—minor children, spouses, and perhaps aged parents—should be the only family preferences. Family reunification yes, family reunion no. Emphasis on technological skills for immigrants will improve our weak economic productivity and level of competition with foreign countries. Skilled immigrants reduce wage differentials and economic inequality, whereas unskilled immigrants contribute to the economic injustice of greater income inequality in the United States.

WELCOMIST: Your position is hidebound, stereotypically prejudicial to human rights, and contrary to the motive forces that made this country uniquely great, a land of opportunity for everyone irrespective of national origins. We do not need to fear change. A mobile, developing population and economy lead to a higher standard of living. Your position represents and promotes "declinism" and a politics of fear. A moratorium or an immigration ceiling of 300,000 would damage our economic prospects as well as contradict our cultural values and our human rights standards. In contradistinction, a politics of hope declares that immigrants revitalize the American Dream and remind us of new frontiers to explore, which has always been part of our heritage. We should not discriminate against the ambitious poor who have risked much to come to a foreign land.

The facts are that immigrants are enterprising. They go into our inner cities and generate economic activity by starting small businesses, providing services, and creating jobs. Professor Julian Simon has provided economic statistics that show that immigrants do not displace low-income American workers. Nor do they overuse welfare since most immigrants are young males. The average immigrant family costs $1,400 in welfare and schooling compared to the average native cost of $2,300. It is our elderly Americans on Medicare and Social Security who are the most expensive regarding government entitlement programs. Within 11 to 16 years, immigrants are earning as much as native-born workers. Immigrant children, far from being a burden on our public schools, are revitalizing them because many do better in school than their American-born counterparts. As a group, foreign-born children living in the United States for 5 to 10 years have a grade point average of 2.58 compared to 2.44 for American-born children. They spend more time on homework. However, as immigrant children get "Americanized" and partake of our American popular culture their better performance declines to the American-born level. We should be more worried about what we are doing to ourselves than what immigrants from the outside are doing to us. Likewise, family breakdown, unproductive labor, and crime have American, not immigrant, roots.

Clearly, immigrants do not contribute to, nor are they to be confused with, the so-called "underclass" in the United States today. Most immigrants are not the ones stuck in a cycle of poverty from generation to generation. It is native-born Americans who lack the spark of energy and the strong family environment and who are strongly attracted toward immediate gratification rather than long-run planning (saving, sacrificing, deferring, etc.). In fact, immigrants are an answer to our declining standard of living. We need an expanding labor force so that American jobs are not exported. Inexpensive labor is a benefit to American consumers who gain from lower prices as a consequence.

The recommendation that we go to an immigration policy that certifies 150,000 immigrants on the basis of labor skills has proven cumbersome and unworkable in the past. Getting employer certification is the problem. Far better would be the development of a point system as proposed by the economist Barry Chiswick (see his testimony before the U.S. House of Representatives Judiciary Committee's Subcommittee on Immigration, March 1, 1990). Canada and Australia use a point system. Skills, education, job training and experience, and knowledge of English would be given points as well as the existence of family kin who could provide financial sponsorship. Every year we would establish a threshold level of points related to our economic situation that would be the basis for admitting whatever number of enterprising immigrants that are desirable. Congress could set a minimum and maximum, leaving to a special commission the determination of the specific annual number.

Nevertheless, much greater numbers than you propose would be feasible because cold, naked economic productivity is not the only standard. We all know that individuals do better when they have supportive families. There is no reason why we cannot have 400,000 to 500,000 family-based immigrants each year. It is not "nepotism" to reaffirm the tradition of family togetherness, which is the main stimulus for good citizenship and economic productivity.

Simple, practical measures can be devised to take charge of our refugee program so we can be the humanitarian country we proclaim ourselves to be. The backlog of refugee applications should be handled by an asylum corps comparable to those in countries such as England, France, and Germany. To impose a $130 visa fee on persons seeking asylum, as the Immigration and Naturalization Service (INS) wants, is to penalize thousands of legitimate asylum seekers. Denying them work permits for 150 days is grossly unfair and will only encourage more abuses of the system such as joining the underground economy or using false identification. The right to asylum is guaranteed under international law and in treaties signed by the United States. Quick, full hearings for asylum applicants is the best deterrent to fraud and the illegitimate asylum seekers who simply want to get into the United States and disappear.

Rather than adapting a punitive, "get tough," law enforcement mentality and policy, we need to realize we are dealing with human beings who are doing exactly what we would be doing if we were in their situation. Given the broad expanses of our country and our wealth (actual and potential), we can afford to be generous toward new immigrants. The establishment of a national identity card sounds like what a highly regimented, totalitarian state would impose on its subjects. A "dog tag" identification system would be analogous to the Jim Crow laws used to target black Americans, although this time it would be primarily Latinos. Your recommendation of a *bracero* program is tantamount to a "rent-a-slave" Mexican program. The unionization of farm laborers and improvement of farm laboring conditions would be impeded. Why not expand the existing H-2 program, which properly puts the burden on employers to petition for temporary immigrant labor?

RESTRICTIONIST: We are more respectful of human rights if we determine whether we truly are better off accepting millions of more people. Immigration now counts for one-third to one-half of our population growth. The Census Bureau projects that by the year 2025 around 50 million persons will be added to the United States population if we do not impose limits on immigration. A population explosion of too many people without the resources to accommodate them is contrary to a *qualitative* notion of human rights. And do we benefit other countries when we encourage a "brain drain," which is to say accepting the most qualified professionals from other countries? Why do we not propose economic development aid packages to countries such as Mexico, which will have the dual purpose of improving the labor conditions in foreign countries where there are large numbers of potential immigrants to the United States and also open the door to American exports, which will benefit American workers? Free trade (not including the absolutely free movement of laborers) makes everyone better off. Certainly letting into the United States a lot of immigrants from depressed areas of the world does nothing for their own countries.

Can anyone believe that we now have a millionaire-investor category for immigrants? We will admit 6,800 immigrants per year if they invest $1 million in our economy or $500,000 in a rural or high unemployment area. Is this a drug dealers' bonanza or what? Most of the so-called political refugees seeking asylum really are attracted to the better U.S. economy and way of life. We have no obligation to such people, and we should not spend millions more to have an asylum corps to handle this surge of applicants. Rights of people have to be balanced by obligations. We have removed Vietnam from the asylum list and we should remove most, if not all, countries from the list. In a world that is increasingly becoming more democratic, there will be fewer legitimate asylum seekers. More freedom fighters need to remain in their own countries to fight for democracy and the improvement of economic conditions there.

There is an underclass of 15 million Americans concentrated in the inner cities of our population centers: Miami, Los Angeles, Washington, D.C., Denver, New York, Chicago, Boston, etc. Immigrants are a drain on our welfare system because we are now into the second wave of immigration with extended families joining young males. All the more reason to revise our immigration criteria. It is inappropriate to bring up Social Security and Medicare because they clearly are not welfare. The recipients and their employers have paid into these programs and are thereby entitled. The state of Oregon took matters into its own hands by linking job training and English language skills in order to cut in half cash welfare benefits that were going to recent immigrants. There are proposals in California to deny welfare payments to immigrants. On the November 1994 ballot in California was a Save Our State (SOS) initiative that denies undocumented children access to public schools and removes undocumented persons from AFDC and MediCal benefits. (This proposition passed but has been thwarted by the courts.) These benefits are a "magnetic lure" to immigrants according to California Governor Pete Wilson, who also claims that California spends $2.3 billion on illegal immigrants. Who can be surprised that 62% of Californians favor SOS, according to a *Los Angeles Times* poll.

The economist Donald Huddle of Rice University in Houston claims that U.S. taxpayers paid $121 billion in public assistance to immigrants in 1993, but only received $77 billion in taxes from legal and illegal immigrants. The net loss was $44 billion in 1993. Aid to Families with Dependent Children (AFDC) for illegal immigrants alone cost U.S. taxpayers $820 million in 1992. Immigrants are not an economic or taxpayers' bargain. Three states, Florida, New York, and California, are suing the United States government for failing to redistribute federal money to these states that are heavily affected by immigration. The INS has clearly failed to control immigration. Certainly the federal government, which collects immigrant taxes, could be responsible enough to grant funds to ease the economic burden that these states endure.

It is not only increased welfare expense (Food Stamps, AFDC, Medicaid, etc.) but also the heavy financial drain on our educational and criminal justice systems that immigrants are causing now. In 1992, immigrants cost $2.8 billion for bilingual education, $12.8 billion for primary and secondary education, and $2.4 billion for public higher education. Twenty-five percent of the student population in New York, Florida, and Texas is non-English speaking. The dropout rate among Hispanics is 36%. In 1986, 36% of all immigrants had less than 12 years of education, compared to 15% for American-born persons. How can we expect that they will benefit by upward mobility? And even when you subtract the taxes paid by immigrants in California, totaling $720.7 million, you still have a net cost of $1.86 billion. 7.2% of all native Californians receive public aid; for immigrants the figure is 10.4%. In the past our economy did not penalize as heavily the underprepared and unskilled. Today it is different.

In California, 35% of all felons are immigrants. It cost California in 1992 $500 million to arrest, try, and imprison immigrant criminals. Twenty-five percent of federal prisoners are immigrants at a cost of $500 million a year for incarceration. We are now encountering youth gangs among immigrant groups. The significant increase in Asians in Grand Rapids, Michigan has brought crime and violence. Organized crime among immigrant groups is not uncommon regarding drugs, gambling, and prostitution. Chinese, Japanese, Jamaican, Russian, Israeli, and Nigerian crime syndicates have developed since 1985. It is sad, but nevertheless true, that immigration is adding to our criminal justice problems.

Our country is primarily WASPish, or White, Anglo-Saxon, Protestant, with 70% to 80% of Americans descendant from Western European cultures. We should not assume that cultures from other parts of the world will easily and naturally assimilate, especially if we accept unqualifiedly huge numbers without any breathing spaces (such as a moratorium on immigration for an extended period of time) that we benefitted from in the past. Certainly it is sobering to reflect upon the ominous implications of ethnic conflict over bilingual education, the Los Angeles riots in which a majority of rioters were Latinos not blacks (one-third of 6,000 persons arrested were illegal aliens), conflicts with Koreans in New York City and Laotians in Wausau, Wisconsin, the World Trade Center bombing by immigrant terrorists, Vietnamese shrimpers on the Texas coast, and Chinese vessels filled with illegal aliens heading for slave sweatshops in the United States.

There is nothing desirable in and of itself to have America be a replica of the entire world. What reason do we have to believe that Third World immigrants from Latin American, Asia, and Africa will be amenable to Western liberal democracy when their countries of origin have little politically and culturally to prepare them for our liberal democracy? Furthermore, when ethnic identity and cultural separatism are so much the fashion among our opinion elite, there is just not the same commitment to Americanization that we had in the past.

Our country today faces exceedingly difficult problems, with overpopulation among our underclass (immigrants have very high fertility rates), the heavy strain on our public services by poor people, and the absence of good paying jobs to uplift the underclass. What cheap immigrant labor provides is a supply of persons that discourages employers from upgrading their work environments for Americans who cannot live on depressed wages, underemployed jobs, jobs without health benefits, and miserable working conditions. From 1973 to 1991 the real wages of American workers fell, and the main cause was cheap immigrant labor perpetuating poor job conditions such as low wages and low productivity. For example, we have a shortage of nurses in the United States, which leads to the importation of nurses from foreign countries. But there are plenty of Americans who would go into or stay in nursing if there were training programs for them and if the work and pay conditions were improved.

Surplus immigrant labor also encourages our industries to stay low tech. In Los Angeles the labor market in 1977 had 2,500 unionized black janitors. But in 1985 the number had dropped to 800. Immigrants depress wages and displace low-income American workers, especially unionized labor that tends to be more expensive for employers. No wonder business leaders champion open borders. They do not care about human rights in a qualitative sense; they only want to increase their economic profits.

WELCOMIST: Your remarks play well to those who are afraid of change (the politics of fear). But such fearmongering will not succeed. Most Americans know what made this country great, and it was an admixture of a variety of nationalities. We are not limited to White, Anglo-Saxon, Protestant Western Europeans. That is our great and noble experiment: to be a teeming house of nationalities, creating our own unique, blended American nationality over time. What works for us could be called a kind of "pluralistic assimilationism." What we have in common, an abstract universalism, is our liberal democratic political constitution and capitalistic economic structure, which together provide a context of beliefs promoting change and progress. On the other hand, the context and substance of our people are more like an ethnic particularism, which gives us a strong sense of personal, family, and community identity in a world that can be otherwise quite cold, impersonal, and bureaucratic.

Those who believe there is some population bomb related to immigration fail to see how people have adjusted over time to new environments. Modern technology is a decentralizing factor enabling more Americans to live dispersed rather than on top of each other in urban areas. We do not risk overpopulation but underpopulation of our labor force. To avoid a population decline and to expand our economy, one million immigrants a year is about right. Environmental problems are not related to overpopulation numbers but to what we are doing in relation to the environment. The danger of our economic decline exceeds any danger of overpopulation and environmental collapse. We need an immigration policy that promotes our economic expansion. Most business leaders favor open borders in order to expand our economic pie so that more Americans can share in expanding economic wealth.

The real point of reference in this debate is not overall costs, since obviously those who are below a middle-class standing will cost more. We need to compare low-income immigrants and natives and realize how the latter cost more over time. Secondly, there are hidden, indirect benefits—the multiplier effects of immigrant labor, immigrant spending, and immigrant taxes. George Borjas writes that there is not a "single shred of evidence of an adverse effect on earnings and employment opportunities" caused by immigrants when you look at the aggregate, rather than highly selective specific cases. One study showed little effect on the earnings of nonimmigrants when a 10% increase in Mexican population occurred. The labor force participation rate is little affected by immigrant labor.

The Urban Institute report on immigration released in May 1994 challenged Professor Huddle's methods and conclusions. Huddle underreported incomes of immigrants and the taxes they paid. Immigrants make significant contributions to Social Security, unemployment insurance, and gasoline taxes, all of which Huddle ignores. In all, about $50 billion of contributions to our economy was ignored. Immigrants' net contribution is in the range of $30 billion a year, the amount in taxes they pay over and above the cost of public services for them. Furthermore, Huddle based nearly $12 billion in costs on worker displacement caused by immigrants, assuming without hard evidence that every 100 low-skill immigrants cause 25 native workers to lose their jobs and not get other jobs!

As long as the United States has a growing economy there is a positive role for immigrants. The flow of immigration could be tied to economic growth prospects. Of course, the Urban Institute admits that some state and local governments need a fairer share returned to them of the money immigrants contribute to the federal government. This redistribution would help defuse local taxpayer hostility towards immigrants.

RESTRICTIONIST: We are not prepared to handle the number of immigrants you propose to let into the United States. The story of immigration's woes in Wausau, Wisconsin (as told calmly and moderately by Roy Beck in *The Atlantic Monthly*) makes it clear that we have a volume and capacity problem. No one, be they members of the federal government or of voluntary agencies promoting immigration, wants to assess the environmental, infrastructural, economic, and social consequences to communities when rapid and concentrated population growth via immigration occurs.

The rage of multiculturalism dividing Americans into hostile ethnic groups can only be exacerbated by high levels of immigration. We are no longer the type of economically developing country that needs a cheap, unskilled labor supply. Controlled economic development, low population growth, and cultural assimilation are the only rational bases for an immigration public policy. There is no world in reality or in possibility where removing all boundaries, barriers, or hurdles will ordain a heaven of human rights flourishing. Consequently, it is our obligation to work within limits. How much better it would be for most people to stay put and exercise their energies to the fullest wherever they find themselves.

WELCOMIST: Your position strikes us as too elitist, namely: "We have achieved ours and now all you others should achieve yours, preferably elsewhere." The shining example that is the United States of America offers quite another alternative: hands clasped across the world. Other people in the world can participate in our flourishing and, in fact, keep it culturally and economically proceeding at a healthy pace. Human rights are universal propositions based on universal experience. Human rights are not to be relativized and marginalized by some overriding socioeconomic, property-ownership privilege declared by those restrictionists who have claimed the mountain top.

BIBLIOGRAPHY

Allen, Jennifer. "Fly North." *New Republic* (December 27, 1993): 9-10.

Auster, Lawrence. "The Forbidden Topic." *National Review* (April 27, 1992): 42-44.

Barnes, Fred. "No Entry." *New Republic* (November 8, 1993): 10-14.

Bean, Frank, et al. *Opening and Closing the Doors*. Lanham, MD: University Press of America, 1989.

Beck, Roy. "The Ordeal of Immigration in Wausau." *Atlantic Monthly* (April 1994): 84-97.

"Becoming American, Bad Habits and All." *New York Times* (February 23, 1994).

Bender, David and Leone, Bruno, eds. *Illegal Immigrants: Opposing Viewpoints*. San Diego: Greenhaven, 1994.

_____. eds. *Immigration: Opposing Viewpoints*. San Diego: Greenhaven, 1990.

Borjas, George. *Friends or Strangers?* New York: Basic Books, 1990.

Bornemeir, James. "Immigration Cost Study Draws Fire." *Los Angeles Times* (June 28, 1994): A3, A19.

Bouvier, Leon and Gardner, Robert. *Immigration to the United States: The Unfinished Story*. Population Bulletin, Volume 41, November 1986.

_____. *Peaceful Invasions*. Lanham, MD: University Press of America, 1988.

Brand, H. et al. "Inequality and Immigration." *Dissent* (Summer 1994): 404-413.

Briggs, Vernon. *Mass Immigration and the National Interest*. Armonk: Sharpe, 1992.

Brimelow, Peter. "Time to Rethink Immigration." *National Review* (June 22, 1992): 30-46.

Buchanan, Pat. "America has a Right to Preserve Its Identity." *Conservative Chronicle* (August 28, 1991).

Cohen, Warren. "The Millionaire Immigrants." *U.S. News & World Report* (June 10, 1991): 54.

Dowie, Mark. "Bring Us Your Huddled Millionaires." *Harper's* (November 1991): 58-59.

Edmonston, Barry and Passel, Jeffrey, eds. *Immigration and Ethnicity*.

Washington, D.C.: Urban Institute, 1994.

Enchautegui, Mary. "Effects of Immigration on Wages and Employment of Black Males." Urban Institute Research Paper (May 1993).

Fix, Michael and Passell, Jeffrey. "Report on Immigration." Washington, D.C.: Urban Institute (May 1994).

Fukuyama, Francis. "Immigrants and Family Values." *Commentary* (May 1993): 26-32.

Glazer, Nathan, ed. *Clamor at the Gates*. San Francisco: Institute for Contemporary Studies, 1985.

_____. "The Closing Door." *New Republic* (December 27, 1993): 15-20.

Gurwitt, Robert. "Back to the Melting Pot." *The Social Contract* (Fall 1992): 17-21.

Harrison, "American and Its Immigrants." *National Interest* (Summer 1992): 37-46.

"Immigration." *Editorial Research Reports* (June 1, 1986): 431-451.

"Immigration Reform: Pros and Cons." *Congressional Digest* (October 1989): 225-256.

Jencks, Rosemary, ed. *Immigration and Nationality Policies of Leading Migration Nations*. Washington, D.C.: Center for Immigration Studies, 1993.

Keely, Charles. *U.S. Immigration Policy: An Analysis*. New York: Population Council, 1979.

Kinsley, Michael. "Gatecrashers." *New Republic* (December 28, 1992): 6.

Lacey, Daniel. *The Essential Immigrant*. New York: Hippocrene Books, 1990.

Lamm, Richard and Imoff, Gary. *The Immigration Time Bomb*. New York: Dutton, 1985.

Lowell, Lindsay and Papademetriou, D. "Introduction: Immigration and U.S. Integration." *Policy Studies* (Summer 1992): 76-85.

Miles, Jack. "Blacks vs. Browns." *Atlantic Monthly* (October 1992): 41-68.

Moore, David. "America Feels Threatened by New Immigrants." *Gallop Poll Monthly* (July 1993): 2-16.

Morgenthau, Tom. "America: Still a Melting Pot?" *Newsweek* (August 9, 1993): 17-23.

Muller, Thomas. *Immigration and the American City*. New York: New York University Press, 1993.

Reich, Robert. "Friends or Strangers." *Washington Monthly* (February

1990): 53-60.

Rohter, Larry. "Florida Takes Fight On Immigration Policy to a New Battlefield." *New York Times* (February 11, 1994): A1, A8.

Rosenblatt, Roger. "Sunrise, Sunset." *New Republic* (December 27, 1993, 20-23.

Rothstein, Richard. "Immigration Dilemmas." *Dissent* (Fall 1993): 455-462.

Salinas, Peter. "Take a Ticket." *New Republic* (December 27, 1993): 13-15.

Simon, Julian. *The Economic Consequences of Immigration*. Cambridge: Blackwell, 1989.

_____. "Why Control the Borders?" *National Review* (February 1, 1993): 27-34.

Skerry, Peter. "Borders and Quotas: Immigration and the Affirmative Action State." *Public Interest* (Summer 1989): 86-102.

Sontag, Deborah. "Illegal Aliens Put Uneven Load On States." *New York Times* (September 5, 1994): A8, A14.

Stein, Dan, ed. *Immigration 2000*. Washington, D.C.: FAIR, 1992.

_____. "Why America Needs A Moratorium on Immigration." *The Social Contract* (Spring 1993): 55-56.

Suro, Roberto. *Remembering the American Dream*. Washington, D.C.: Brookings, 1994.

Tanton, John and Lutton, Wayne. "Immigration and Crime." *The Social Contract* (Spring 1993): 159-167.

Wattenberg, Ben. *The First Universal Nation*. New York: Macmillan, 1991.

Wattenberg, Ben and Zinsmeister, Karl. "The Case for More Immigration." *Commentary* (April 1990): 19-25.

Weidenbaum, Murray. "Leviathan in Rio." *National Review* (April 27, 1992): 44-45, 56.

Weiner, Tim. "U.S. to Charge Immigrants a Fee When They Seek Political Asylum." *New York Times* (February 17, 1994): A1, A12.

TWO

AFFIRMATIVE ACTION REVISITED

Over thirty years ago, in 1963, affirmative action had its beginnings as a policy to remedy the long history of sexual and racial discrimination. Today affirmative action is under heavy fire and threatens to become a severely divisive and acrimonious bone of contention. California once again leads the way with a possible 1996 proposition to end all affirmative action policies at the state level. In addition, the courts are questioning affirmative action policies more closely. And talk radio is stirring up the issue at the grass roots. Has affirmative action gone too far? Do we need affirmative action anymore? Do people really understand what affirmative action is? Why not make public policy on the basis of socioeconomic need and disadvantage rather than sex and race? In general, is there a kind of mean-spirited countermovement in American politics, based on an American nationalistic core of rugged individualism, against any kind of government social policy that benefits anyone in particular on the basis of sex and race?

No doubt this flare-up over affirmative action is a preparatory battle, as each side measures the consequences, in advance, for the upcoming 1996 presidential election campaign. President Clinton needs to hold on to his Democratic base, and the Republicans see affirmative action as a wedge issue that could possibly separate 1992 Clinton voters from incumbent Clinton in the 1996 election.

In the affirmative action debate two sides have squared off in American politics. One side favors the renewal of affirmative action and governmental social policy and wants to carry on the battle for civil rights. The other side, in the name of civil liberties, advocates retreat from government social policies that are contrary to the so-called American norm of individual self-sufficiency. As is usual, what at first blush is a basic, politicized public policy issue turns out upon closer examination to be a much deeper matter of our cultural ideals and sense of social justice.

THE DIALOGUE

CIVIL RIGHTS: The political attack on affirmative action by so-called angry white males rests on a fundamental misunderstanding of what affirmative action means in policy and in practice. Affirmative action applies to the civil rights of women, minorities (specifically African-Americans, Hispanic-Americans, and Native Americans), and the handicapped. All of these groups have historically suffered acts of discrimination and are, as a consequence, disadvantaged in terms of equal opportunities. The major beneficiaries of affirmative action to date are women. Do angry white males not care about the fate of their working mothers, wives, sisters, and daughters? Or is it that attacks on affirmative action are really scapegoating racial and ethnic minorities? Why do we have to personalize this issue when we should need only enlist our sense of justice to see this as fairly promoting equality of opportunity, an agreed-upon, overall, common good?

CIVIL LIBERTIES: The major problem with affirmative action is that it deals with people as categories or groups rather than as individuals. Our country was founded on individual rights and liberties, not group rights and liberties. You ignore that many individuals not covered by affirmative action laws have been discriminated against and lack equality of opportunity also. Affirmative action unfairly privileges certain categories of Americans while it forgets about any other Americans who are disadvantaged. It is not just white males who have had enough of affirmative action. Many Asians and Jews see affirmative action as a threat to their opportunities. A number of black persons are leading the fight against affirmative action in California; they resent affirmative action policy because it stereotypes them as needy and not able to make it on their own merits.

    The zealous promotion of affirmative action is beyond what the civil rights movement and the Civil Rights acts were all about. Civil rights meant ensuring everyone their political right to vote and participate in our civil or political society. When the civil rights movement attained these fundamental objectives this movement then advanced to the area of social and economic interests and outcomes. However, the civil libertarian stresses the importance of individual rights and equality of opportunity. You conceal an attempt to achieve equality of outcome by advocating equality of opportunity. The mobilization of government to carry out social and economic transformation is a very radical matter about which there will be deep controversy. Affirmative action laws and policies have not worked without compelling racial and sexual quotas and timetables. A significant majority of 65% to 70% of Americans opposes affirmative action. Even in the communities targeted by affirmative action, the majority in favor of affirmative action is below 60%. The time has come to fight and penalize racial and sexual discrimination without resorting to affirmative action quotas.

CIVIL RIGHTS: The reason a majority of Americans have turned against affirmative action is the scapegoating politics of misrepresentation regarding what affirmative action actually is. Examine the 1994 campaign ads of Senator Jesse Helms! Whole groups are being scapegoated; there is no real commitment to looking at women and minorities simply as individuals seeking equality of opportunity. Until we reach the day when we are economically sex and color blind (assuming that such invisibility is a completely desirable goal), we will have to take head-on the importance of groups. Women and minorities are constantly defined by their sexual and racial group attributes, which of course amounts to sexism and racism. That is why affirmative action exists, to overcome this racism and sexism.

Affirmative action means four different things. I am confident that most Americans will support at least three of these four definitions, if only we make the proper kinds of distinctions among them. First, affirmative action originally only advised all employers and admission officers to consider whether equally-qualified women and minorities should be given the break when the composition of the workforce, school, or management level underrepresented women and minorities. Underrepresentation is a rough measure of the female and minority population in an area, or a rough measure of the available women and minorities for an occupation or career. All that was asked is a favorable, affirmative consideration of women and minorities in light of past, if not prevailing, unequal opportunities. The only time sex, race/ethnicity, and handicap would be relevant was after a judgement of the qualifications of applicants. A woman, minority, or handicapper would have to be among the finalists on their own individual merits.

Second, affirmative action policy measures the commitment of public sector and private sector employers by examining their pool of applicants.

Employers should advertise far and wide to ensure a representative pool of applicants. In no way does affirmative action policy require the hiring, admitting, or promoting of women and minorities. Such a quota plan actually is unconstitutional under the *Bakke v. University of California Medical School at Davis*, 1986. This evaluation of employers' pools is a good faith test of an employer's concern or affirmative intentions. Such an employer would hire a qualified women or minority if available.

Third, affirmative action quotas are constitutional as an ex post facto remedy for actual sexual and racial discrimination when proven in a court of law. What other remedy is there that changes a systematic pattern of discriminatory behavior? Yes, such quotas will disadvantage some white males, but previously the employer had discriminated in favor of white males. Justice requires a court-ordered quota and timetable plan to correct for and compensate past wrongs. Such court-ordered affirmative action plans have a time limit. People who are caught discriminating deserve this punishment.

Fourth, and most controversially, affirmative action policy has led to "goals and timetables" to improve women's and minority representation in the workforce and in schools. In most cases these are voluntary plans in the private sector. In the public sector, affirmative action goals and timetables may be required. Goals are not quotas because there is not a set, determined, number of women and minorities that must be hired, admitted, and promoted. Instead, there is a goal or target figure which may be underachieved, hit, or surpassed. This definition establishes affirmative action in the strongest sense because it is premised on the strategy that real, quantifiable change should occur. At this point everything depends on how strong a person's belief is in the need for affirmative action as a remedy given a fairly intractable economic reality of sexual and racial discrimination.

The civil rights movement naturally advanced from strictly political issues (voting and office holding) to economic issues (open housing, jobs, bank loans, etc.). There is no doubt that economic issues are more heated and controversial because people feel and believe that if someone else succeeds, they lose. We have to correct this zero-sum frame of mind with a positive-sum (I-win, you-win) attitude. Are we not all better off when qualified women and minorities get what they deserve? Can a society fulfill its potential if certain categories of people are systematically discriminated against? If this expression of civil rights is really just promotion of socioeconomic interests, then these are the socioeconomic interests of us all, assuming that we have a vibrant sense of social justice.

CIVIL LIBERTIES: Your definition of affirmative action is disengaged from the years of experiences that people have had being told that they did not get the job, the promotion, the admission to a school because they did not have female or minority status. There is a seething resentment and animosity about this "reverse discrimination." Workers have had to deal with underqualified, affirmative action employees. What happened to the norm of merit, i.e., hiring, admitting, or promoting the most qualified person? How can we be better off as a society if "bean counting" rather than merit is the way we make decisions.

There are so many disturbing incidents, especially in the mandatory affirmative action programs of governments, where government agencies and public schools have been required to fill positions with women and minorities. In order to fill positions with women and minorities, the new affirmative action standard is "minimally qualified," not the best or greatest qualifications. Such an affirmative action practice undermines our central belief in the American Dream that a person who works hard will succeed rather than just getting entitlements on the basis of sex, race, or ethnic status, all of which we have no choice about.

In practice, the term "goals" is but a euphemism for "quotas." Agencies and businesses that contract with governments know they will be judged on the basis of their numbers. Everyone knows that certain job positions must be filled with women and/or minorities. Even the *Bakke* case, which bans quotas, admits considerations of gender and race, if you do not admit openly that these are the sole or predominant factors for a decision.

CIVIL RIGHTS: The term "reverse discrimination" is a complete misnomer when talking about affirmative action. Affirmative action is a positive, not a negative, policy to correct for past and present discrimination. Yes, some white males may not get jobs that they once got without having to compete fairly with women and minorities. And that is the rub. The anger over affirmative action is the anger of those who now have to compete in a structurally changing economy where many white males no longer can just get a good job without considerable classroom, book learning.

The fallacy being committed here is the fallacy of equivalence. Are women and minorities on the same level playing field as white males when they go for a job? Do not white males on average have more opportunities and connections than women and minorities? Which ones are the disadvantaged relatively speaking? Who has experienced a long legacy of sexism and racism?

The facts are that sexism and racism are still alive in our economy. Studies involving apartment managers, bank loan officers, and car dealers demonstrate that a white couple gets more favorable treatment than a black couple about 60% of the time, even though both couples present themselves with the same type of jobs, incomes, assets, and middle-class appearances. The rules of the game are different for blacks and Latinos. Clearly, women are taken advantage of in many situations. A recent study proves that the glass ceiling exists—women can see where they could be in upper management, but they cannot get there. Women have over 40% of all jobs in the workforce, but they have less than 5% of senior management positions. Women and minorities are seen as a threat to upper management. Rarely do they receive close mentoring and encouragement to rise to the top of their profession.

Your talk about merit presumes that some meritocracy exists or should exist. The hard facts are that the good ol' boy network and upper class advantages and connections determine who is going places. Rarely does pure merit on the basis of credentials and performance decide who gets the job or promotion. You have to get along to go along, and many women and minorities are excluded from the socializing that establishes the grounds for climbing career ladders. At the present time we have all kinds of special preferences for veterans, for alumnae, for whoever knows whom, and so on. White males especially in the middle and upper classes have more connections, more opportunities, and more advantages. Affirmative action is only barely able to correct for these prevailing institutionalized biases.

CIVIL LIBERTIES: Your argument degenerates into victimization status, which is hardly the appropriate basis for people finding and taking the initiative to better themselves. Consequently, there is a knee-jerk dependence on government to solve individual and group problems. Indeed, the courts should severely punish real sexual and racial discrimination. In fact, Shelby Steele justifiably proposes that we make sexual and racial discrimination a criminal act subject to jail sentences. The threat of punishment backed up by test-casing people noted for discrimination (apartment managers, bank loan officers, employers, car dealers, etc.) would be more consistent with the sense of fairness found in American public opinion.

Affirmative action has backfired on its proponents because it has gone too far and has alienated many supporters of sexual and racial justice. The backlash factors are: (1) women and minorities will be hired only for low-level, segregated positions with little chance of promotion, all of which satisfies the "bean counters" or "number crunchers"; (2) there will be resentment within the workforce toward qualified women and minorities who are mistaken for unqualified workers hired only because of their race and/or sex; and (3) affirmative action programs have been manipulated by nonminorities for their own economic advantage flouting the original purpose of affirmative action set-asides. For example, windfall profits have been made by white males who fronted women or minorities to get radio, television, cable, or cellular phone licenses from the Federal Communications Commission's affirmative action preference programs that supposedly promote diversity. Programs that reward minority contractors, almost irrespective of the higher costs, have been discovered to be front operations with kickbacks to white males. These big deals do little to help the most socioeconomically disadvantaged, especially when these deals only benefit already well-placed women and minorities.

In addition to the backlash factors, there is evidence that many women and minorities who benefit from affirmative action do not need it since they have the education and credentials to be hired on their own nonsexual and nonracial merits. Affirmative action simply drives up the bidding war between employers for these advantaged women and minorities. Middle-income white women may be the greatest beneficiaries of affirmative action. As a consequence, disadvantaged (really down and out) women and minorities do not benefit as much from affirmative action. (In fact, affirmative action may contribute to the widening economic gap within minority groups, exacerbating relations within these minority groups.) We rely too much on affirmative action to bring about upward economic advances, and when this does not succeed because affirmative action is a limited tool, then there are demands for more extreme affirmative action measures that only contribute to a stronger backlash. The time has come to find alternatives to affirmative action.

There are reasons why many women do not advance despite affirmative action. Some choose not to put in the 50 to 60 hours a week to build a career because they want to have a strong family life. Other women are socialized to accept less. Some women prefer not to take on the greater responsibility and greater burdens that come with promotions. So it is not just a case of the "glass ceiling" of sexual discrimination. It makes no sense for a business enterprise or any organization not to want to benefit from the talent and productivity of women, but it may make a lot of sense for women not to participate in the male rat race to get ahead.

CIVIL RIGHTS: The backlash factors that you allude to can easily be corrected by having a well-tailored affirmative action program. You cannot just hire women and minorities and expect that they will naturally fit in. The workforce has to be educated regarding a responsible affirmative action policy so that women and minorities are not cold shouldered or discriminated against after being hired. Also employers could have "promotion from within" plans and job shadowing so that all employees know how they can advance within a company. Thus, segregated employees and dead-end jobs could be avoided. All of this is consistent with good employee morale, irrespective of women and minorities.

As for alternatives to affirmative action, what do you have in mind? Why not reparations? The Japanese-Americans who were interned during World War II and lost all their property were recently paid $1.2 billion. Native Americans over the years have received billions for broken treaties and atrocities. African-Americans who were in slavery for 246 years deserve reparations also.

CIVIL LIBERTIES: We need alternatives to affirmative action because affirmative action does little for those who cannot be in the pool of qualified professionals. In other words, we need to stress education and job training. Let's place more emphasis on Head Start and community development projects so we do not lose so many young people to unemployment, poverty, crime, and early death. We cannot expect more equality of outcome if we do not address equality of opportunity in education, family, and neighborhood.

If we are going to stay with affirmative action we should make it sex and race neutral. In other words, we should make affirmative action apply to socioeconomically disadvantaged persons no matter what their race, ethnicity, or sex. Then there would be no grounds for a backlash from white males or other groups who are not eligible for affirmative action as it now stands. Such an affirmative action approach would not be overturned by the courts because a "socioeconomically compelling" law does not solely rely on preferential categories of race and sex such as set-asides and numerical goals and targets. How could disadvantaged women and minorities be hurt by changing affirmative action away from race and sex? Recent Supreme Court decisions (e.g., *Adarand Constructors Inc. v. Pena*, 1995) have moved in this direction by applying a "strict scrutiny" test (asking whether there was explicit, proven discrimination) and requiring a "compelling government interest" test (general socioeconomic disadvantage).

Affirmative action was originally intended to be temporary and short term. The time has come to build cross-racial, cross-sexual alliances to promote what is best for the disadvantaged rather than suffer the political conflict and possible failure that inevitably results from black-white, female-male divisions. Dr. Martin Luther King specifically advocated a Bill of Rights for the Disadvantaged, while rejecting a Black Bill of Rights.

CIVIL RIGHTS: Your alternatives definitely need to be carried out, but without abandoning affirmative action and without diluting and diverting affirmative action away from those groups who have uniquely suffered from severe discrimination, namely women and minorities. Without programs targeting the problems that women and minorities confront, then change and progress will be diminished for them. Furthermore, you do not properly gauge what is going on today in American politics. The uninformed public opinion dynamic is to cut off all who are disadvantaged. There is a strong belief that government at any level should not (or is unable to) promote any form of socioeconomic justice. Therefore, people should be cut loose to sink or swim on the basis of their own efforts. Such is the per(verse)suasion of Social Darwinism or survival of the fittest.

Can I believe that you really want to prosecute discrimination? Most glaringly disturbing is the fact that the Equal Employment Opportunities Commission has a backlog of 90,000 cases. So much for the record of the federal government to prosecute sexual and racial discrimination cases. There is a real breakdown in will and commitment to achieve concrete results. Two-thirds of the new employees in the work force from 1992 to the year 2005 will be nonwhite, and they deserve better protection and fairer opportunities.

A civil rights, affirmative action approach has been moderately successful, more than doubling the African-American middle class and breaking down occupational barriers for women. We still need affirmative action to enable women and minorities to be promoted into middle- and upper-management positions. There are 166 separate federal affirmative action programs and 9 million persons have benefitted from affirmative action. We do not need to destroy these programs that have initially had such a good track record. As President Lyndon Johnson succinctly put it, "You do not take a person who for years has been hobbled by chains, liberate him, bring him to the starting line of a race and then say, 'You are free to compete with all others,' and still justly believe you have been completely fair."

CIVIL LIBERTIES: Quoting President Johnson is a good idea because he refused to take affirmative action programs in the direction of quotas. President Nixon did that so he could then campaign against quotas. But the most important thing President Johnson was saying was that we need to find the best means to prepare all our people (especially the disadvantaged) for the workforce. This means conscientious efforts to upgrade public education, link K–12 education with workforce needs, provide real job training (and retraining) programs, and so on. I do not believe that American public opinion is against government programs that show real, concrete gains as opposed to open-ended, preferential entitlements. The decision by the University of California Board of Regents in July 1995 to end all affirmative action programs in the University of California system is a step in the right direction. To admit minority students who have a 51% graduation rate (compared to the 81% graduation rate of whites and Asians) is unfair to these minority students who then have to deal with personal failure. Many of these minority students are not from disadvantaged backgrounds anyway.

Dismantling affirmative action programs will also reduce the costs of complying with these programs costs that result in fewer job prospects. For example, businesses face great bureaucratic paperwork costs to comply with affirmative action laws. The more money spent on paperwork, the less money there is available for expansion and jobs. Also there is the further problem of governments having to forego the lowest bid on government contracts in order to award contracts to minority businesses. The taxpayers do not get the best deal for their money.

CIVIL RIGHTS: Once again it is not the affirmative action policy that is the problem in universities, but the failure to devise an affirmative action program that succeeds. Many universities do nothing to help disadvantaged students make the transition from deprivational environments to a university environment. The failure rate is high because there is little personal needs assessment and program tailoring. Why should not public universities have a commitment to benefitting broadly all people? A fact rarely publicly addressed is that the financial burden of public university education is borne more heavily by taxpayers who will never receive any higher education advantages. Likewise, when it comes to awarding government contracts, the government has a moral responsibility (distributive justice) to insure that the taxpayers' largesse is spent and distributed broadly rather than simply to make the rich richer. Nationwide we are talking about billions of dollars in affirmative action set-aside programs that can be incubator funds for minority and women's businesses to develop. The major difference between your side and our side is that we see the need for government to redistribute taxpayers' funds to create a fairer, more egalitarian society.

BIBLIOGRAPHY

Ayres, Drummond. "Conservatives Forge New Strategy to Challenge Affirmative Action." *New York Times* (February 16, 1995): A1, A11.

Belz, Herman. *Equality Transformed: A Quarter Century of Affirmative Action*. New Brunswick, N.J.: Transaction, 1991.

Berkman, Harvey. "Clinton Report Makes Case for Affirmative Action." *National Law Journal* (July 31, 1995): A11.

Bernstein, Richard. "Moves Underway in California to Overturn Higher Education's Affirmative Action Policy." *New York Times* (January 21, 1995): B7, B8.

Bok, Derek. "Admitting Success: The Case for Racial Preferences." *New Republic* (February 4, 1985): 14-16.

Carter, Stephen. *Reflections of an Affirmative Action Baby*. New York: Basic Books, 1992.

Chideva, Faral. "Equality? I'm Still Waiting." *New York Times* (March 11, 1995): op ed page.

Cohen, Carl. "Naked Racial Preference." *Commentary* (March 1986): 24-32.

Cohen, Richard. "Civil Rights Battle Is Won: Curb Use of Affirmative Action." *Washington Post* (January 31, 1995): A15.

Eberhard, Jennifer and Burks, Richard. "Rutgers, Race, and Reality." *New York Times* (March 11, 1995): op ed page.

Editorial. "The Nuclear Wedge Issue." *New York Times* (February 28, 1995): A12.

Glazer, Nathan. "The Affirmative Action Stalemate." *Public Interest* (Winter 1988): 99-114.

_____. *Affirmative Discrimination: Ethnic Inequality and Public Policy*. New York: Basic Books, 1987.

Greenhouse, "Affirmative Action Case Seems to Perplex Court." *New York Times* (January 18, 1995): A12, D20.

_____. "High Court Rules for Ex-Employee in a Job Bias Suit." *New York Times* (January 24, 1995): A1, A9.

Hacker, Andrew. "Affirmative Action: The New Look." *New York Review of Books* (October 12, 1989): 63-68.

Holmes, Stephen. "Affirmative Action, Yes, Though Not Now As Is." *New York Times* (March 10, 1995): A9, A21.

_____. "Review of Affirmative Action Gains Support." *New York Times*

(February 27, 1995): A10, A13.

Lockhart, Charles. "Socially Constructed Conceptions of Distributive Justice: The Case of Affirmative Action." *Review of Politics* (Winter 1994) 29-49.

Lynch, Frederick R. *Invisible Victims: White Males and the Crisis of Affirmative Action.* New York: Greenwood, 1989.

Kahlenberg, Richard. "Class Not Race." *New Republic* (April 3, 1995): 1-27.

Kilborn, Peter. "Women and Minorities Still Face Glass Ceiling." *New York Times* (March 16, 1995): C22.

Kindrow, G. "Affirmative Action Hiring: A Case Study." *Harpers* (July 1991): 27-35.

Maxwell, Bill. "Angry White Men." *Grand Rapids Press* (March 19, 1995): E5.

O'Neil, Dave. "Affirmative Action in the Labor Market." *Annals* (September 1988): 88-104.

Page, Clarence. "Affirmative Action Debate Waged at the 'Fairness' Front." *Detroit News* (April 9, 1995): 3B.

Purdum, Todd. "Senator Deals Blow to Affirmative Action." *New York Times* (March 10, 1995): A8, A16.

Raspberry, William. "Racism's Lost in the Bias Debate." *Grand Rapids Press* (March 19, 1995): E5.

Reed Adolph. "Assault on Affirmative Action." *Progressive* (June 1995): 18-20.

Reed, Leonard. "What's Wrong with Affirmative Action." *Washington Monthly* (January 1981): 24-31.

Rosenfeld, Michael. *Affirmative Action and Justice.* New Haven: Yale University Press, 1991.

Roelofs, Ted. "Reexamining Affirmative Action." *Grand Rapids Press* (April 9, 1995): E1, E4.

Schwartz, Herman. "In Defense of Affirmative Action." *Dissent* (Fall 1984): 406-414.

Sowell, Thomas. *Preferential Policies: An International Perspective.* New York: Morrow, 1990.

Steele, Shelby. "Affirmative Action Must Go." *New York Times* (March 1, 1995): op ed page.

Wilson, William Julius. *The Truly Disadvantaged.* Chicago: University of Chicago Press, 1987.

THREE

POLITICAL REDISTRICTING:

PRINCIPLES AND/OR POLITICS?

Every ten years after each decennial census the issue of reapportionment and redistricting occurs in our fifty states. Reapportionment and redistricting are not the same thing since there can redistricting or drawing new district lines without changing the "portion" of representatives allotted. Clearly, the redistricting process by state legislators, state governors, and state and federal courts (if required) is a highly charged, political matter: "to the victor goes the spoils." Can politics ever be taken out of politics and still have anything left?

Despite the inherently political nature of redistricting, there are principles involved. Frequently, the courts resort to principles to guide and apply norms to this political practice. Even if we discovered a god(dess) among us who was entirely neutral and disinterested, there still would be political winners and losers. The outcome still would matter. Nevertheless, we need not despair because we are not in a world all principles, nor all politics. Principles and politics interrelate and that is why we dialogue.

THE DIALOGUE

PRINCIPLES (Leave it be): The recent failed nomination of Lani Guinier
to be President Clinton's Director of the Office of Civil Rights and recent
Supreme Court decisions challenging political redistricting that benefits
minority, disadvantaged groups have brought to the forefront the
controversial nature of realizing political change through manipulating
political representation. At the heart of liberal democracy is the problem
of representation, not just participation. Everyone can participate (vote
in elections), but will everyone be represented among the decision makers
who hold real political power?   Furthermore, does the principle of
representation in democracy require that everyone have more than just a
voice and a vote?

It is one thing to have the right to vote (a central principle of
democracy) and another thing to demand as a right (an entitlement? one's
self-interest?) to get your own way. In a free democratic society there
will be more than voicing and voting; there will also be the protected
right to associate and the uncensored freedom of the press to propagate.
But there are still no guarantees that you will get your own way, be likely
to be in the majority, and never have to suffer the pangs of defeat.

Perhaps many people confuse a representative democracy operating
on the basis of majority rule with a pure democracy requiring unanimous
consent. It is true in a *pure* democracy every person must agree. Consent
must be always unanimous for a decision to go into effect. And perhaps
there are some issues of conscience (e.g., slavery and war) that require
complete agreement, otherwise the dissenter must leave such a society
(emigrate or be imprisoned/enslaved).   But we do not have a pure
democracy, nor would it be desirable given human limitations.
Communist regimes ruthlessly enforced a pure democracy in form,
namely, unanimous voting for only party-approved candidates.

However, in an impure, *representative* democracy (note in a pure
democracy every adult citizen would be a legislator and never would
alienate her/his voice and vote to any representative), we operate on the
practical principle of majority rule. People deliberate and persuade in
order to arrive at majorities, and yes the process should not be quick and
cheap. Certainly we need to extend the greatest likelihood for the largest
(most inclusive) majority. Representation always will be tenuous and
unsure since it is an alienation and a distance between the represented
(who embody the will of the people) and the representatives (hopefully,

those found wise in judgement).

POLITICS (Let us transform): Your principles abstract from and impoverish the reality of the political practices of democracy and representation in the United States. The whole history of representative democracy in the United States has been the struggle of individuals and groups to get political power and to exercise it. Now that women and minorities have formed powerful groups seeking substantive representation on the basis of their defined interests, we are told that we should put ourselves above our interests in the name of some abstract (white male?) principle of impure, representative democracy.

What needs close examination and analysis is the actual workings of majority rule. In reality, majority rule means the fixed, permanent, and continuous rule of the majority homogeneous group in the United States today. We have an electoral system (winner takes all in single-member districts) that guarantees the dominance of this homogeneous majority. It is not for nothing that Republicans and the Department of Justice under the Reagan and Bush administrations aligned with minority groups (blacks and Latinos) to create racially homogeneous districts. Put as many blacks and Latinos in their own separate districts and all other districts (naturally a majority of them) would be white, suburban, and Republican-inclined. This neosegregation gets both Republicans and minorities elected, but allows Republicans to attain a decisive majority over minorities and Democrats when in office.

Whoever controls, politically speaking, the redistricting process gets to define political outcomes for a generation or more. Is this a political plot, or what? If you truly believe in a political process that creates a broad-based, consensual majority and not just a limited, white Republican majority, then you will look at alternatives to our present political system of representation.

PRINCIPLES: Before considering whatever proposals you have to change the political process of representation, we need to be clear about the rules of the game in political redistricting. We believe there are fair and neutral political principles at stake that are not reducible to just plotting partisan political interests and political power. We go to the Supreme Court to find the principles that serve as criteria in the political process of redistricting. There are four such principles or guidelines: (1) "one person, one vote," which means that legislative districts within states are to be as close to mathematical equality in population as is possible; (2) all districts must be contiguous, i.e., there can be no districts separated and unconnected; (3) strange-shaped districts are suspect because, as much as possible, districts should recognize natural boundaries, political boundaries (county and city lines), and communities of interest; and (4) no districts should be drawn that divide up and dilute the concentrated strength of minorities (especially African-Americans and Hispanics) who have been discriminated against in the past and/or are now disadvantaged.

The Voting Rights Act of 1965 requires districts of equal population size and no discrimination against the voting power of racial and ethnic minorities. It is the interpretation of the 1982 amendment to the Voting Rights Act of 1965 that has started the violation of the criteria listed above. The 1982 amendment made it clear that minorities should have no fewer opportunities to participate and elect representatives of their choice. The implementation of this amendment after the 1990 census led to "racial gerrymandering." In other words, strange- and unreal-shaped districts became acceptable to guarantee "majority-minority districts." For example, the 12th congressional district in North Carolina covers 160 miles across North Carolina connecting four different cities by no more than a sliver of land following three different interstate highways! Such a serpentine district was labeled "bizarre" by Justice Sandra Day O'Connor. A North Carolina resident quipped, "If you drove down the interstate with both doors open, you'd kill most of the people in this part of the district." In 1993 in the Supreme Court case *Shaw v. Reno*, a five to four majority of the Court ruled that it was unconstitutional and contrary to the 14th Amendment's equal protection of the laws to devise districts segregated by race. There would have to be some sufficient justification constituting a "compelling government interest" to deny white citizens their voting rights.

The only way this racial gerrymandering could succeed was for the Republicans to play out their "racial card" for 1992. The more minorities (blacks and Latinos) they could stuff into central city, majority-minority districts (by definition a majority-minority district is 60% to 65% minority population), the more lily-white the suburban districts would be for Republicans to dominate. In the thirteen states with new majority-minority districts in 1992, Republicans picked up twelve seats. This was the result of increasing majority-minority districts from 38 in 1990 to 52 in 1992. The result has been called "voluntary resegregation" and the "new political reservation system" because minority elected officials now are isolated without the possibility of forming many coalitions with their natural Democratic allies.

POLITICS: Since this country started to draw district lines, we have had political designs to "gerrymander" districts for political power advantages. Minorities are only asking that they too have the kind of political leverage that white majority Americans have always had when Democrats or Republicans drew political district boundaries. The Supreme Court has wisely recognized that *both* partisan and racial gerrymandering deserve careful judicial scrutiny in order to determine whether there is discrimination. In the case of race, majority-minority districts may be created if there are: (a) a sufficient concentration of numbers of people discriminated against; (b) an established pattern of racial bloc voting exists; and (c) white bloc voting defeats minority candidates. If we truly lived in a country where there was no institutional, structural racism and sexism, then it would not matter whether women and minorities had their own representatives.

It is not just the whole history of racism and sexism. The prevailing power structures today still prevent minorities and women from getting public policy *outcomes* in accord with their interests. A *Congressional Quarterly* study revealed that white representatives supported Reagan-conservative legislation 63% of the time while black representatives supported such legislation only 28% of the time. It is falsely assumed that the civil rights movement needed only to extend the right to vote to all women and minorities and then nothing else would need to be done. Just having the right to vote does not mean that those who vote will be in the majority after all the votes are counted, never mind being in the majority vote of those in office who legislate. Majority rule all along the line persists in keeping women and minorities out of power when the majority rejects the interests of women and minorities.

As a consequence, there is a need for remedies that overcome the power of the majority rule when it is used to bolster the sexism and the racism of the white majority. You failed to mention the Supreme Court cases in the 1960s that overturned the way states were rigging redistricting to preserve the power of incumbents and people in rural areas. *Baker v. Carr* in 1962 established the legal, constitutional basis for adjusting state legislative districts to accommodate large population shifts in the state of Tennessee. Redistricting no longer was just a political decision that the courts would choose to avoid to review. In 1964 in *Reynolds v. Sims* and

Wesberg v. Sanders the Court affirmed the principle of "one person, one vote" and made this principle applicable to congressional districts as well. Some congressional districts at that time had a population ten times larger than other congressional districts.

A sense of justice requires that each person who votes have the same voting power as any other person voting in an election. It is no surprise that in 1986, in *Thornburg v. Gingles,* the Court ruled that it is unconstitutional to redistrict with an intent to dilute minority voting strength. If a redistricting scheme constantly prevents bloc minority votes from ever electing the representatives of their choice, then bloc minority votes are not equal in power and influence to the majority vote. What other remedy can there be for such racial discrimination than the drawing of district boundaries to include as many minorities as necessary to achieve majority-minority districts?

The severity of racial disenfranchisement is often ignored. Not since Reconstruction had there been a black congressmember from Louisiana, and there had been no black congressmembers from North Carolina in this century. For example, in 1991 25% of the population in New York City was Latino, yet Latinos had only 4% of the seats. An X-shaped district was drawn only a block wide at one point to pool Latino votes in Manhattan, Queens, and Brooklyn. The Congress that met in 1993 had 24 new majority-minority districts comprising 15 more African-Americans and 9 more Latinos. Now there are a total of 20 Latinos and 32 African-Americans in Congress. Previously white males were overrepresented in Congress.

We need to move to an election system that is based on proportional representation, which is to say, representation based on ethnic/racial and gender proportions in the population. Then we can achieve truer equality and justice.

PRINCIPLES: The key phrases of your argument are "intent to dilute," "constantly prevents," and "bloc minority vote." There must be a clear, demonstrable intent proved in a court of law and not just an unfavorable result. A result unfavorable to some group could be accidental, or if intentional, not at all based on racial or sexual discrimination. Furthermore, to show an injustice you have to prove that a minority bloc is *constantly* in the minority, that is, always losers in elections. The tyranny of the majority only exists if there are permanent minority losers. Of course, extremists and fanatics who are antidemocratic and do not deserve to ever be in any majority do not count in favor of a tyranny of the majority charge. Furthermore, why is it assumed that minority voters vote as a bloc? Is there not diversity of voting preferences and diversity of interests among minorities? Is it politically healthy to segregate minority voters in districts that are predominantly one race, or one ethnic group, or one party?

The Supreme Court has made a serious mistake getting involved in the politics (*Davis v. Bandemer*, 1986) and race issue (*Thornburg v. Gingles*, 1986) of political redistricting. No doubt the Supreme Court is reconsidering "racial gerrymandering" not only because of public opinion backlash, but also because race-mandering may unjustifiably privilege "race." In 1994 federal courts in Georgia and Louisiana (as a result of the *Shaw v. Reno*, 1993) found racial gerrymandering unconstitutional in these states since there was no other (overriding) justification for certain districts than race. Equal rights is one thing almost everyone agrees about, but race-specific remedies are deeply controversial. In 1995, the Supreme Court found in *Johnson v. Miller* that race cannot be the predominant factor in drawing district lines. Thus Georgia's 11th congressional district was declared unconstitutional. The Court is now requiring that other factors are needed to balance with majority-minority district creation, namely, communities of interest, geographic communities, and even incumbent protection.

As for partisan gerrymandering, two political scientists, Andrew Gelman and Gary King, have found that partisan gerrymandering tends to increase electoral responsiveness since it shakes up the existing system. Partisan gerrymandering is not simply an incumbent protection plan since political parties tend to try to maximize their partisan support in many districts (greed), not just in a few, which dilutes the strength of incumbents. To get more seats you create more districts, which necessarily have smaller voting margins. Also, incumbents fear too great electoral safety in their districts since it encourages political primary competition from within their own party. Consequently, partisan gerrymandering (especially in an era of weakening political party affiliation) does not create a "lock" for political parties. Racial gerrymandering, however, is an entirely different matter than partisan gerrymandering since the former is much more successful and biased in guaranteeing uniform and uncompetitive racial results.

Is not proportional, descriptive representation via majority-minority districts a kind of quota system of legislative seat set-asides? Do we need to believe that white people are the intractable enemy of minority interests? Governor Wilder of Virginia and Senator Carol Mosely-Braun of Illinois among others disprove the belief that majority white voters will not elect black candidates.

POLITICS: It would be a better world if there were no racism and African-Americans, Latinos, and others did not have to congeal into voting blocs for self-protection. But there is no other choice when you are beleaguered. There is a distinctive set of values that are achieved when minorities and women have representatives who are descriptively the same race, ethnicity, and gender as themselves. First of all, there is the belief that it is easier to make oneself understood when you are dealing with someone who has shared the same experiences racially, ethnically, sexually, economically, and politically. You can feel just where the shoe pinches.

Secondly, there is the role model factor. Clearly, the disadvantaged and the discriminated against need the psychological boost that comes from identification with someone just like them who has succeeded against the odds.   There is nothing peculiar about descriptive or delegate representation. A whole book has been written by Richard Fenno on the homestyle characteristics of *all* members of Congress, who naturally express and witness the similarities they have with the folks back home. Psychologically, it is natural for all political participants to gravitate toward those who are mirror images of themselves or with whom they can establish bonds of identity. It is of special, overriding importance, given the horrible discrimination that certain racial and linguistic groups have suffered in the United States, that they have their own representatives who can address the needs of their disadvantaged constituents.

Once the white power structure at the state/local level had to accept majority-minority districts and the presence of minorities in legislative bodies, the rules and powers for officeholders were changed. Minority representatives have been frozen out of budgetary decisions and legislative deal making. That is why extraordinary measures have to be devised to ensure that minority elected officeholders can actually represent their constituents and make a difference once elected.

Recent Supreme Court decisions are much more tenuous than you let on. For example, the same day *Johnson v. Miller* was delivered striking down Georgia's 11th congressional district, the Supreme Court upheld California's nine black and Hispanic congressional districts. Both *Shaw v. Reno* and *Johnson v. Miller* were five-to-four decisions. Only two justices in that majority (Scalia and Thomas) are absolutely opposed to "race-based" policies. Consequently, seven Justices are willing to accept the constitutionality of government remedies to correct for racial discrimination. In a sense we are back to *Bakke*, which is to say, that we have to do a better job fashioning majority-minority districts so they are constitutionally upheld.

PRINCIPLES: The principle one should be striving for is an integrated, color-blind society. Your recommendations for redistricting lead to voluntary resegregation—provoking hostile, us versus them, divisions in our common society. What is most at stake for all of us are the substantive issues of politics and what is called virtual or trustee representation. Just because someone is descriptively representative of us, which is to say the same race, ethnicity, and gender, does not necessarily mean these representatives will serve the best substantive interests of their mirror constituents. In fact, a recent study by Carol Swain, reveals that liberal white representatives serve black interests just as well as black representatives. If Republicans are permitted to dilute the liberal Democratic vote by concentrating as many liberal Democrats (especially minorities) in as few districts as possible, then black representatives will not be able to build coalitions to constitute a majority in legislatures. This is a classic case of a group that would do better for itself as a whole if they did *not* pursue their narrow group self-interest.

POLITICS: Unfortunately, we are stuck in a situation where who knows what is better: to elect a marginalized minority officeholder, or to elect a number of officeholders who owe "something" to minority voters while not being minorities themselves? No longer is it enough just to have the right to vote. We have to have the success of actually electing someone who previously would never have been elected.

Besides the creation of majority-minority districts we could also experiment with cumulative or preference voting, something that U.S. corporation stockholders, some U.S. voting jurisdictions, and other countries use. Cumulative voting means at-large, multimember districts that enable people to have as many votes as there are candidates to be elected from an at-large district. In other words, if there are five elected officials for one district, then each voter will have five votes that can be cast all for one person or split up any way the voter chooses. This kind of preference, weighted, and cumulative voting registers voter intensity. To take an example, in the past the white majority vote prevented any minority candidates from winning in rigged, at-large districts that diluted the minority vote, keeping the minority in the permanent, losing minority. Cumulative voting changes all of this and is better than carving out single-member districts and segregating the minority vote in majority-minority districts. Cumulative voting enables *any* intense group to concentrate its voting power and to elect its representatives who otherwise never would get elected. Cumulative voting is clearly race-neutral (whereas majority-minority districts clearly are not) and only favors those groups who succeed in organizing voters.

PRINCIPLES: You fail to consider some extremely negative consequences that come from your scheme of cumulative voting. While on the surface cumulative voting is race-neutral, its consequences are just as severe, if not more severe, than majority-minority districts. Not only will the black vote count as an intensely concentrated bloc, but all kinds of extremist groups are possible especially to counteract the black vote's success. David Duke had his limited state/local successes for good reason. The KKK, the NRA, antiabortionists, fundamentalists, capital punishment advocates, and all kinds of locally intense interest groups will flower electorally in ways they cannot even imagine now. Who knows what extremists are out there just waiting for this cumulative voting opportunity? Most proportional representation schemes lead to multi-party, faction-ridden politics where disagreements are magnified and decision-making paralyzed.

Cumulative voting encourages the kind of passionate factionalism that Madison feared in a democracy as democracy's most natural and dangerous disease. Even when minority candidates are elected, they will be isolated in legislative bodies. Consequently, minority status cannot become a majority factor precisely because your electoral scheme, cumulative voting, divides the body politic. You have not found the Madisonian means that "extends," "broadens," and unites us, despite our natural diversity of interests.

POLITICS: The truth in politics, in fact the major axiom in politics today, is that those who are organized have political power. We need to encourage and broaden the possibilities of organization for those who are presently unorganized in order that more Americans have political leverage. Politics is inevitably about "interests" and their aggregation. Yes, there may be at first more "factions" or interest groups, but they will soon see the need to build coalitions with one other. That is why the consequences you fear are not likely; they are only participatory, expressive, democratic consequences. Extremists will be isolated and fail because they cannot build the coalitions necessary for vote concentration and success. Cumulative voting is much more likely to build cross-racial coalitions than our present winner-takes-all, single-member district election system, and cumulative voting does not isolate and segregate as do majority-minority district election systems.

There will be circumstances where we confront third stage problems. At the first stage, you remember, voting rights had to be won by women and minorities. At the second stage, just electing women and minorities had to be fought for. At the third stage, substantive decisions by legislative bodies benefitting women and minorities have to be gained. At each stage there is the problem of winning for those not in the majority. A tyranny of the majority means the permanent exclusion of those who never constitute a majority at the second and/or third stages.

Special provisions need to be enacted at times to make it possible for minorities to win and succeed. For example, why not a minority veto when it comes to certain legislation of extreme interest to minorities such as civil rights and welfare policy? There can be supermajority requirements (two-thirds or three-fourths majorities) to protect minorities from majority tyranny. In many instances the U.S. Congress has supermajority provisions (e.g., ratifying treaties, proposing constitutional amendments, passing laws without any amendments being made on the floor of the House or Senate, removal of office of the President or a federal judge). There can be plural executives to include minority representation at crucial and powerful levels of decision making. An activist government and group power are what disadvantaged minorities seek since they cannot rely on their individual initiative alone to raise themselves up.

PRINCIPLES: The problem with your "politics" is that it is so powerfully interest-based. You resurrect specific racial, ethnic, and gender interests assuming they are necessarily contrary to the interests of the majority of our society. Thus there is no way to avoid conflict, hostility, and division. Your interest group politics fabricates and provokes a tyranny of the majority. Civil rights issues up to the point of not being special preferences and social welfare policy up to the point of working for people are solid majority-supported policies. Sure we will argue over what a specific preference is and what is needed in civil rights. And we will disagree over how far social welfare policy should go. But these are natural differences of degree, not fundamental, ideological "lines drawn in the sand."

What we need in our politics is not more, heated-up interest group wheeling and dealing. We need to create a public space for rational deliberation and persuasion, with the hope of transcending our narrow self-interests in the effort of finding the public good. Lani Guinier, for example, has no overriding, transcendent notion of the "public interest." She assumes a kind of government that will have to "satisfy" all kinds of interests without any normative criteria except intensity. The emphasis is entirely on results or outcomes rather than on procedural ("due process") justice. Government has the role of being a major provider rather than simply getting out of the way so individual initiative can prosper.

Your proposals for a minority veto or a supermajority vote sound similar to the great slaveholder advocate John Calhoun, who wanted to give the South an absolute bloc vote if need be to stand in opposition to the bloc of Northern states and the bloc of Western states. Each of these three blocs of states would have an absolute veto. Calhoun called this the theory of concurrent majority, and it was conceived to prevent a tyranny of majority. It is odd that Lani Guinier never mentions Calhoun in her book, *The Tyranny of the Majority*. This is positive proof how promoting group interests can backfire if the "wrong group" coalesces and has predominance. We do not know exactly (especially beforehand) what a "wrong group" is in a democracy. That is why we rely on the procedures of majority rule that appeal to the best judgement of the citizens' representatives.

POLITICS: The comparison to Calhoun causes no difficulty since Calhoun's bloc voting plan could be appreciated from a race-neutral standpoint. Also I have no problem with the white minority in South Africa having similar voting advantages as a protected minority. More importantly, your idealistic turn, resorting to some transcendent vision of the public good, puts a mask over the very ugly reality of hard core racism and sexism in our society. All of this needs to be brought out into the open. Such racism and sexism is pervasive, institutional, well-entrenched, and more sophisticated than ever in achieving its exclusive objectives. All this talk about aspiring to the public good is either naive or a form of dissimulation. Women and minorities are mightily frustrated, especially after the Clarence Thomas–Anita Hill affair. How many more Willie Hortons, Rodney Kings, Lani Guiniers, and Jocelyn Elders do we need to have before you get the point?

Mechanisms have to be devised in politics if our politics is going to mean anything and change for the better. Note how public opinion polls across the board give high disapproval ratings to our political representatives. A more inclusive politics, including women and minority voices, is the necessary basis for political transformation.

I am a realist who recognizes the very real power of group interests. Individuals politically only make sense and have political power if organized in a group. Consequently, it is natural to recognize group rights, and group rights are a natural extension of individual rights since individuals constitute groups.

PRINCIPLES: You charge that racism and sexism are endemic, and they everywhere obscure and falsify what is happening in American politics today. But political developments reveal a different understanding. For example, three major cities no longer have black mayors—Los Angeles, Philadelphia, and New York. A fourth city, Detroit, has a new black mayor who is anything but racially confrontational. Americans in cities and elsewhere are looking for strong managers and good government types who can run our cities efficiently, clean up corruption, provide basic services, and promote economic development. Racially strident mayors (Washington, Young, Berry) or even race relations expert mayors (Dinkins and Bradley) no longer have majority credibility. The prominence for a while of General Colin Powell's presidential candidacy rested on his command/managerial skills rather than on any Jesse Jackson type, exhortatory rhetoric. Other nonblack minorities (especially Latinos) are also switching to good-government mayors. Jesse Jackson's rainbow coalition did not flourish and is not feasible. The successful black public official today is not a race leader but an accommodationist who will work with businesspeople and reach out to the white suburbs.

Your expansion of individual rights to group rights politicalizes and exacerbates issues on the basis of race, gender, and ethnicity. The lady statue of justice is blind. It is not for nothing that we have a long legal history of individual rights; we want to recognize all people as individual human beings rather than as discriminatory categories of people.

POLITICS: The business establishment tries to control our cities and in many ways can threaten the tax base of a city. The so-called good government forces you appeal to are predominately probusiness, white, middle- and upper-class people. What you see happening is a backlash against facing race and poverty issues. When the general public realizes that managerial efficiency does not build a spirit of loyalty and belonging, which is necessary for community development and empowerment, then there will be a return to mayors who provide more than just basic services and fiscal responsibility. A strong mayor provides the patronage and public jobs that bind people to the good of the city. Chicago Mayor Richard Daley Jr. knows that he has to be this kind of political mayor (as well as a good manager) to achieve longevity in office. The question is whether mayors, be they white or black, include the broad diversity of ethnic groups in their governing and decision-making process. Special procedures and special yardsticks have to be used to ensure broad representation. All mayors and other political leaders recognize the group nature of our political society. People think politically in terms of group interests, and politicians know they have to satisfy such groups in a democracy.

PRINCIPLES: But concentrating on group affiliation ignores the issue overlap from group to group. This is the basis for coalition building and producing the largest possible majority hopefully comprising the "public good." Your kind of politics leads to calculations on the basis of "what is in it for my group" and a kind of cynicism about the "public good" (can we afford this?), rather than reasoning that stresses "how can we define issues to include as many groups as possible" on the road to "the greatest good of the greatest number."

BIBLIOGRAPHY

Ang, Douglas. *Real Choices/New Voices: The Case for Proportional Representation*. Berkeley: University of California Press, 1993.

Applebome, Peter. "Suits Challenging Redrawn Districts That Help Blacks." *New York Times* (February 14, 1994): A1, A12.

Cook, Rhodes. "Map-Drawers Must Toe the Line in Upcoming Redistricting." *Congressional Quarterly* (September 1, 1990): 2786-2793.

Duncan, Phil. "Black Representation and Redistricting." *Congressional Quarterly* (August 19, 1989): 2198.

Elving, Ronald D. "Redistricting: Drawing Power With a Map." *Editorial Research Reports* (February 15, 1991): 98-111.

Fenno, Richard. *Homestyle: House Members in Their Districts*. Glenview: Scott Foresman, 1978.

Gelman, Andrew and King, Gary. "Enhancing Democracy Through Legislative Redistricting." *American Political Science Review* (September 1994): 541-555.

Greenhouse, Linda. "Supreme Court Spars on Validity of District Based Solely on Race." *New York Times* (April 20, 1993): A1, A12.

_____. "Court to Hear New Challenge to District Drawn for a Black." *New York Times* (December 9, 1994): 1, 7.

Grofman, Bernie. *Political Gerrymandering and the Courts*. New York: Agathon, 1990.

Guinier, Lani. *The Tyranny of the Majority*. New York: Free Press, 1994.

Klein, Joe. "Principle or Politics." *Newsweek* (June 14, 1993): 29.

Lemann, Nicholas. "Race, Reform, and Urban Voters." *New York Times* (November 4, 1993): op ed page.

Lichtman, Allan. "Quotas Aren't the Issue." *New York Times* (December 7, 1994): op ed page.

McCoy, Frank. "Racial Politics and the High Court." *Black Enterprise* (November 1993): 25.

Meachem, Jon. "Voting Wrongs." *Washington Monthly* (March 1993): 28-32.

Pitkin, Hannah. *The Concept of Representation*. Berkeley: University of California Press, 1967.

Rush, Mark E. "In Search of a Coherent Theory of Voting Rights."

Review of Politics (Summer 1994) 503-523.

Scott, Matthew. "Redistricting Expected to Increase Black Influence." *Black Enterprise* (March 1992): 16.

Sunstein, Cass. "Voting Rites." *New Republic* (April 25, 1994): 34-38.

Swain, Carol. *Black Faces, Black Interests*. Cambridge: Harvard University Press, 1993.

Thernstrom, Abigail. "By Any Name, It's a Quota." *New York Times* (December 7, 1994): op ed page.

_____. "Guinier Miss." *New Republic* (June 14, 1993): 16-19.

FOUR

IQ, POVERTY, AND RACE:

FOR WHOM THE BELL CURVE TOLLS?

What does social science research, especially that involving statistics, tell us about equality and inequality in American society? What political conclusions do we draw from such social science evidence regarding public policy enactments? Some scholars point to environment, which is to say socioeconomic circumstances, to identify the root causes of poverty and inequality. Other, more controversial, scholars consult intelligence and heredity (I.Q. and genetics) as the dominant factors explaining economic success and well-being. Is intelligence really distributed in a "bell curve" with the inevitable result that we have a caste-like, pyramidal society?

Many writers have begun to talk about the growing and fixed underclass including the greater number of those falling from the middle class into the ranks of the poor. Are we seeing the formation of a sharply distinct, two-class society of haves versus have-nots, with the middle class shrinking? Is there anything we can do in regard to the demands of an advanced capitalistic society which is increasingly sophisticated, technological, and based on brain power? Are we dealing with a class-based dilemma, or is race (also) a legitimate factor in this division of America? These questions haunt the highly controversial book by Richard Herrnstein and Charles Murray, *The Bell Curve*.

THE DIALOGUE

COGNITIVE ELITE: The world we live in and our future world will require and depend on more intelligence exhibited by people in the labor market. Brains now overwhelm brawn. Consequently, demonstrated intelligence will be highly rewarded, and those who cannot meet such high intelligence demands will be left behind. A cognitive elite will rule in every sector of our economy. Structural economic change, which is to say going from a blue collar manufacturing economy to a white collar, technological economy, is the irreversible path of our historical, socioeconomic development. In the past such a premium on intelligence was never required for wage earners or for career economic success. People of all kinds mingled and integrated with each other. We never had to tap into the full extent of people's intelligence in the cognitive sense. But times have radically changed. Now we are achieving a full-fledged, meritocratic society.

Already this cognitive elite is distinguished and demarcated by its special, exclusive neighborhoods, schools, workplaces, leisure spots, etc. Outsiders and inferiors are prohibited except as service personnel. Accordingly, we as a society no longer can afford to ignore the issue of intelligence and IQ, the major determinants of success and productivity in our increasingly sophisticated society. A taboo and unofficial prohibition previously was placed on genetics and intelligence research, ignoring the evidence that IQ and heredity outweigh socioeconomic environment especially now that we have a sophisticated society that has: (a) demanded cognitive stratification, and (b) has diminished inequality of opportunity, environmentally speaking.

SOCIOECONOMIC CLASS: Your comments contain some observations as to the general characteristics of our advanced capitalistic society which are not greatly in dispute since we all know the statistics of the decline in the blue collar manufacturing sector in the United States and Western Europe and the disappearance of many urban, entry-level, low-skill jobs. No longer can a young person afford to just get a high school diploma, and even an undergraduate degree is not enough in many cases. Education and training will have to be lifelong for workers to stay abreast of rapid change. But is this solely a matter of "intelligence"? Loosely speaking, sure we have to expect more intelligence via more education. What is this "intelligence"? Is it captured by standardized test scores and

IQ results? Even though there may be a good match (correlation) between test scores and IQ on one hand and then occupational advances and income on the other hand, nevertheless what makes our existing society the unquestioned norm for excellence? Have not many outstanding people throughout history failed to fit in (e.g., Socrates, Christ, Buddha, Thomas More, H.D. Thoreau)? There is a glaring neglect and stolid conservatism (on the part of *The Bell Curve* proponents) in their failure to question radically our society and the kind of narrow-minded "intelligence" it demands.

There are many kinds of intelligence: artistic, scientific, moral, philosophical, etc. The authors of *The Bell Curve* fail to see and affirm this multiplicity, and the political consequence is a threat to the foundation stone of the American republic as defined by Thomas Jefferson in the Declaration of Independence: "all men are created equal". What equality means here is "equal human worth" despite diversities of intelligence and any unequal physical and mental endowments. This is the basis for political equality (we are all equally citizens—"one person, one vote") and equality of opportunity, which taps the full potential of human beings, all of whom are equal in integrity.

The most shocking aspect of Herrnstein and Murray's book is that they state that equality of opportunity has been fairly well achieved in the United States, therefore most remaining differences are heritable and genetic. Again, the fascination with statistics, such as the median education for blacks being 12.8 years and for whites 12.6 years, does not prove that these groups have the same opportunities. Quantity does not mean quality. Socioeconomic factors leave low-income people (whether black or white) at a tremendous disadvantage in their upbringing and socialization process. Intelligence is simply not a fixed, one-dimensional property; it is a process. We are in actuality nowhere near factoring out socioeconomic environments so that only heredity is left to explain differences. Of course, we will never be able to isolate environment and heredity because we cannot put people into laboratories like white mice. In reality, nature and nurture interact from the beginning; they are inextricably mixed. Again, we need to acknowledge our common humanity irrespective of any *relative* stratification that modern society engenders.

COGNITIVE ELITE: We have no complaint with your emphasis on multiple intelligences, the human factor, and the importance of dissidents in relation to modern society. All that is fine and well except for the omnipresent fact that all of this is less important and relevant because of the unavoidable demands of our modern society. It is our contention that few people disagree (although most people are unwilling to face the consequences) that our society is forming a cognitive, technocratic elite and that this will determine people's various standards of living. By "intelligence," we mean: (a) the ability to learn and generalize from what we learn, and (b) the capacity to infer and to apply relationships from experience. This type of intelligence allows a person to adopt readily to his/her environment.

Alarming facts and figures demonstrate a growing underclass of adolescents with antisocial norms such that physical violence, immediate gratification, and predatory sex have become ways of life. Just about 30% of all live births or 1.2 million children in 1991 were born to unmarried women (over half, 707,572, to white women). Only 35% of these women are high school graduates (down from 48% in 1981). Also, 69% of these women had incomes of less than $20,000. In addition to all this, we have a government ready to subsidize heavily such behavior, and a culture and a society unwilling to stigmatize and penalize this behavior. We have to be "politically correct" and *not* call this the "illegitimacy" peril. Cannot we expect that this illegitimacy rate will continue to snowball? All of this destructive behavior strongly correlates with intelligence.

As for SES (socioeconomic status), you know that it is possible statistically to separate out SES variables leaving heredity as the only factor left to account for differences. When psychometricians do this, they find a range of 0.40 to 0.80 (40% to 80%) that is heritable when explaining intelligence. This conclusion is simply mainstream science. In addition, we have found that it is very difficult to change our environment, which nurtures intelligence in such a way as to increase IQ. Outside interventions (e.g., government social programs such as Head Start) do not make any significant and lasting changes for the better. A person's IQ at age 8 is not going to change much for the better throughout his/her adulthood.

SOCIOECONOMIC CLASS: We do not have to accept and agree to live in a technological, cognitive-elite-dominated society. There is no reason why we should put more and more emphasis on work, technical intelligence, and the high-powered rat race. We certainly could choose (and there are signs that many are choosing) to spend more time on leisure and play to become more fully human rather than molded by a one-dimensional, all-work existence. There are strong integrational and cross-cutting forces in American society bringing together people of all walks: the mass media, sports, popular culture, Americanization, political participation, religion, etc. There is no irreversible, across-the-board trend to a segregated society of enclaves based on IQ. It is curious that the kind of intelligence that Herrnstein and Murray trumpet is exclusive, divisive, and elitist. Is there not another kind of intelligence (the real kind?) that unites people because the more intelligent people are, the more capable they are relating to others and benefitting others?

Basically, your use of standardized intelligence tests is meant to find an overpowering absolute that would negate any social programs (especially government ones) to reform the human situation. In this respect you go in the direction of a Calvinistic (predestination) genetics that denies the American political culture belief in amelioration, progress, the unleashing of individual energies, and change. What would be the consequences of following your cutbacks (if not termination) of government social programs directed at poverty-stricken women and children? You wrongly conclude that removing so-called subsidies would force people to change their behavior. We believe that such people are more likely to resort to abortion, abuse of children, underground economy activities, and despair. Despair means that they will have less incentive to get out of poverty. If we really want to improve their lot in life, then our governments need to devise new social programs and benefits (e.g., child care, job training) that are positive incentives.

Likewise, IQ tests are not as unchanging as you contend. In *The Bell Curve* it is acknowledged that there has been significant progress at the lower end of the IQ scale (albeit doubts that further progress can be made). Do you dismiss outright the remarkable improvement in IQ scores among American immigrants (especially Jews)? Why is there no consideration of the studies in Europe showing significant improvement in IQ over time when early childhood education, motivation, and test-taking skills are improved? No wonder there is such a great range, 40% to 80%, in what you think counts for heritable intelligence.

Your understanding of "intelligence" is severely restricted to intelligence tests. There are many other factors pertaining to intelligence such as:

(a) educational opportunities and resources

(b) commitment and motivation for learning
(c) family support
(d) peer support
(e) community support
(f) nutrition
(g) health
(h) organization skills and discipline
(i) effective teaching
(j) stimulation at early ages by one's parents and culture.

This complex of factors makes whatever is determined by intelligence tests to be quite unstable especially if we create the kind of experimental, innovational environment that you do not want to invest in.

COGNITIVE ELITE: Our evidence shows that IQ is relatively stable and fixed, and furthermore we do not see any kind of new educational programs offering dramatic changes. Nevertheless, *The Bell Curve* makes an important distinction that has been lost sight of in the full-scale attack on its argument: "Measures of intelligence have reliable statistical relations with important *social phenomena*, but they are a limited tool for deciding what to make of any given *individual*." (italics added) In other words, we are talking about whole groups and general conclusions, not particular individuals. When it comes to some particular individuals, the possibilities for improvement may be considerable. Therefore, we should have environments and educational systems that get the most of students' potentials. However, we have done just the opposite since the 1960s. We have uplifted the lowest achievers and brought down the gifted to mediocrity. No wonder parents with money choose private schools (including those parents who are public school teachers) to develop the highest talents of their children.

Not many critics of *The Bell Curve* have paid heed to the following quote: "If the reader is now convinced that either the genetic or environmental explanations [of ethnic differences in IQ] have won out to the exclusion of the other, we have not done a sufficiently good job of presenting one side or the other. It seems highly likely to us that both genes and the environment have something to do with racial differences. What might the mix be? We are resolutely agnostic on that issue; as far as we can determine, the evidence does not yet justify an estimate."

We are not Calvinistic geneticists promoting a determinism unwarranted by the evidence. No matter whether you emphasize nature (heredity) or nurture (environment), intelligence is statistically, relatively constant for groups of people, so the experts assert.

SOCIOECONOMIC CLASS: The passage you quote from *The Bell Curve* is common, along with a lot of other passages, *qualifying* matters and offering *escape clauses* when critics try to pin Herrnstein and Murray down. Why go to such pains to discount outside intervention if nature is not so determinist? To say that individuals are not to be confused with groups (and the bell curve involves groups and averages, not individuals and their particular scores) still cannot avoid two terrible consequences: (1) employers and university admissions personnel want to use such "intelligence" measures because they are narrowly so predictable, and (2) racial and ethnic groups now become characterized as more or less intelligent than other groups.

It is true that the courts since the 1970s have prevented employers from using IQ tests (see *Griggs v. Duke Power*, 1971) unless there is a "manifest relationship" between the job requirements and the standardized test. Nevertheless, most employers now use standardized, psychological profile tests, and they look for general measures of aptitude, trainability, teamwork potential, and other positive motivational factors. The groundwork has been laid for possible racist uses of standardized tests.

It is our central contention that standardized intelligence tests primarily measure motivation, test readiness, and reveal adjustment potential. A tautology exists in this area (similar to the reductionist tautology of Social Darwinism, "survival of the fittest"; of course, the fit survive if survival is defined solely as the consequence of being fit). Intelligence tests are loaded or rigged to reveal precisely the "intelligence" that testers want to call "intelligence." No wonder that Herrnstein and Murray tout the success of military testing as a great indicator of military job performance. A regimen exists here irrespective of testing for specific job tasks, and unfortunately, these are the tests that the courts are willing to allow. Thank God for those who do not fit into such a conservative, authoritarian mold.

COGNITIVE ELITE: Your position smacks of the 1960s, flower child, let's head-for-the-commune syndrome that has its roots in romanticized anarchy. Testing is very important for institutions, organizations, and employers to perform and produce at the highest possible levels. To have a well-functioning society and economy we need to put people to the test competitively since this brings out the best in them. Your position supposes some arcadia of grazing sheep and cattle with no contests, demands, and challenges.

We are not opposed to finding dignified places in our society and economy for everyone. That is why we strongly recommend that people take up the thought-provoking dilemmas covered in *The Bell Curve*. The lesser talents and abilities of persons can be accommodated.

SOCIOECONOMIC CLASS: Now is the time to discuss the other consequence of relying so heavily on standardized intelligence tests. Herrnstein and Murray make it clear that on average Asians score 3 points higher on intelligence tests than whites, but blacks score 15 points lower than whites (a full one point standard deviation). To put it even more strongly, the average white person scores higher on IQ tests than 84% of the black population, and the white/black differences are greater when going to higher SES levels. Only 37% of the black/white gap is explained by SES, and much of SES is a result of intelligence, so Herrnstein and Murray contend.

There are all kinds of problems with such an analysis beyond a simple fact that cannot be ignored: this is fodder for racists to promote white supremacy and Asiatic xenophobia. To simply state these so-called "statistical facts" is a heavy psychological blow to African-Americans, who have struggled and suffered long and hard in order to be treated with equal promise and dignity.

Why do you think, in the first place, that "race" is a meaningful category or concept? Is not it true that there is no such thing as a pure race, and no such thing as an individual who is racially unmixed? All races have been subject to intermixture (white people especially are the most mixed up), so how can any strictly *racial* conclusions be reached? The same goes for genetic makeup. In so many ways we are the result genetically of a fortuitous, or not so fortuitous, genetic package. What we *do* with this genetic package is what counts!

The greatest differences are within groups, not between groups. The Herrnstein and Murray statistical range of differences from 0.40 to 0.80 applies *within* groups, not *between* groups. So why even use the term "race"? Also, it is a fallacy to go from supposed heritable factors within a group to comparing different groups on the basis of heritability. How do Herrnstein and Murray account for the fact that blacks in the northern part of the United States score higher on average than whites in the South?

In addition, the overseas military children of German and black-American parents score as well as the children of German and white-American parents.

The central difference between us is that you think we can do less since we inherit such a genetic package as well as our SES, and we think we can do much more; that is, human nature is a field of quite limited possibilities. We contend that the SES component has a big effect on IQ tests and genetics. If you do not nourish and use it, you can lose it.

A debating tactic of Herrnstein and Murray (which you mimic) is the reliance on so-called experts in psychometrics and on what certain technical journals have published. There is no such "expert" agreement, and Herrnstein and Murray know this well because they have never submitted their arguments to any scholarly journals where they would be put to the test of peer review. In fact, Charles Lane has researched the so-called scholarly sources of Herrnstein and Murray and the trail leads to well-known racists and racial/eugenic publications.

On top of all of this, the evidence quoted by Herrnstein and Murray is limited to meager evidence based on separated twins and siblings (some of which may have been falsified by Cyril Burt) and gross generalizations from the National Longitudinal Survey of Youth, which could easily be given opposite interpretations. *The Bell Curve* refuses to acknowledge the controversy among knowledgeable scholars and the alternative interpretations from the same data, except to dismiss all of this as not what the "intelligence research community" validates.

COGNITIVE ELITE: The hard statistical factors about significant IQ differentiations among the races must necessarily be put on the table for consideration if we are to come to terms with our modern society and economy. We are not racists, and if there are any sources we use that are racist they are not racist in the strictly data aspects of their research. A campaign has been underway to discredit Herrnstein and Murray by all kinds of underhanded, left-wing, McCarthyite tactics such as guilt by association, verbal slurs, and suppression of research that challenges liberal, egalitarian pieties.

The human dignity and worth of all people is not at stake in the linkage of intelligence and race. Racists will be racists no matter what we say or publish. We are not racists, and the only way we can counter the wrong-headed racist consequences of IQ data is to present the data openly for public discussion. If we provoke liberals to devise better educational and governmental programs that raise the cognitive abilities of groups, then we will have served a very useful purpose.

Take, for example, the very serious problem of dysgenesis that all kinds of people want to ignore. Dysgenesis is the social phenomenon of "likes" mating such that there is less and less mating between people of different cognitive capabilities. People of high cognitive ability are mating with each other to an extent unlike any other time in our history, and they are having fewer children because of the high "opportunity costs" of having children. Low cognitive ability people are mating more exclusively with each other and enjoying high fertility rates. Also, immigrants are a large factor in our U.S. population increases, and the latest stock of immigrants represent low skill people and their families. Therefore, we do have to be wary of a decline in our population quality. Linked to such a decline will be more antisocial, norm-violating behavior, e.g., more crime, more welfare dependency, more illegitimate births, more homelessness, etc.

SOCIOECONOMIC CLASS: Your remarks about population quality and dysgenesis are ugly and racist. You are inviting those who favor a scientifically-engineered eugenics policy to have widespread popular credibility. Democracy is based on a belief in the judgment and sense of the common people who are relatively equal and compatible with each other. Your IQ musings threaten the very basis of democracy, which is a faith in the people's common sense to express the will of the people.

The Bell Curve throws a bucket of ice-cold water on the political efforts of those who wish to improve the socioeconomic status of people by enlisting the efforts of those same people who obviously do not have their own cognitive plan to lift themselves up. In most cases the lack of such a cognitive plan is not a fault of genes, race, or cognitive ability, but rather the denial of incentives and opportunity to put people's capabilities to work productively. Yes, there always will be those among us who never develop their talents, but that is a call for action, not fatalistic resignation.

COGNITIVE ELITE: It is naive to believe in the advanced stages of our society and economy that an elite does not rule and does not need to rule. The mass of people do not even want to rule; they want to be told (and then immediately experience) what is best (most pleasurable) for them. The intelligent inherit the world. These are the facts no matter how unpleasant they may be for your own euphemized world view. Perhaps we could have more success with people's inherent abilities if we put into place the adoption of newborn babies, removing them from environments that negate their supposed potentialities. Yet such an adoption policy would be very expensive and would override fundamental parental rights. Does anyone have anything better to offer than dependency-causing, government welfare programs?

BIBLIOGRAPHY

Beardsley, Tim. "For Whom the Bell Curve Tolls." *Science* (January 1995): 14-16.

"The Bell Curve Symposium." *National Review* (December 5, 1994): 32-61.

Browne, Malcolm. "What Is Intelligence and Who Has It?" *New York Times Book Review* (October 16, 1994):3, 41, 45.

Carvajal, Doreen. "Rutgers' President Endangered in Furor Over Race Remark." *New York Times* (February 11, 1995): 9.

Dickens, William T., Kane, Thomas, and Schultze, Charles L. *Does The Bell Curve Ring True?* Washington, D.C.: Brookings Institution, 1996.

Fraser, Steven, ed. *The Bell Curve Wars.* New York: Basic, 1995.

Goertzel, Ted. "The Myth of the Normal Curve." *Humanity and Society* 5 (1981): 14-31.

Gould, Stephen Jay. "The Bell Curve." *New Yorker* (November 28, 1994): 139-150.

___. *The Mismeasure of Man.* New York: Norton, 1981.

Herrnstein, Richard and Murray, Charles. *The Bell Curve.* New York: Free Press, 1994.

Hofer, Myron. "Behind the Curve." *New York Times* (December 26, 1994): editorial page.

Holt, Jim. "Anti-Social Science." *New York Times* (October 19, 1994): editorial page.

Jensen, A.J. "How Much Can We Boost IQ and Scholastic Achievement."

Harvard Educational Review 39 (1969): 1-123.

Kamin, Leon J. "Behind the Curve." *Science* (February 1995): 99-103.

Kaus, Mickey. "The End of Equality." *New Republic* (June 22, 1992): 21-27.

___. *The End of Equality*. New York: Basic Books, 1992.

Lane, Charles. "The Tainted Sources of 'The Bell Curve'." *New York Review of Books* (December 1, 1994): 14-19.

"Mainstream Science on Intelligence." *Wall Street Journal* (December 13, 1994): A18.

"Measuring Intelligence." *Economist* (January 6, 1995): 69-71.

Mehler, Barry. "In Genes We Trust." *Reform Judaism* (Winter 1994): 10-14, 77-79.

Morgenthau, Tom. "IQ, Is it Destiny?" *Newsweek* (October 24, 1994): 53-62.

Murray, Charles. "The Real 'Bell Curve'." *Wall Street Journal* (December 2, 1994): editorial page.

"Race and I.Q." *New Republic* (October 31, 1994): 4-37.

Richardson, Ken and Spears, David, eds. *Race and Intelligence*. Baltimore: Penguin, 1972.

Ryan, Alan. "Apocalypse Now." *New York Review of Books* (November 17, 1994): 7-11.

Seligman, D. *A Question of Intelligence: The IQ Debate in America*. New York: Birch Lane Press, 1992.

Snyderman, M. and Rothman, S. *The IQ Controversy*. New Brunswick: Transaction Books, 1988.

Tucker, William H. *The Science and Politics of Racial Research*. Champaign: University of Illinois Press, 1994.

Woolridge, Adrian. "Bell Curve Liberals." *National Review* (February 27, 1995): 22-24.

FIVE

FEMINISM: THE CONFLICT OVER

DIRECTION OF THE WOMEN'S MOVEMENT

The women's movement began in the United States in 1848 at a small chapel in Seneca Falls, New York. Elizabeth Cady Stanton delivered a speech about the wrongs done to women which only women could understand in the depths of their deprivation. Over the years Susan B. Anthony collaborated with Stanton to open up opportunities for women in education and employment. Their greatest energy was put into achieving a constitutional amendment that finally in 1920 gave women the right to vote. With such political and civil rights success, the women's movement went into somewhat of a demise until the 1960s, when the feminist movement arose. Simone de Beauvoir's *The Second Sex* and Betty Friedan's *The Feminine Mystique* inaugurated a second wave of consciousness raising among women, this time a more socioeconomic movement (and therefore more radical) directed at how women are treated institutionally throughout society. These second-wave feminists were well educated, yet their opportunities and achievements made them more aware of psychological, economic, and sociological oppressions. Even with many more doors open for them, something fundamental was not as it should be for women.

Today there are many versions of feminism and, in fact, an important and healthy debate is going on among women and their versions of feminism. It is unfortunate that "feminism" has taken on negative connotations, since very significant women's issues deserve to be discussed and debated in a more positive light. Does equality mean sameness across the board, or does equality mean difference, albeit treating fairly and respecting equally those women who are different? Is there a feminist consciousness, or a set of characteristics that we can call uniquely "feminist"? If so, does this constitute something we can call a "feminist culture"? If not, then is being feminine simply a social construct and convention, and even men if properly habituated can be "feminists"? How do "black feminists" (called "womanists") relate to the feminist movement? What is it, with all their sameness and differences, that "feminists" want?

THE DIALOGUE

LIBERAL FEMINIST: To understand what "feminism" is about (the term "feminism" was coined in the first decade of this century) we need to consult the untidy and conflicting internal history of feminism itself. This history can be explained by way of three stages. The first stage was manifestly political/legal in the strict, specific sense of voting participation in politics and legal recognition of women (the right to own property, etc.). This stage can be called the civil, individual rights wave. It is best known in terms of the suffragette movement (Elizabeth Cady Stanton and Susan B. Anthony) that culminated in the Nineteenth Amendment in 1920 giving women the right to vote.

After a period of quiescence, a second stage or wave occurred in the 1960s. It was the consequence (somewhat related to World War II when many women replaced men in the workplace) of the increasing number of employed women and the importance of a second income for middle-class achievement. Women's issues became economic and social or, to put it differently, politics now had an economic and social agenda that questioned whether there were barriers and obstructions to the fulfillment of political rights and opportunities already granted. Prior to the 1960s, the labor movement and a substantial number of women opposed women's equality with men if it meant that certain protections for women such as labor laws (e.g., maximum number of hours required to work in a week) would no longer be upheld. By the 1960s technological changes and the desire of most women to take on work, even if physically strenuous and dangerous, virtually removed the opposition to across-the-board job equality.

In 1963 the Equal Pay Act was passed to insure that women received the same pay when doing the same jobs as men. Also, the process was begun to remove the classification of jobs by sex so that job segregation (by arbitrary classification) would come to an end. The passage of the Civil Rights Act of 1964 and the establishment of the Equal Employment Opportunity Commission made it possible to expand in a practical and legal way women's rights, opportunities, and equality. On the down side, an Equal Rights Amendment to the U.S. Constitution was proposed in 1972 but fell short of passage by three states. Likewise, comparable worth legislation (equal pay for different jobs if equal in worth to the employer) passed in many states but never became a national law, never was upheld by the federal courts, and never was applied outside the area of state public/government employment.   Affirmative action programs also expanded, but a backlash occurred and restriction of these programs seems unavoidable in the 1990s.

The lesson seems to be that when going from political and civil rights to social and economic change, there inevitably will be increased conflict and opposition. Males are not generally threatened by the right of women to vote and have legal rights, but when you go on to jobs and pay and what seems like preferences, then a strong backlash can occur. Individualistic, capitalistic premises of allocational justice based on merit now are overridden by group, socialistic designs based on distributive justice for the needy and disadvantaged.

We are now in the third stage or wave of the women's movement, which can only partly be described as a divisive and conflicting period. It is not unredeemable capitalist society or patriarchal males that are the primary problem. Rather, a widening gap between radical feminist and postmodern feminist leaders on one side and ordinary women (including moderate, liberal feminists) on the other side has derailed the women's movement. Feminists are at war among themselves, and the direction of the women's movement is in doubt. We need to take a closer look at the many issues and attitudes that now divide the liberal and radical feminist leadership.

The liberal feminist position (and this reveals why we are called equity feminists) is that women deserve a level playing field with men, and they need the same rights and opportunities that men have. Let gender-blind competition occur among everyone in a fair and civil way. Men should not be threatened by women's advances; most men are married and directly benefit from women's advancement (not only their wives but their mothers and daughters also). There is no need to believe that this is a zero-sum (nothing or all) affair; we all benefit as a society (I win-you win) when the most qualified get their due reward and everyone can develop his/her potential to the fullest. Liberal feminists see no divisiveness and want no divisiveness regarding men who have favorable attitudes toward women. If misogyny existed in the past (and it did), there is no justifiable reason to replace it today with misandry.

RADICAL FEMINIST: Your historical overview of the feminist movement fails to be self-critical and conceals the limits and shortcomings of such a lukewarm liberal-democratic position. Your vaunted equality of opportunity has not brought about significant changes in the lives of women today. For example, women still make 59 cents for every dollar men make. One in four women can expect to be raped. The self-esteem of young women around the ages 11 to 15 is lower than that of males at those same ages, and evidence shows that teachers give more attention to young males. Because of the "beauty myth" women are heavily forced into cosmetics, weight-loss programs, anorexia, and unnecessary surgery. The real failure of liberal feminism is its acceptance of the capitalist, patriarchal system as it is, as if gradual, piecemeal reforms (that do not offend the male power structure) will improve the lot of women and win the support of the male power elite. Radical feminists want to transform the system and even develop a new, nonpatriarchal language to alter fundamentally our society and economy.

It is amazing how your rendition of history displays none of the indignation that characterizes true feminists. There has been over 2,000 years of patriarchy, female suppression and subordination, and a whole androcentric world and language to enforce women's slavery. Women have even been duped to collaborate in their own enslavement. Some women have learned how to maneuver and manipulate in order to have survival power only. Only in the twentieth century have women been "allowed" to develop both their sexual (family) life and their intellectual (education) life. Liberal feminists are a perfect example of just surviving while engaging in internal self-denial. Women have to recover their dignity by privileging their own culture and breaking out of the confines of private, domestic existence.

To give an example of the fundamental difference between liberal and radical feminists, we would never propose "stages" in the history of the feminist movement. As Peggy McIntosh has pointed out, we should look at qualitative, interactive *phase*s in the progressive development of feminism. These phases are very personal-historical for women. There are five such dynamic phases capturing the experiences of more than half the world's population, namely women. The first phase is womanless history or silence. Women are silenced to the isolated, alienated private sphere of the household, no doubt their punishment for Eve's evil in the Garden of Eden. If it is not women's evil sexuality that is the factor silencing women, then it is the power and control that males can enjoy by keeping women locked up in the household. Some radical feminists have resorted to a new term, "herstory," to counteract the invisibility and dismissal of women during this first phase of history.

In the second phase of our history only great, exemplary women are acknowledged. They, of course, are the exception, and that is why they are singled out with little threat to male power. This kind of tokenism perpetuates the nonentity status of all other women. Many textbooks today that sidebar women are only at this phase. In the third phase, women become a problem since they do not go along with not being recognized. They get angry. Anger and rage is at the heart of being a feminist. If all individuals have certain inalienable rights and we are all created equal, then why are women subordinated to men and excluded from so many activities in which they could shine before the world? From "ouch" experiences, women then have "click" experiences. Women challenge the establishment that controls who gets heard and who can act in public. The exclusive male canon of writers who control history and constitute our literary heritage is questioned. A growing solidarity among women occurs as forms of male resistance result. In many ways most of us today are still in this "betwixt" phase three.

In phase four women break the pyramid of male power and open up the hitherto private world of women. Women are valid humans who have had the lonely task of perpetuating the human race, albeit in silence and out of the way. Women now constitute history, a history that is rewritten and reconstructed to include the different value systems of all women. Radical projects are pursued, such as language transformation, doing science in a feminist way, and the different ways of learning (epistemology) among women. In the fifth phase (a phase we have certainly not reached), history will have been redefined and restructured to include all the diversity of women and men, and no longer will power (who dominates whom) be an issue. Perhaps we will have achieved a truly complementary society for men and women, but not androgyny or the loss of male-female difference.

The most salient issue between liberal and radical feminists is the "radical" position that a total transformation of the prevailing patriarchal system is required. Sexism (and racism) are institutional, endemic, and irreversible if only compromises and piecemeal gains (crumbs) are the objective. Liberal feminists believe that if they can just get a level playing field (equity), then everything will turn out fairly. But this position fails to fight for the particular unique *identity* of women qua women. That is why radical feminists are known as *difference* feminists. Only in this way will women be recognized and valued. Furthermore, it is naive and outrageous to believe that the backlash against feminism is caused by disagreement among women, rather than by the rearing of the ugly head of the male power establishment. Liberal feminists cannot see the trenchant patriarchal system perhaps because they so much want to join it.

POSTMODERN FEMINIST: Both the liberal (equity) feminist and the radical (difference) feminist do not carry to the full logical conclusion their own history tale of feminism. In other words, they do not adequately deconstruct the past to realize ultimately where we have arrived in the present and where we are heading in the future. All of history is the struggle for power; every aspect of life is political, meaning that the political analysis of the forces of power at play is the only way to understand who is doing what to whom. We need to rip the mask off and demystify such notions as individual rights, equality, progress, and any other linguistic terms that assume something substantive and essential. A new language and set of terms as proposed by the radical feminist will not change the irreducible reality that every term and every move is a matter of power or powerlessness. Anger alone changes nothing and may lead to self-destructive types of behavior.

Everything is relative and in flux. You have nothing to lose, and some enjoyment to gain, if you attack (deconstruct and unravel) any and all attempts to fixate, stabilize, and permanentize things. The enjoyment is in the battle of exposing and discombobulating any structures and systems. In the end the individual roams free to do as s/he pleases. There is no male essence and there is no female essence (counteressence). The false consciousness of the radical feminist is to assume that women are unique and superior when in fact they are power-driven animals like all the rest of the human species. Only the postmodern feminist is the true pluralist and diversitarian in the best sense of what we favor—a carnival milieu. There are always going to be a diversity of men and women going every which way.

As postmodern feminists we do not advocate just one path, the liberal democratic, pragmatic way of gradual piecemeal change, nor do we accept the very judgmental female ideology of the radical feminists. The world is made up of all kinds of people and choices. We instigate more choice and alternatives and more variety. In this way we are more respectful of individuals than any other feminists. To us difference means infinite variability (no two fingerprints are the same) and not just gender differences since "gender" is as bogus a concept as "race" is.

WOMANIST: The story of the history of feminism told by the liberal feminists and the phases of feminism delineated by radical feminists ignore the determining role of the black civil rights movement, which paved the way for the second wave of feminism and resurrected the powerful explanatory phenomenon of "cultural identity." Great numbers of black women in the labor force first confronted balancing work and family and single parentage before white women had to deal with these concrete dilemmas. Many people know how backhandedly "sex" was inserted in civil rights legislation with the intention of killing that legislation. All in all, the feminist movement learned a lot about movement politics from the civil rights movement, yet rarely is this indebtedness explicitly acknowledged. In effect, black women are doubly neglected and made invisible by the white male power structure and the white-dominated feminist movement.

As a result, there are deep fissures between white feminists and black feminists, which is why Alice Walker coined the term "womanist" to capture the distinctiveness of black feminism. To be precise, white feminists have excluded the basic experiences of black women since white feminists tend to be middle class or better and solely preoccupied with matters of sex to the exclusion of race and class. Black women cannot afford this luxury because racism and poverty, not just their sex, have been their concrete oppression. Womanists want to make salient the struggle against racism and economic disadvantage while still acknowledging that sex and white patriarchy are major problems also. White women as well as white men have been part of the racist system of oppression. Consequently, the gross failure to take up the fight against racism causes deep, abiding suspicion.

Specifically, we womanists call attention to the weak support that feminists gave to Shirley Chisholm's presidential campaign in 1972. Apparently, Gloria Steinem, Bella Abzug, and Betty Friedan preferred keeping alliances with the white male power structure and the Democratic Party establishment. There has also been over the years an absence of black women in the leadership circles of the National Organization of Women (NOW). In the campaign for the Equal Rights Amendment (ERA) there was little effort to mobilize the support of black women. White feminists have not been receptive to Angela Davis. Yet these same feminists can claim that NOW is the NAACP for women! It rankles black feminists that the white feminist movement has coopted slogans from the civil rights movement. As the black power movement faded, the feminist movement rose in prominence. White feminists have had much more access to the mass media to present their concerns. Finally, in the literature of the feminist movement it is common to find an undertreatment of black issues and black feminism. Note in Alison Jagger's landmark book, *Feminist Politics and Human Nature*, only 17 of the 400 pages in this book deal with black feminism.

LIBERAL FEMINIST: What you all are unwilling to face, since you are part of the cause of this, is that three-fourths of American women want to strengthen and improve women's status in American society, but only one-third call themselves feminists. Thirty-nine percent of women blame feminists for making it harder for them to work and have a family at the same time. These women are pragmatic and relativistic, while your positions are ideological and absolutistic. You call for some socioeconomic transformation that few women support, and it is not because of fear and ignorance. Most women do not harbor the deep antagonism and despair that radical feminists have.

Your so-called facts about the oppression of women are simply myths and propagandistic lies. Women on average make 72 cents for every dollar a man makes (not 59 cents). And if you correct for age, to reveal how significant the progress has been in the past two decades, then women aged 16–25 make 92 cents for every dollar a man makes. Much still needs to be done, especially in the area of socialization (rather than the capitalist economic system, which is rational enough to reward talent be it female or male). Young women today are still being socialized in their families and schools to lower their sights to low-paying jobs and careers. We need to change attitudes and bring about a new generation of go-getting women who will make opportunities for themselves. And yes we do have to focus on the much more serious, socioeconomic plight of black women faced with a cycle of poverty and dependency. Government welfare programs lacking incentives and ghetto segregation have sapped the energies of black women.

Furthermore, there is no hard evidence that one out of four women will be raped. Rape is a serious problem, but such high figures just cannot be verified. The reports of low esteem among adolescent girls and teachers paying more attention to boys have also been exposed as lacking foundation by Christina Hoff Sommers in her book, *Who Stole Feminism?* There are so many crazy stories being peddled (e.g., that women get beat up more on SuperBowl Sunday than on any other day of the year), and this does tremendous harm to the credibility of the feminist movement. We have to delineate very carefully and accurately the discrimination against women and then fashion practical policies to overcome this discrimination. Most women (and most Americans) are pragmatic, not ideological. They reject the absolute relativism of postmodern feminists and the totalistic critique of both the postmodern feminists, radical feminists, and womanists. The democratic capitalist system is not totally discriminatory and corrupt.

Basically, we disagree with postmodern feminists because we contend that they have abdicated responsibility for practical, political change in favor of some kind of anarchistic free-for-all. We do believe there can be (and already has been) meaningful change and progress. There is no reason to become so pessimistic that only destructive and individually pleasurable behavior can be sought. Not all of reality is reducible to power. There is persuasion, reciprocity, empathy, and sharing, all of which point to forms of female-inspired mutuality that bring people together for positive activities. Of course, we believe in cross-gender and cross-racial cooperation and solidarity, which distinguishes us from radical feminists who tend to be gender (gynocentric) separatists. Why not an androgynous society if this means men and women crossing over to realize characteristics that were once stereotypically male and female?!

RADICAL FEMINIST: The problem with liberal feminists is that they accept at face value the statistics and methods of the male-defined world. Consequently, everything seems much better than it actually is. The liberal feminists know that less than half the crimes committed are reported and included in the statistical crime measures. As regards rape, there is even less reporting because women do not want to be "man-handled" in the criminal justice system after their rape. Furthermore, we have a more expansive definition of rape than the liberal feminists and male-controlled criminal justice system will countenance. We consider any resisted, rejected, sexual violation of women to be rape. We listen carefully to the personal narratives of women rather than bookishly consulting government data.

Likewise with the pay gap, official statistics do not consider the underemployment of women and the greater intermittent employment of women because of domestic, child-rearing responsibilities. This results in a much lower average wage difference for women than the Census Bureau's 72 cents. Talking about socialization obstructing women's development is too abstract and social scientific. And it can backfire. In fact, this socialization argument was successfully used against women who claimed in a court case that Sears was discriminating against them in job opportunities. We contend that it is better to go into the workplace, classrooms, and families to assess personally the frequently subconscious and subtle forms of denying women (gestures, attitudes, words used, tones of voice, etc.) to devise a better measurement of the reality that drains women of their resources and worth. Liberal feminists along with male social scientists heavily criticize this "subjective" evaluation; of course, both these groups have vested interests to protect.

We wholeheartedly agree with black feminists or womanists that the whole system is corrupted by sexism and racism. We tend to believe that the fight against patriarchy will automatically overcome racism and socioeconomic deprivation. That may be naive, but we alone among feminists recognize the importance of "difference," which means that we are open to hear and listen to the diverse voices of Hispanic, black, Asian, Native-American, etc. peoples. Our concept of difference includes cultural differences that produce different experiences and stories. The lovely mutuality that liberal feminists speak about (cooperation, empathy, solidarity, sharing, etc.) has its source in being female. Males are competitive, aggressive, individualistic, self-interested, and rationalistic (ergo, suspicious of feelings). Women are cooperative, peaceful, nurturing, healing, connecting and relating, and self-sacrificial. Radical feminists promulgate an ethics of care to counter the abstract, rule-based norm of justice imposed by males. Liberal feminists fail to see the importance of this distinction and are not true to what is a foundational difference between men and women.

Carol Gilligan's research shows the variations in responses between men and women when they are confronted with decision-making scenarios. Women who hear their feminine voice are concerned about relational realities and making connections with others. Men are more autonomous and removed. Consequently, women are more personal, they take responsibility for caring, and they see themselves in a web of involvements (interrelations) with others. On the other hand, men are competitive, rule-following, and more concerned about their own pseudo-objective stand or position. Women have a built-in sense of empathy tied to real-life situations; men see themselves as separated, with strong primary obligations to their own selves.

As a consequence, we women favor a politics of personal identity to overcome the terrible duality women experience being mother/wife in the private realm and then being "other," an outsider, in the public realm. Politically and legally women are equal to men, but socially and sexually they are different. Frequently, women are interrupted, ignored (tolerated), or excluded rather than accorded respect. Women need to turn to other women first to achieve their personal collective identity. Language transformation means ridding our language of male terms, and religious transformation means that some feminists will turn to earth goddess worship, which is to say the feminization of God. That is why we certainly think the world would be a better place if feminized.

Consequently, we favor "politicalizing the personal" and "personalizing the political". The boundaries between the public and private spheres need to be broken in favor of feminist values rooted in the private sphere of the family. Once this occurs in the realm of values, then we will have broken the resistance males have to sharing in family, child-rearing responsibilities. Likewise women will be more accepted in what is now the public sphere of politics and business. The glass ceiling (that women only can look through but never penetrate) separating those who make decisions and those who carry out decisions will be shattered. We, of course, do not expect some androgynous outcome. We are not naive about our transformational project. Males will always be males, but why do they have to have the balance of power?

WOMANIST: Black feminists cannot be held responsible for the alienation of the feminist movement from stay-at-home women, working/struggling women, and men. In fact, womanists have always sought collaboration with progressive black men to overcome racism. In addition, black women have had closer relationships to poor women because they share their experiences, and black women have had a different relationship to our black men than white women have had to their white men. Black men have been as much (if not greater) victims of white patriarchy as white and black women. Consequently, black women have sought solidarity with black men (not to let even a straw stand in their way). Black women have been stronger ("de mule uh de world" in Zora Neale Hurston's words) and more successful on average than black men because the labor market has been particularly discriminatory against black men. Black women have benefitted from the education so strongly encouraged by black mothers, and black women have fitted into the changing labor force. Black men are considered dangerous and evil by the white power structure including white women. Note how white feminists who talk about rape do not mention the nasty racism that targets and frames black men as habitual rapists. White feminists forget how many black women have had to work as servants for upper-class white women who denigrated black women. So there is this special angle of vision called by Patricia Hill Collins the "outside/inside" standpoint of black women. We have been kept outside the progress of white women's development in the twentieth century, yet we experience so much within the white power structure as lowly servants ("flies on the wall"). Therefore, for us the whole system is the common enemy, not just because it is white, patriarchal, and sexist, but because it is also racist and economically repressive. White feminists do not consistently focus on this three-fanged paradigm of interlocking oppression by race, class, and gender. Thus solidarity among all feminists is lacking. An interlocking race, gender, and class analysis and revolution is necessary and unavoidable if real justice is to be sought.

POSTMODERN FEMINIST: There are no foundations or essences. Therefore, there are no fundamental differences between men and women regarding care and unconcern for others, peace and war, cooperation and competition, etc. Some men have been in charge and certainly have a lot more to account for in the course of history. But we are talking history not human nature. There is no determinate human nature; there is no more than human potentiality for self-constructed outcomes. Radical feminists and liberal feminists want to hold on to some transcendent morality when in fact there are only human social constructions and the powerful who enforce such constructions. Our project is to destabilize the powerful so that more and more individuals can have their own crafted selves. Womanists such as bell hooks and Patricia Hill Collins agree with our deconstructivist project regarding biologically determined concepts such as race as well as gender-determined concepts. Realizing that we confront only social constructions, a more thoroughgoing revolution is possible.

We do not draw lines and boundaries because everything is artificial and we reject all determinism. We consistently oppose all authorities and any incipient authoritarians. Liberal feminists and radical feminists have authoritarian urges written into their respective dogmas of gender neutrality and gender uniqueness. Actually the category of gender is less revealing than the category of socioeconomic class. Those with wealth, and the power that comes from wealth, act more consistently than those whom we define by gender alone. This is especially the grievance that African-American "womanists" have against the middle-to-upper class, white feminist movement. Those in the lower socioeconomic class, including African-American women, have not been heard, and of course "race" has been ignored because race is not gender differentiated. Many African-American womanists do not want to wage war with their African-American male counterparts because this only divides their broader campaign against racism. Feminists need to be completely open to anyone (irrespective of gender) who wants to deconstruct.

LIBERAL FEMINIST: We reject the position of radical (difference) feminists that females have inherent (biologically or through socialization and history), special propensities that need to be promoted and presumably protected. This position commits the same error as male supremacy, except now it will be female supremacy. We reject the awful stereotypes of women being weaker (caring), passive (peaceful), irrational (emotional), and accordingly in need of special protection. We know that this dichotomization of polar attributes has a long history, and on this point we agree with the postmodern feminists (although not with their methods) that this binary, symbiotic relationship should be broken. It is odd that radical feminists engage in such bipolar analysis and thinking when they charge males with this logocentric fallacy.

Of course, postmodern feminists leave us in no better position because their pluralism entails an anarchical individualism and atomization such that there is no basis for women (and also for men and women) to come together to achieve social betterment. There are no grounds of solidarity and common political action. It is everyone for himself and herself. This is Hobbes' state of nature—a perpetual war of everyone against everyone else. Womanists are too anticapitalistic, which is to say socialistic, and the promoting of class antagonisms as well as racial antagonisms tends to result in implacable divisiveness and hostility. We, on the other hand, are optimistic about political alliances and political change. Nevertheless, this requires rational persuasion, compromises, and continual debate. We advocate political and economic career advancement within an open, liberal, democratic, free-market society. In such a capitalistic society, advantages and opportunities multiply—we just have to guarantee that women have chances equal to men.

RADICAL FEMINIST: We do not uncritically support such bipolarity of the sexes on the basis of generalizable characteristics pertaining to the sexes. The origin of such characteristics is in the sexual/economic division of labor, which we seek to transform in favor of the feminine pole since that pole represents more than half the human race and has kept the human race alive. We are not biological determinists (and we are mightily aware of the potential racism and sexism of such determinism). Furthermore, we are the only feminists who see the need to rid ourselves of individualism, be it the individual rights position of the liberal feminists or the atomized individualism going every which way of the postmodern feminists.

The alternative to individualism is a communitarianism or collectivism. The history of male oppression (patriarchy) and the strong (almost innate) commitment of men to individualism and autonomy make it extremely difficult to imagine such a communitarianism or collectivism including men. (We leave it to the optimistic liberal feminists to develop males' feminine side.) Women because of their confinement to the private domestic sphere and having been treated as "other" than men, totally responsible for birthing and nurturing the young, have socialized within them a sense of relatedness, connectedness, healing power, and compassion. We believe there are strong stirrings in the black community for soul-sister solidarity and mothering. These white and black female yearnings are rejected by most men, so women establish a solidarity among themselves. For some women it is natural to become lesbians, although such bonds among women need not be based on sexual intimacy.

The ravages of male individualism construct a tenuous society based on the unlimited pursuit of self-interest, greed, acquisitiveness, war, selfishness, incivility, and alienation. It does not matter how equal the chances and opportunities are for women under such an exploitative capitalism. Liberal feminists rally to the male model of success when actually true women want solidarity, not some go-it-alone autonomy to compete on equal terms with men. Politically, many radical feminists head in the direction of socialism (not male capitalism) because there is a caring community there based on the social needs of the disadvantaged and oppressed. Socialism relies on the collective judgment of what is best for the common good, otherwise known as distributive justice, to raise up and redistribute to those who have not adequately shared in the goods of a society. There is concern for the particular needs of persons rather than the pursuit of things to enhance selves.

WOMANIST: The radical feminist comes close to resurrecting the myth of matriarchy in the black community by emphasizing soul sisters and mothering. There are also soul brothers. We are well aware of sexism and antihomosexual tendencies among black men. The civil rights movement was so strongly black male dominated that black female voices were often suppressed despite the fact that the civil rights movement was inspired by a woman, Rosa Parks, and the March on Washington was proposed by a black woman. The biggest problem that black males face is not the strength and energies of successful black women. Precisely because of the socioeconomic oppression of the white male capitalist system and the long legacy of slavery, the black male has not been able to fulfill his natural family responsibilities. But the lifting up of black males in the fight against racism does not mean the putting down of black women. The whole dynamics of this everyday intraracial struggle are beyond the experiences of white feminists. Black feminists strongly support Afrocentrism, which is to say the reconceptualization of African-American experiences, something only people of African-American culture can carry out. We all face as women the same conditions and experiences of sexism, but we womanists also have to respond to racism and classism. It would do the white feminists well if they too took more concern for the socioeconomic oppression of low-income white women.

POSTMODERN FEMINIST: We reject any kind of socialism and collectivism as authoritative impositions on individuals, restricting their free energies and the healthy diversity that would characterize a society of free individuals. That there are more than ten kinds of feminists is an occasion for great applause: liberal (equity) feminists, radical (difference) feminists, postmodern feminists, lesbian feminists, eco-feminists, poststructural feminists, personal development/therapy feminists (Steinem), mothering feminists, womanists (Walker), New Age feminists, antipornography feminists (Dworkin), goddess worship feminists, Jewish feminists, Slavic feminists (Drakulic), and other feminists *ad infinitum* we hope.

A carnival of pluralistic voices allows everyone to pursue their own particular inclinations. It is not biology, history, the "other," or any obstruction and determinism that defines us. We define our own individual selves however we choose to construct ourselves. Have no fear, find the courage to construct your own identity, and constantly be vigilant regarding those who want to construct systems, dogmas, hierarchies, and authorities in order to impose their values on you. Personalize and subjectify all that is political (power) and ferociously resist the politicalization (domination) of your subjectivity. Privatizing the public sphere is the ultimate act of liberating and unleashing individual energies.

LIBERAL FEMINIST: We know that black feminists have suffered from racism and greater socioeconomic disadvantage. But have not Asian women and Jewish women and darker-skinned Hispanics also suffered from racism as well? What is it that is unique about the black experience, on both the negative and positive sides? And the concept of "blackhood" that many black feminists espouse is also in need of deconstruction, isn't it? Much of what womanists argue (e.g., Afrocentrism) seems to go in the direction of separatism. It is hard to see what the grounds are for a working alliance with black feminists if they are going to be so racially and economically ideological.

The ravings of the postmodern feminist leads to a kind of anarchy of freewheeling desires without the minimum structure and order necessary for individuals to reach achievement in their efforts and then maintain their achievements. From that wild libertarian extreme we then go to the other extreme, radical feminism, where socialism empowers bureaucrats to socially engineer outcomes by redistributing goods from those who succeed to those who do not succeed. And these extremists believe they are doing justice—the justice of the unbridled self versus the justice of the all-powerful state?

There is an in-between position avoiding such extremes, namely, reform capitalism, whereby individuals are extended equality of opportunity (e.g., public school system) and get to compete in a free market where opportunities multiply for those who exert themselves in a continually developing society. Let us not forget that capitalism and democracy break down traditional society, which had kept individuals in fixed places. Women were restricted to being dependents of men, isolated in the household, and unable to develop their full potentialities. With technological developments (contraception and safe abortion) women now have the power to choose whether they will be mothers or not, or when they will be mothers. We need to preserve this right of privacy (the choice of contraception and abortion) and not let the state (the public realm) intrude. Were not there many communist/socialist countries that had state regulations rewarding reproduction (e.g., USSR, Romania) or severely restricting reproduction (e.g., China)? Of course, we do not want to privatize totally the public realm because the public realm (government) in a liberal reform capitalism has a role to protect individual rights and free competition, provide incentives for economic development, enact safety and health regulations, and offer educational opportunities. There are some things that individuals alone or as a group are unable to achieve without the power and programs of government.

The radical feminist is wrong in assuming that there are attributes (e.g., care, nurture, cooperation) that uniquely and primarily characterize women. Many men have, or could have, these attributes. We count on this change or redirection of men's personalities to realize more sharing of nurturance of children and household tasks. If women are so uniquely different and superior as radical feminists contend, then what hope do we have to redress sexual inequalities and get more male responsibility and sharing? Such sexual differences stand in the way of practical, everyday equality.

RADICAL FEMINIST: Both the liberal feminists and postmodern feminists fail to acknowledge the evidence that supports "difference" feminism. For example, a study of men's and women's reactions to facial expressions of sadness and joy reveals that men are less sensitive to sadness in women's faces and women are better able to recognize sadness in men's faces. Brain scans reveal that men and women use different parts of their brain when doing similar activities, suggesting that men are more involved in direct action and women in symbolic action. Likewise, women in legislatures act more as facilitators and moderators, whereas men like to take stands and put their mark on things. Men are more controllers, while women seek broad consensus. Because legislators are dominated by a male style of legislating, women are found to be less effective, decisive, and credible. Of course, this legislative game is biased against women. In the business world also women are frequently misperceived as soft and compliant. If they are not this way, then they are accused of being "too male." Over the matter of the Persian Gulf War there was a 25% gender gap between men and women, with greater numbers of women favoring peace. Further research should bring out even more characteristic differences.

The general problem with the liberal feminist position is that its equity program of equalizing matters between men and women has come to an end today with a mixture of successes and failures. To advance further to correct for all the disadvantages and injustices women are subject to, there must be policies that directly target and benefit women as a group. The liberal feminist emphasis on individual women's rights and opportunities has primarily benefitted already well-positioned, white middle- and upper-class women. But system change and transformation have not occurred. In three areas of public policy—social welfare, pornography, and women's pay—we have to go beyond liberal democratic policies and address women qua women, specifically dealing with their special needs.

In social welfare policy, poverty has been quite feminized, and we need to devise a woman's solution. It would be great if men became responsible in terms of using contraceptive devices and supporting their children rather than believing that this is a woman's problem. Realistically, we are not going to change male behavior and attitudes greatly, although we should never stop trying. We need a radical, grass-roots solution and that can only mean the building of women's communities to provide prenatal education, day care, preschool education, and support networks. Women who have been through dire circumstances can instruct teenage women to take control of their bodies and future, to have a life plan such that feminine reproduction does not become a wrecker of one's opportunities for self-sufficient living. Yes, government and corporation funding of child care to insure higher quality and plenty of access would be quite important. But relying on outside, impersonal bureaucracies can encourage dependency and a failure to make the effort of will to change one's own life. Only in feminist organized families, groups, and communities will people find the inner resources to take on the world. Alone most of us are as if nothing.

As for pornography, the liberal, individualist position of mutually consenting adults and free speech has done nothing to keep eros and violence under self-control. We need to look at pornography directly. Its main motif is the subjection, exploitation, and violation of women by men. And, of course, the sexist belief is that this is what women like and want, if it is not just said to be their fitting fate. If we cannot get laws banning pornography on the basis of the civil rights of women (as Canada has enacted and enforced), then at least we can educate women and men to draw the line between healthy sexual expression and violence. A laissez-faire, free-market approach does not protect women. Since men and women today compete in the marketplace much more equally, ironically the male drive to lord it over women in the vulnerable area of sex is even more threatening and vicious. We need to resurrect feminist community standards of decency.

Comparable worth (equal pay for different jobs equal in worth to each other) is a necessary next stage to overcome the sexual segregation of women in low-paying jobs. Comparable worth will target women to overcome their economic/job victim status. Women's worth is at stake; corporations are already doing job evaluations to determine women's contribution to the corporation's economic success. The fact that women for centuries did unpaid labor in the household is no excuse for underpaying women in the workplace. Women are no longer enslaved in the family, yet women especially bring values from the family that can humanize the workplace. Only when women assert their collective difference will women get the recognition they have long deserved.

WOMANIST: Black feminists agree with the radical feminists regarding a distinctive feminist ethic of caring. We also agree that we should avoid abstractions and deal with concrete experience (in the form of personal narrative and stories) as the loci for feminist meaning. There are differences among feminists, but if there is ongoing dialogue among feminists, not excluding the voices of nonwhite feminists, then coalitions and solidarity will form. Womanists are not separatists. The liberal feminists, paralleling their alliance with the capitalistic system, would marginalize us once again by falsely accusing us of separatism. The fact is that nonwhite feminists should have their own autonomous groupings, yet keep in touch, by dialoguing, with all feminists.

Black feminists tend to see pornography and drugs alike as external threats to the building of sound communities among African-American people. Pornography is a multibillion dollar capitalistic enterprise drawing resources from the black community. As for welfare reform, the Republican plan to turn welfare money over to the states (decentralization) is a plan to put the eventual financial burden for welfare on the states. The white power structure will be in control, and we expect that the defining of welfare as a black welfare queen problem will result in increased racism and the deprivation of low-income blacks struggling in hostile employment and educational environments. This mean-spirited, punishment mode of dealing with the welfare system is what is causing black separatism. Only black self-help will be left to deal with these problems. No wonder the Reverend Louis Farakhan led the million man march to Washington.

POSTMODERN FEMINIST: Women (and men) deserve to be liberated, not defined, especially by others. The only acceptable definitions are one's own self-definition. Women need to reverse the male domination defining and characterizing pornography. In some ways pornography is a healthy safety valve for sexual expression and may be a part of sexual therapy using fantasies rather than actual violence. If women engage in self-regulation, they will be able to protect themselves without the heavy authoritarian hand of the state, which is unable to distinguish between pornography with and without redeeming, individual value. Some women (such as Camille Paglia) want to celebrate sexual danger. Women are not so weak as to need state censorship protection. Clampdowns on pornography tend to affect homosexual material (e.g., in Canada), and in general, discriminate against dissent. All porn is political.

In the area of social welfare, we fear the overbearing impact of maternalism, which stifles women's independence and self-sufficiency. The present-day welfare system is matriarchal and keeps women in a womb of dependency. There need to be more monetary incentives that reward women for getting off welfare dependency. The present system creates despair and negligence. Education and training liberate without a doubt, but so many welfare mothers need development of their motivational faculties. Comparable worth is an excellent policy as long as it does not engender a redistributional war between men and women, while the wealthy managerial elite sit on their pots of gold and look on this sex war with amusement. I do not know why radical feminists are not advocating more worker takeovers and workers' cooperatives to break the system of corporate managerial control with their outrageous salaries and perks irrespective of their business' profits.

LIBERAL FEMINIST: The postmodern feminist stumbled on a central problem when she said that radical (difference) feminists carry their gender difference to the point of conflict and war between the sexes. State-enforced preferences for women regarding pornography, welfare programs, and women's pay will only increase the backlash and gender gap that extreme versions of affirmative action have caused. We certainly favor liberating women by providing child care, health care, better paying jobs, and education. These programs have to be enacted with male collaboration to stress the neutrality and gender-free nature of these programs and the world we want to live in. Males cherish autonomy, and they have a world that makes autonomy more realizable for them. We advocate autonomy for women and in the process believe that men will respect women for their autonomy (not for strident demands for special preferences). The development of a private morality among women against pornography is the surest (morality springs from personal habituation within families) and the safest (no resort to government censorship) way to isolate and stigmatize pornography. Women are not helpless victims. If there were no market for pornography, its presence would recede.

RADICAL FEMINIST: Perhaps the central question we feminists have to answer is our understanding and evaluation of the family. For better or worse this has been the nucleus and the haven for women. Many of the moral values we find characteristically female are related to the family—care for relationships, nurturance, reconciling interests, cooperation, safety, and togetherness. Are not the care and education of children our most important responsibility, and why should this great task become some awful burden assigned primarily to women?

Some radical feminists believe the family is not just a convention and a temporary union of free autonomous individuals upon reaching the age of reason. We do not hold to the rationalistic, autonomous man theory. We believe humans are social by nature and supportive (social) associations lead to the fullest development of our human potential. No go-it-alone logocentrism for us. All rights and obligations flow from collective associations. Individualism and freedom outside the conditions of social order make women more vulnerable than men, although not that many men succeed in the career rat race either. We look to feminism for a transformation of our individualistic society such that collective principles (belonging, togetherness, solidarity, healing) enliven us. Human flourishing is more attuned to such a social morality than it is to economic acquisitiveness.

LIBERAL FEMINIST: We are strong defenders of the natural rights of individuals irrespective of any social formations. All social organizations, including the family, are conventions (constructions). Yes, we need to reconstruct the family, but for the sake of greater individual freedom for women because it is in the family that female oppression has been rooted. Whether or not women marry and start a family is their choice. Women should not have to sacrifice a career or feel guilty about dividing their time between career and family. Programs providing flex time and parental (not just maternal) leave are very important to get more male (father) involvement in child rearing. Furthermore, we need to get more government-funded child care with government regulations that insure high standards and educational environments. We need more recognition of the value of child rearing and the diversion of resources toward child care. Certainly our economy will be more productive and wealthy if we prepare our children for their unavoidable, sophisticated, technological future. It is the concern for individuals, not the loss of such individuality in collective associations, that should be our guiding principle. Provide an adequate economic base of opportunities and individuals will take it from there.

POSTMODERN FEMINIST: There are all kinds of families and groupings that will characterize our future. Same-sex unions, polygamy and polyandry, sperm banks and test tube babies, single-mother families, temporary marriages, and so on already are being experimented with. We leave it to individuals to decide what works for them. It is weakness and dependency to resort to collective bodies to control us. Radical feminists want to impose a new moral absolutism because they fear diversity. Morality means limits, and we celebrate the unlimited.

RADICAL FEMINIST: Liberal feminists kowtow too much to males. The marginal return you receive for this subservience can only keep women marginalized. Do not you believe that women have special differences that constitute cultures of their own that can transform the world for the better? Do not we have to construct feminist cultures to oppose the "rape culture" of men?

LIBERAL FEMINIST: Radical feminists adopt an oppositional, blame-the-other consciousness that ignores the human condition of imperfection, dissatisfaction, and ineluctable tragedy. Can we blame men for the deficiencies of human existence? Does this really provide the appropriate leadership of the women's movement? To assert that women have a culture all their own based on the separatism of your difference criteria is to carry feminism in the direction of lesbianism. It is not that lesbianism is totally objectionable (homophobia), but rather that the greatest number of feminists do not choose this sexual preference, and they see lesbianism as more of a lifestyle than a culture. Lesbians can also express a lot of hatred of men. What is a matter of private individual choice and experience should not define the feminist movement as a whole when lesbians are no where near the majority. We favor the liberation and fullest realization of women's sexuality, but that is a personal and private matter that should not skew the feminist movement in the direction of some antimale binge.

POSTMODERN FEMINIST: Let 10,000 feminist blossoms bloom. All of a sudden the liberal feminist has erected her own difference, the bifurcation of the public from the private, as a basis for writing lesbians out of the feminist movement. Yet some of the most active and successful feminists are lesbians at the grass-roots level keeping the feminist movement alive.

RADICAL FEMINIST: Women need to reclaim the public space and renegotiate its boundaries. Males favor the abstract public self, disembodied citizenship, juridico-legal terms for deal making, impersonal bureaucracy, and autonomous, individual rights. A female-gendered citizenship would be quite different since women foreground their attachments to private feelings and allegiances, their bodies, and kinships (to other sisters and to family). Women favor face-to-face relationships and sisterhood groups that will take intimate care for personal development. The public sphere now will be infused with concerns that previously were relegated and circumscribed to the private sphere so they would go unmet. Government and the political process do not have to be distant and cold. The nurturing and healing characteristics of women can transform politics into an activity that provides a wide range of public goods to achieve a higher and more equal standard of living for all Americans. For example, if we can pay men for all their soldiering, why cannot we pay mothers and provide them with pensions? Many women are in poverty as the result of divorce. Why should not men be required after divorce to maintain women and their children at the same higher standard of living that most divorced men have? We have failed to take seriously in a political fashion the private realm of oppressive burdens placed on women in child-rearing.

WOMANIST: What has been occurring among you feminists is too typically Eurocentric and adversarial. On the other hand, a good dialogue does not produce winners and losers, and differences are respected at the same time that common grounds for understanding and practical action are reached. As feminists we all agree that we need to find diverse, self-definitional, and self-valuational knowledges. From our collective, past-imposed silence, we will rescue our subjugated knowledge. We African-Americans will recreate a distinctive oral culture as found in the blues, which is not entertainment but profound feelings and hopes. A different aesthetics is found in African-American quilt-making, stressing contrasts and unpredictability rather than the uniformity of Eurocentric quilt-making. There are many emerging black women writers who are resorting to an Afrocentric epistemology that has many resemblances to recent feminist epistemology. The Afrocentric contribution, of course, varies since African-Americans have had their own everyday experiences. But the conceptual epistemological framework that overlaps with feminist epistemology is: (1) motherwit wisdom and personal experience rather than formal booklearning; (2) a dialogue mode (spontaneous call and response is the Afrocentric mode of dialogue) connecting speakers and testing their knowledge claims; (3) an ethic of caring that stresses empathy and personal expressiveness; and (4) an ethic of personal responsibility that links persons with one another. Black feminist thought is one particular angle of vision; out of many angles of vision come generalizations and a kind of universal understanding of oppression.

LIBERAL FEMINIST: We reject the breakdown of the boundaries between the public and private spheres (which we want to keep separated) because the consequences will be disastrous. If the public sphere were opened up to all the subjective interests and drives of women and men, the conflict and the impossibility of reaching consensus would discredit politics. Radical feminists favor a politics of personal therapy that cannot possibly accommodate all the competing interests of individuals. Politics and government must be limited to gender-neutral, practical, public policy making, leaving it to individuals outside of politics and government to find the best responses to their particular, diverse needs. The radical feminists would freight government with tremendous projects inconsistent with the notion of limited liberal-democratic government. Politics has no final solutions; government serves to insure an environment where liberated individuals (irrespective of gender) can use their own freedom and power to determine their own lives. The radical feminists propose government interference to correct for the mistakes (diverse) individuals make;   at the same time such government intervention would discourage individuals from using their talents and energies to improve their own lives without government support. Where will government get all the money to fund the expensive women's support programs advocated by radical feminists? It is amazing the degree to which child-rearing has been converted to a political/economic payoff rather than a moral/educational activity of love. Radical feminists have denigrated motherhood and have given feminism a bad name among many women.

RADICAL FEMINIST: By keeping women's problems of gross inequality in the private and individual sphere, liberal feminists are upholding the oppressive, antimothering status quo. This is the real denigration of women to dependence on an impersonal welfare bureaucracy and on absentee males who minimalize their obligations to their offspring. It is only by empowering women as a group (not just individuals) that we can get real political and economic change.

BIBLIOGRAPHY

Atwood, Margaret. *The Handmaid's Tale*. New York: Simon and Schuster, 1986.

Bambara, Toni Cade. *The Black Woman*. New York: Random House, 1980.

Bem, Sandra Lipsitz. "In a Male-Centered World, Female Differences Are Transformed Into Female Disadvantages." *Chronicle of Higher Education* (August 17, 1994): B1-B3.

Christ, Carol and Plaskow, Judith, eds. *Womanspirit Rising*. San Francisco: Harper and Row, 1979.

Collins, Patricia Hill. *Black Feminist Thought*. New York: Routledge, 1990.

Daly, Mary. *Beyond God the Father*. Boston: Beacon Press, 1973.

Dietz, Mary. "Context Is All: Feminism and Theories of Citizenship." *Daedalus* (Fall 1987): 1-23.

Disch, Linda. "Towards a Feminist Conception of Politics." *PS* (September 1991): 501-504.

Eliot, George. *Middlemarch*. Boston: Little Brown, 1900.

Elshtain, Jean Bethke. "Contesting Care." *American Political Science Review* (December 1994): 966-970.

____. "Feminism and Politics." *Partisan Review* (Spring 1990): 181-191.

____. "Sic Transit Gloria." *New Republic* (July 11, 1994): 32-36.

Faludi, Susan. "Blame It on Feminism." *Mother Jones* (September/October 1991): 24-30.

Firestone, Shulamith. *The Dialectics of Sex*. New York: Morrow, 1970.

Flax, Jane. *Disputed Subjects*. New York: Routledge, 1993.

Fox-Genovese, Elizabeth. "Beyond Individualism: The New Puritanism." *Salmagundi* (Winter/Spring 1994): 79-94.

____. *Feminism Without Illusions*. Chapel Hill: University of North Carolina Press, 1991.

____. "Feminist Rights, Individual Wrongs." *Tikkun* 7.3 (May-June 1992): 29-34.

Gibbs, Nancy. "The War Against Feminism." *Time* (March 9, 1992): 50-55.

Giddings, Paul. *When and Where I Enter: The Impact of Black Women on Race and Sex in America*. New York: Morrow, 1984.

Gilligan, Carol. *In A Different Voice*. Cambridge: Harvard University Press, 1982.

Goldberger, Nancy Rule, et al. "Women's Ways of Knowing." in Shaver, Phillip and Hendrick, Clyde, eds. *Sex and Gender*. California: Sage, 1987.

Gordon, Suzanne. "Every Woman for Herself." *New York Times* (August 18, 1991): editorial page.

Held, Virginia. *Feminist Morality*. Chicago: University of Chicago Press, 1993.

Hirschmann, Nancy. "Freedom, Recognition, and Obligation: A Feminist Approach to Political Theory." *American Political Science Review* (1989): 1228-1244.

hooks, bell. "Black Students Who Reject Feminism." *Chronicle of Higher Education* (July 13, 1990): A44.

____. *Yearning*. Boston: South End Press, 1990.

Hunter, James Davison and Sargent, Kimon Howland. "Religion, Women, and the Transformation of Public Culture." *Social Research* (Fall 1993): 545-582.

Ireland, Patricia, et al. "Backlash Against Feminism." *Time* (March 30, 1992): 8-10.

Jagger, Alison. *Feminist Politics and Human Nature*. New Jersey: Rowman and Littlefield, 1988.

James, Henry. *The Bostonians*. New York: Dial Press, 1886.

Jones, Kathleen Jones. "Citizenship in a Woman-Friendly Polity." *Signs* 15 (1990): 781-812.

Kaminer, Wendy. "Feminism's Identity Crisis." *Atlantic Monthly* (October 1993): 51-68.

Kolata, Gina. "Man's World, Women's World—Brain Studies Point to Differences." *New York Times* (February 28, 1995): B5, B8.

LaRue, Linda. "Black Liberation and Women's Liberation." *TransAction* (November-December 1970): 61-64.

Lehrman, Karen. "Women's Hour." *New Republic* (March 14, 1994): 40-45.

Lerner, Gerda, ed. *The Creation of Feminist Consciousness*. New York: Oxford University Press, 1993.

Lewin, Tamar. "Furor on Exhibit at Law School Splits Feminists." *New York Times* (November 13, 1992): 14.

McIntosh, Peggy. "Interactive Phases of Curriculum Re-vision: A Feminist Perspective." *Working Paper #24*. Wellesley, Massachusetts: Center for Research on Women, Wellesley College, 1983.

McGinn, Colin. "Mothers and Moralists." *New Republic* (October 3, 1994): 27-31.

Mansbridge, Jane. *Why We Lost the ERA*. Chicago: University of Chicago Press, 1986.

Morrison, Toni. "What Black Women Think About Women's Liberation." *New York Times Magazine* (August 22, 1971): 15, 63-66.

Nussbaum, Martha. "Feminists and Philosophy." *New York Review of Books* (October 20, 1994): 59-63.

____. "Justice for Women." *New York Review of Books* (October 8, 1992): 43-48.

Okin, Susan M. *Justice, Family, and Gender*. New York: Basic Books, 1989.

Owen, Diane and Zerilli, Linda. "Gender and Citizenship." *Society* (July/August 1991): 27-34.

Pettigrew, L. Eudora. *Women's Liberation and Black Women*. Paper delivered to National Association Convention of Black Psychologists, August 1974.

Patai, Daphne and Koertge, Noretta. *Professing Feminism*. New York: Basic Books, 1994.

Rohde, Deborah ed. *Theoretical Perspectives on Sexual Differences*. New

Haven: Yale University Press, 1990.

Roiphe, Katie and Lehrman, Karen. *The Morning After*. Boston: Little Brown, 1993.

Schabu, Diana. "Sisters At Odds." *Public Interest* (Winter 1995): 100-105.

Schneir, Miriam, ed. *Feminism In Our Time*. New York: Vintage, 1994.

Smitherman, Geneva. *Talkin and Testifyin': The Language of Black America*. Boston: Houghton-Miflin, 1977.

Snitow, Ann. "Pages From a Gender Diary." *Dissent* (Spring 1989): 205-224.

Sommers, Christina Hoff. *Who Stole Feminism*? New York: Simon and Schuster, 1994.

Stone, Deborah. "Of Alms and the Woman." *New Republic* (December 26, 1994): 27-31.

"Studies Split On Sex Gap in Treating Heart Patients." *New York Times* (April 14, 1992): B6, C9.

Sunstein, Cass. "Porn of the Fourth of July." *New Republic* (September 9, 1995): 42-45.

Tannen, Deborah. *Gender and Discourse*. New York: Oxford University Press, 1994.

____. "You Can Talk Your Way Through the Glass Ceiling." *USA Today* (December 15, 1994): 11A.

____. *You Just Don't Understand*. New York: Morrow, 1990.

Tronto, Joan. *Moral Boundaries*. New York: Routledge, 1993.

Walker, Alice. *In Search of Our Mothers' Gardens*. New York: Harcourt Brace Jovanovich, 1983.

Wolf, Naomi. *Fire With Fire*. New York: Random House, 1993.

Wolfe, Alan. "She Just Doesn't Understand." *New Republic* (December 12, 1994): 26-34.

Wright, Robert. "Feminists, Meet Mr. Darwin." *New Republic* (November 28, 1994): 34-46.

Young, Iris M. *Justice and The Politics of Difference*. Princeton: Princeton University Press, 1990.

SIX

A DISABILITY CULTURE?

TO MAINSTREAM OR NOT TO MAINSTREAM?

Is there a distinctive and unique culture that would apply to the handicapped, disabled, physically and mentally challenged? The difficulty in choosing a term for these groups of people reveals the diversification of its members and the struggle over sameness and difference, inclusion or separation regarding themselves and others outside their groups. If being handicapped constitutes a culture of some sort, then joining the mainstream becomes a questionable enterprise without some qualification. Are we using "culture" here to mean a lifestyle as opposed to a whole history of customs, a distinct language, and a body of knowledge?

Again the central question is the degree to which, if at all, a group of people should have their personal and private conditions count (for special consideration?) in the public sphere where we all may interact. Should we enact laws and make policies to ensure the "survival" of such cultures or subcultures? Does it follow logically because prejudiced people have made so much of certain people's personal characteristics (sex, race, physical ability, etc.) as a deviation from their almighty "norm," that we should now highly stress those same characteristics, albeit in a very positive sense, in order to compensate for such prejudice or to protect such groups, rather than neutralizing and voiding such characteristics as not having relevance in public for the most part? These are tough questions which require a great many specific considerations and qualifications in the back-and-forth of dialogue.

THE DIALOGUE

OURSTREAM: The handicapped communities of the physically and
mentally challenged have begun to discern the political, social, and
economic need to come out into the open, to organize, to demonstrate,
and to achieve objectives that guarantee the rights of disabled persons to
receive their due recognition and respect. (We prefer that the term
"disabled" be always used as an adjective and that we be referred to as
"persons" or a "community.") There is considerable diversity within the
disabled community. Consequently, we need the following, broad
definition of who we are: (1) from birth physically and/or mentally
disabled persons; (2) by happenstance (accident, disease) persons
physically and/or mentally disabled; (3) mentally ill persons; (4)
developmentally (learning) disabled persons (slow learners, dyslexics,
attention deficit disorder syndrome persons, etc.); 5) chronically ill
persons; and (6) alcohol and drug addict persons. Today 45 million
people or 18% of the population in the United States are disabled persons.
From 1970 to 1988 the number of people reporting impairments and
activity limits increased 50%, increasing as a percentage of the overall
population from 11.8% to 13.7%.

Contrary to what nondisabled persons believe, there is no objective,
fixed, uncontroversial, medical definition for disabled persons. In general,
we can state that if you are a disabled person you are unable on your own
to perform some basic and essential life functions. But the "inability" may
be more in the environment of barriers and restrictions and in the attitudes
of people that claim you cannot be independently abled. Some disabled
people quickly develop a psychology of defeat when confronted by
environmental and attitudinal obstructions. That is why in the 1970s an
independent living movement began among some disabled individuals who
resented being labeled "cripples" (a Berkeley, California newspaper in
1967 used a caption, "Helpless Cripple Goes to School"). We have had
to fight a client mentality that made us utterly dependent on medical,
social, and governmental services personnel. Instead of some
institutionalized dependency status (the paternalism that asserts "you
cannot succeed on your own"), disabled persons have sought a consumer
choice model. There are alternatives and degrees of independence, all of
which are best worked out among support groups of disabled persons
themselves and not through cold, impersonal bureaucrats.

MAINSTREAM: Now is not the time (and perhaps there never will be the time) to radicalize the disability rights movement. We need to build as many coalitions as possible within and outside our movement. First of all, within the communities of handicapped, there are too many varieties and differences on the basis of age, status, type of disability, needs, resources, and policy preferences. For better or worse, the American environment we are in is highly individualistic, piecemeal, and diverse in responsiveness to the handicapped. Change and reform have been gradual, and you get true recognition by establishing inclusiveness in the mainstream.

Second, we do not emphasize some brand of political correctness when we use terms. Certainly, terms such as "crippled," "deformed," and "retarded" never need to be used, but handicappers and the disabled become the brunt of jokes (e.g., "the vertically challenged" for short people) when they get too picky. Our most pressing concern is with intentions and with what is in the hearts of people. For the most part, nondisabled persons are willing to learn, and we should give them every opportunity to do so, rather than putting them at a disadvantage and loss in some confrontation with us.

Third, we have to stick with what has made us so successful in terms of government legislation and policy, especially the Americans with Disabilities Act (ADA) of 1990. Basically, the ADA prohibits discrimination against disabled persons in employment, transportation, public facilities, and communications. We are not like other rights movements and do not need high visibility. Americans have turned against rights pleaders for seeking special and costly privileges. Right now we have substantial public support because our "affliction" is considered to be involuntary and something obviously deserving of a helping hand. Under Medicare, Supplementary Security Income (SSI), and Medicaid about $500 billion is spent every year on behalf of disabled persons.

Fourth, there are huge costs associated with transforming the world to make it "handicapper friendly", and yet Americans know that the cost of government and taxation is now too onerous. We have to be very careful when proposing public policy to avoid a backlash that would return us to the days when the handicapped were institutionalized, closeted, and hidden from view. Americans love to hear and see a successful ("I overcame the odds") hardship story on the individual level. This approach harnesses support, whereas radical demonstrators and exhorters cause negative responses. The disorderly conduct of demonstrators who chain themselves to buses, blockade offices, and crawl up the Capitol steps sends a media message that turns away the general public from such sights. We need to convey the right image: we are productive, contributing members of society, neither obstructive nor offensive. American political culture rewards the productive who participate in the mainstream, the I-can-do people, and not emotional pleaders who push their cause onto others.

OURSTREAM: Our differences over the right strategy (means) for the disabled rights movement are based on the very different goals (ends) that we have. We want more visible exposure and with that more understanding. We are the only cultural movement that anyone can join at a moment's notice with a disabling accident. The general public needs to know this, by shock effect, if necessary. We do not want to be kept out of the way, stuck at home, or in institutions. We prefer organizations that are run by disabled persons since we want the maximum control over our own lives and that requires support services which promote our psychological identity. Government policy has tended to be a bureaucratic relegation of the disabled community to permanent withdrawal from the labor force because the government does not allow for degrees of productive participation. Instead, you are either a totally disabled person or not a disabled person at all, which means you are given federal and state funds or totally cut off.

This bureaucratic, medical model used by professional service providers angers disabled activists because it is ameliorative (you have income maintenance, now go away) and paternalistic (we know best for you), rather than being corrective (rehabilitation and support services) and autonomy-minded. Income maintenance awards are based on physical/mental impairment rather than the variable ability to work. Accepting this approach to the disabled person diminishes the need to make the environment "disabled-person friendly" and delays changing the attitudes of the nondisabled about what a disabled person is capable of doing. We know that the general public's perception of disabled persons is a greater handicap for us than our own physical/mental disability.

MAINSTREAM: There is all the difference in the world between those born disabled and those who are disabled when older, later in life. The former may believe they have a distinctive culture all their own. Since they have known nothing else, being disabled is their accepted norm.

Among people who are deaf from birth, there is a growing movement for separate cultural recognition. They do not want to be "fixed"; and they consider hearing implants to be mutilation and "genocidal." We understand that people may live in a deaf world with its own integrity (American Sign Language or ASL is a language in its own right and not parasitic on English), and we remain hesitant to be imperialistic regarding the norms of the hearing world. Nevertheless, what will be the prospects of such cultural insularity? There are few employment opportunities when you only know ASL. ASL has no written form and thus has an antibook bias. Can we really say that we have developed a deaf person's potentialities to the maximum, if there is no effort, in some degree, to mainstream her or him into the hearing world? Yes, it is a free country, and we do have separatist peoples such as the Amish, the Hasidic, certain religious cults, and so on. We have to be certain that people are freely choosing such lives, aware of the consequences and not more dependent on government programs because they resisted integration.

Are you sure that there are that many handicappers now not working who would be working if there were a shift of resources to vocational rehabilitation? Are not there deep psychological problems of defeatism, not to mention the fear of failure, and the extreme limits that some of the handicapped have? It is one thing to require that welfare recipients find work because they are able-bodied, but the handicapped may require an enormous array of costly services to do some productive work. Everyone agrees that work of some sort brings a sense of personal accomplishment and integrity, and government disability policy may be wastefully discouraging work. Yet this is a very sensitive area requiring cautious, person-by-person adjustments.

OURSTREAM: Only one-third of the disabled population is now working. Certainly we can get well above the 50% mark. Already the federal government has started to make adjustments (your so-called gradualism) by not cutting the working disabled from Medicaid when they go to work only to lose their health care benefits. Court decisions have prevented employers from not hiring disabled persons because of their particular, greater insurance risks. However, such piecemeal policies do not get at the real big change that is needed, and this will never occur if we persist in using your "stealth strategy" to get government legislation passed.

The stealth strategy did pass the ADA in 1990 without any media campaign. The problem with this strategy in the long run is that it does not change public attitudes (prejudices and stereotypes against disabled persons), and private employers remain uneducated about the ease with which they can change their workplace to accommodate disabled workers. Most important of all, we have a severe implementation problem when it comes to carrying out fully laws and regulations that are enacted.

Frequently, your gradualistic and piecemeal strategy has failed to get specific, concrete definitions such as in the case of "reasonable accommodations" that employers must make for disabled persons. If we do not educate the public and private sector employers, then how will we be able to progress to the key factor, personal assistance services (PAS), that will enable more disabled persons to get into the workforce and improve their quality of life? Personal assistants enable disabled persons to take care of daily bodily functions, household needs, mobility from place to place, and communications. They are subject to the direction of disabled persons to insure that maximum independence is achieved.

We believe the costs of going from long-term care (no work outcome) to rehabilitation services and counseling (different degrees of work as the outcome) will only be higher in the short run. In the long run the example of disabled persons at work making a productive contribution to our GNP and paying taxes will offset rehabilitation services. The sensitivity issue can best be addressed by insuring full representation of disabled persons in the vocational and counseling services being provided. A positive incentives system for going to work would be a blessing for disabled persons because their extraordinary effort should be rewarded. Of course, without a national health insurance system, it is not possible to spread out the burden of costs for dynamic, corrective (not stagnant, ameliorative) measures. We believe that only when disabled persons realize they are members of special communities will they devote their services to each other and not become dependent burdens.

We very much agree with theologians who emphasize the need to perceive God in disabled person terms. We have to annihilate the standard norms of what we all physically should look like and be. Consciousness raising is crucial to the spirit of disabled persons. And the hearing-impaired community activists who want to keep their identity intact are only doing what is essential to their survival and self-worth. About 90% of hearing-impaired people marry other hearing-impaired people. And hearing-impaired parents are proud that their children are born hearing-impaired. They have a special culture of their own which non-hearing-impaired persons do not comprehend. Attempts to integrate the hearing-impaired into the mainstream have put them into zones of silence at severe disadvantage. For example, even the best lip-reading hearing-impaired people can only make out about 50% of what hearing people are saying. Consequently, there are severe limits to their degree of participation without ASL. How would you like to be half out and half in every conversation?

As for all of the handicapped, there is a need to establish a shared sense of political identity, an electoral constituency, and a broad-based interest group movement to insure that government not only passes favorable legislation but also enforces it. Enforcement is a major problem for disabled persons, and right now we are in a political environment that encourages Republicans especially to cut funding for enforcement provisions if they are a regulatory cost burden. A strong sense of being a part of a big umbrella organization will enable us to avoid the budget-cutting ax and to fight terrible stereotypes. Your own advocacy of the "can do" person is a stereotype that harms disabled people. We are not all made out to be heroes; most of us want to be treated just as any nondisabled person is.

Especially is it important to build the solidarity to fight public schools and private sector employers who will not make provisions for disabled persons even though the laws require "reasonable accommodation." We know that private sector employers do not fear damages for not hiring or for firing disabled persons. And the "no undue hardship" clause is an escape clause for them. Most accommodations for a disabled worker cost less than $1,000 and require only some flexibility with work schedules. Because there is no specification of "reasonable accommodation" in the ADA (no doubt our mainstreamer's political compromise), employers are not being properly motivated and educated. Who is going to get this message to them?

MAINSTREAM: What is going on in the deaf community is a good example of the dangers of separatism. Most Americans (who hear) would find it perverse on the part of deaf parents to deny their children all the advantages of hearing, even though this in no way makes deaf persons inferior. It is a grossly improper analogy (used by some people) to say that this would be like offering black parents the possibility of having white-skinned children. Skin color has no relation whatsoever to functional advantages. Those of us who know our limits never want our children to not overcome our limits.

As for ASL, certainly that language makes a lot of sense for claiming primacy, but why not offer deaf children a variety of possibilities such as lip-reading, reading and writing English, and cued speech, which enables hearing parents to communicate readily using signs that help deaf persons distinguish words that look alike on our lips. Cued speech is just transliterated English, whereas ASL is a different language all its own. Going beyond ASL helps further integration into the real world.

Where will the tremendous amount of money to fund personal assistant services come from? Over 8 million disabled persons need PAS; only out 850,000 receive it now. Even if a national health insurance plan were adopted (and it has not been adopted because it goes contrary to the capitalistic individualism of our political culture), there will have to be expenditure restraints. Certainly a more productive handicapped community will offset some of these costs. Gradually, we are moving in the right direction. We believe that 8 million disabled persons will be employed as the direct result of the ADA. Our next move should be to get tax incentives for employers to hire disabled workers.

OURSTREAM: Much of mainstreaming for the hearing-impaired and other disabled people leads to frustrated, unfulfilled adults. Why go through life constantly being reminded of your infirmity and difference when your difference can be a positive attribute shared with others? Over 300 independent living centers provide just that experience. What is needed is not tremendous new expenditures on the part of federal and state governments, but rather a rerouting of existing government money away from nursing homes and professional services that do not promote autonomy at all for disabled persons. Granted the beneficiaries of this "medical model" have considerable political clout, but they can be defeated if an aroused general public sees these groups as being on the government dole, warehousing instead of liberating people. We can put images of dependency in nursing homes (not to forget cases of abuse) right into the living rooms of all Americans.

The development of President Clinton's National Public Service program would create a labor pool of personal attendants for disabled persons at relatively low cost. Employers could be required to pay for some of the costs of PAS, and federal block grants to states could cover some costs as well. Right now about $2.4 billion is spent on community-based PAS at a per person cost of $8,000 to $15,000 a year. On the other hand, $20 billion is spent on nursing homes at a cost ranging from $30,000 to $60,000 per person per year. If the public were educated about the per person cost advantage of PAS, and the economic benefits of filling jobs, then we could make the transformation to disabled person autonomy.

It is amazing how much the disability rights movement has in common with other movements for minorities and the disadvantaged. We all seek equality of opportunity in order to achieve real changes in results. We have suffered systemic oppression. Three-fifths of disabled persons today live in poverty. We are not the problem, the environment is. We have pursued a kind of identity politics and have begun to raise the consciousness of our group members by distinctively taking public stands. We have converted so-called negatives into real positives for purposes of pride and affiliation. We have our own voice and language. We have not melted, assimilated, and disappeared. We too have come out of the home (like women) and out of the closet (like homosexuals). We disdain pity and victimization status just as do Native Americans and African-Americans. We seek an active not a passive voice, and we rely on personal narratives (as do women) to get our message across. We too know that the personal is the political. We have our demonstrations, often called "roll-ins," and we seek full participation and recognition in everyday life.

MAINSTREAM: The "stealth strategy" that we employ is invaluable because it isolates opposition, especially that from the business community, which is very conscious of negative public relations. We use this strategy only because we have tremendous support from political representatives in both political parties, many of whom have firsthand experiences with disability in their own families. Remember, at 45 million persons we are the largest advocacy group, but we are not oblivious of the many "free riders" who benefit from our political successes yet do little in the way of contributions. Most of all, many of our members may disdain the high visibility of "direct action." If we had more solidarity and voting power, then we could afford a more visible campaign.

Public opinion is wary of advocacy movements seeking to start new government entitlement programs and spend more taxpayer dollars. At times, disabled people have not had support from the general public and media when their demands were declared "unreasonable." For example, sidewalk toilets in New York City could not easily be made wheelchair accessible and many people thought it an unnecessary requirement in light of the greater overall public good. We need to finesse the issues of disability rights and programs, which means compromising, taking gradual steps forward, carefully picking our fights, opting for tradeoffs, and reaching understandings with potentially more powerful opponents. This is the art of prudent politics.

Yes, we do have a remarkable number of points of similarity with other struggling, nonmajority groups. But it is not true we have as much homogeneity as these other groups that are based on ethnicity and gender. Heterogeneity runs rampant; there is no overall disability culture despite some deaf persons' separatist commitments; and there are many disabled persons that see their condition as a diminishment of what is "normal" (especially if their disability came later in life). We both favor positive attitudes and actions, but we are a group more likely to wonder how different it might have been for us except for the laws of chance. Some disabled persons will question how alcohol and drug addiction and HIV positive persons can be considered disabled when they most often were engaged in behaviors that they freely chose and knew were risky. Even the ADA singles out the mentally ill. Employers can exclude a person with disabilities who poses a specific risk to the health and safety of others.

There are over 100 disability organizations in existence now, which suggests a considerable amount of diversity and potential for disagreement. A 1985 Lou Harris poll did find that 79% of disabled persons felt they had a common identity with other disabled persons. However, only 45% saw themselves a minority group like African-Americans and Hispanic- Americans.

OURSTREAM: All the more reason to take up the activist struggle to consolidate our forces. A backlash against disability programs is likely, just as there is now a backlash against affirmative action (that partly applies to disabled persons) and immigration. We need to educate the press and, in effect, the general public as well that disabled persons do not fit the stereotypes of pity and "supercrip." That old "custodial, paternalistic model" of impairment needs to be superseded by a model of autonomy with disabled persons being the utility maximizers for their own lives. More media exposure can do something about the negative responses that disabled persons receive because of their personal appearance. We know that discrimination increases the more visible and obvious a person's disability is. A strong sense of our personal identity will elicit not just tolerance but respect.   Consequently, we need to regularize our appearance, not for the sake of pity, nor for the sake of heroic appreciation.   In the end, we want the nondisabled to believe and understand that disabled persons succeed and fail like anyone else.

The civil disobedience practiced by the organization called ADAPT (Americans Disabled for Attendant Programs Today) performs a useful service of attention-grabbing.   Their objectives include denouncing nursing homes in order to get more home aid money from Medicaid by way of diverting to home aid a proposed one-quarter of $64 billion a year Medicaid now spends on these disabling nursing homes.

MAINSTREAM: We have no objection to your remarks but would rather stress interdependence and connectedness between disabled and abled persons rather than radical autonomy.   Autonomy can lead to a kind of defiant separatism, and some ethnic and women's groups clearly have tended in this direction.   We first and foremost aspire to integration, but on terms respectful of difference.   In the disabled community there are greatly divergent degrees of independence desired and achievable (e.g., some disabled persons prefer paratransit such as Dial-A-Ride rather than regular transit, and not all disabled persons want complete control over their personal attendants).   With this variety of needs and wants, we need to build flexibility and understanding into laws and regulations.

A recent demonstration by ADAPT in Lansing, Michigan resulted in unnecessary negative publicity.   Their descent on the governor's mansion when the governor was not there, although his young triplet babies were, was considered threatening behavior by the media and general public.   Such offensive street politics is no substitute for working through normal political channels with civility.

In addition, it was recently reported that federal disability payments are going to alcoholics and drug abusers in prison.   We need to assert strongly that taxpayers should not be giving funds to convicts.   Any other forms of corruption regarding disability policy also needs to be strongly condemned to insure that public opinion does not stereotype disabled persons as deadbeats.

BIBLIOGRAPHY

Albrecht, Gary. *The Disability Business*. Newbury Park, California: Sage, 1992.

Albright, John. "ADAPT Plans to Protest." *Lansing State Journal* (October 23, 1995): 1.

Batavia, Andrew. "Relating Disability Policy to Broader Public Policy." *Policy Studies Journal* 21 (1993): 735-739.

Berkowitz, Edward. *Disabled Policy: America's Programs for the Handicapped*. New York: Cambridge University Press, 1987.

Derthick, Martha. *Agency Under Stress: The Social Security Administration in American Government*. Washington, D.C.: Brookings Institution, 1990.

Dolnick, Edward. "Deafness as Culture." *Atlantic Monthly* (September 1993): 37-53.

Fox, Daniel M. "The Future of Disability Policy As A Field of Research." *Policy Studies Journal* 22 (1994): 161-167.

Hahn, Harlan. "The Potential Impact of Disability Studies on Political Science." *Policy Studies Journal* 21 (1993): 740-751.

_____. "Towards a Politics of the Body: Theory and Disability." *Disability Studies Quarterly* 12 (1992): 20-24.

Johnson, William and Baldwin, Marjorie. "The Americans With Disabilities Act." *Policy Studies Journal* 21 (1993): 775-788.

Lane, Harlan. *The Mask of Benevolence*. New York: Knopf, 1992.

Litvak, S. "Financing PAS." *Journal of Disability Policy Studies* 3 (1992): 93- 106.

McGuire, Jean Flatley. "Organizing from Diversity in the Name of Community." *Policy Studies Journal* 22 (1994): 112-122.

Nosek, Margaret and Howland, Carol. "Personal Assistance Services." *Policy Studies Journal* 21 (1993): 789-800.

Pfeiffer, David. "Overview of the Disability Movement." *Policy Studies Journal* 21 (1993): 724-734.

Scotch, Richard. "Understanding Disability Policy: Varieties of Analysis." *Policy Studies Journal* 22 (1994): 170-175.

Shapiro, Joseph. "Disabled and Free At Last." *Time* (May 17, 1993): 50-52.

_____. *No Pity: People With Disability Forging a New Civil Rights Movement*. New York: Random House, 1993.

Spradley, Thomas. *Deaf Like Me*. New York: Random, 1978.

Stone, Deborah. *The Disabled State*. Philadelphia: Temple University Press, 1984.

Treanor, Richard Bryant. *We Overcame: The Story of Civil Rights for Disabled People*. Falls Church, Virginia: Regal Direct Publishers, 1993.

Watson, Sara. "Holistic Policy Making." *Policy Studies Journal* 21 (1993): 752-764.

Weaver, Carolyn, ed. *Disability and Work: Incentives, Rights and Opportunities*. Washington, D.C.: AEI Press, 1991.

Wiener, Joshua M., Clauser, Steven B., and Kennell, David L. *Persons With Disabilities*. Washington, D.C.: Brookings, 1995.

West, Jane, ed. *The Americans With Disabilities Act*. New York: Milbank Memorial Fund, 1991.

Zola, Irving K. "In the Active Voice." *Policy Studies Journal* 21 (1993): 802-805.

SEVEN

THE COURSE AND PROSPECTS OF FLOURISHING IN OUR AMERICAN CIVIL SOCIETY: A MULTICULTURAL DIALOGUE AMONG A NATIVE AMERICAN, AN AFRICAN-AMERICAN, A HISPANIC-AMERICAN, A WASP, AN ASIAN-AMERICAN, AND A JEWISH-AMERICAN

Dialogues are meant to initiate and provoke a back-and-forth (dialectical) discussion and deliberation. No such discussion and deliberation arrives at any quick and easy end. Dialogues are jumping off points that go on and on, and the listeners (if not the participants as well) are caught up in dilemmas, differences, and points of divergence. Yes, some common ground, perhaps some common ends, and some hard-fought consensus can be achieved, although it seems far, far more important that we achieve understanding (*dianoia*) before we commit to an agreed-upon action (*praxis*). Dianoia is the mind going through matters, which is to say, deliberating, carefully, critically, and openly.

Nothing befits the dialogue mode more than multicultural issues. A free and broad-ranging multicultural dialogue between a WASP, a Jewish-American, an Asian-American, a Hispanic-American, an African-American, and a Native American will provoke and stimulate us to ponder how to bring Americans together in our civil society in order to face our particular cultural differences and our unavoidable social interrelations. There is so much diversity and difference within each of these individual groups that it is impossible that any one of these speakers alone could wholly represent his/her own group. Nevertheless, they give some common voice for their groups, and if there can be some common unity within a group, then possibly there can be some common unity among groups across our civil society.

The following dialogue along multicultural lines explores the positive contributions of a variety of cultures that constitute American civil society. Where and how do our differences and disagreements cause us to go our separate, distinctive ways? Where and how may we come together because we are all Americans? Are we really seeing and hearing each other?

To recapitulate the multicultural schema presented in the prologue, logically speaking, there are four possibilities for each of the six speakers in the following dialogue, given unity, the one, and diversity, the many:

I. Assimilationism (or homogenization); THE MELTING POT

II. Unity first but including (tolerating and respecting) diversity; THE TOSSED SALAD (the bowl is more important than the contents)   E PLURIBUS UNUM—from the many, one

III. Diversity first while searching for some unity in the long run if necessary and desirable; THE TOSSED SALAD (the contents are   more   important   than   the   bowl)   CULTURAL PLURALISM—within one, the many

IV. Separatism, every ethnic group goes its own way, since admixture is loss and self-destruction; THE TV DINNER (all stay in their own compartments) SELF-DETERMINATION —Balkanization

Consider how six American ethnic speakers—a White Anglo-Saxon Protestant (WASP), a Jewish-American, an African-American, a Native American, a Hispanic-American, and an Asian-American—express themselves in light of these four logical possibilities.

Analytically speaking, there are four ways that we can choose to investigate and characterize the condition of the American people. We can choose to use the concepts of *race*, or *ethnicity*, or *class*, or *individual personhood*. Potentially the most dangerous of these four concepts is race, and potentially the most limiting (atomistic) is individual personhood. There may be a strange polar connection between racism and individualism insofar as deracinated individuals come to stand directly opposite those that stand on their "race," and refuse to be seen and heard as just individuals. "They are just like me since each is an individual," says one; the other says, "They cannot understand and experience what I have since they are not one of my kind." The problem with the concept of race is that it overrides and cancels the search for a greater truth in favor of some irreducible biological or genetic explanation. (Some people use "race" to mean culture or ethnicity, but is not this usage confusing, causing more problems than it is worth?) The problem with the concept of the individual is similar because irreducible individuality makes it difficult to understand on what basis, other than the accidental, we have anything in common since we are all individuals uncommonly. As a result, both concepts encourage particularism and apartness but at two different levels, the one (the individual) and the many (the groups).

The criterion of race is quite unusable for explaining human affairs. It is not true that crime and unemployment are more prevalent on the basis of race, e.g., being black in the United States. When you adjust for environmental factors such as employment, family situation, and age (among black people there are many more young males vulnerable to unemployment and crime), there are no significant statistical crime differences between the black and white population. Unemployment and crime need to be studied in a socioeconomic (class) or ethnic/cultural sense. Race is irrelevant. The economist Thomas Sowell makes it quite clear that the differences within any ethnic group are greater than any differences between one ethnic group and the larger society. Hence, the focus of our study should be on the internal dynamics of that group and not on the basis of invidious distinctions such as the deviancy of any one race or group. Racism magnifies nonrelevant differences and assumes that factors, such as IQ tests, are some fixed measure. We need only know that the Jewish people given IQ tests in the United States during World War I had lower results than any other group, whereas today they are among the highest. Obviously, the acculturation process (how Jewish people responded to living in the United States) was the decisive process, which we need to examine. As regards political and social affairs, the term "race" (biologically and genetically) is virtually meaningless.

So why not deal with all Americans simply as "individuals" without putting everyone into any predetermined (prejudicial) category? Why does one individual have to be responsible for all Hispanics, all Protestants, all Native Americans? The burden is too great. Why cannot I be understood solely for who I am and what I am? The rejoinder is: "No man [person] is an island." A Robinson Crusoe dies bereft of humanity. On these individualistic terms, alienation and loss seem unavoidable. Atomistic individualism has no substance or content to it (thus T.S. Eliot's "hollow men"), although some individuals may choose to go this far in order to reconstruct themselves. But who among us is not indebted to some inherited socioeconomic group (class) or some cultural tradition (ethnicity)? We may choose to make of our inheritance whatever we desire. Yet choices are bounded by certain contexts and circumstances.

A grand debate exists between those who would use "class" (socioeconomic status) as the best way to explain differences in the United States and those who would use the construction or "myth" of ethnicity and culture (so sociologist Stephen Steinberg contends). Culture or ethnicity is mythical because it is falsely assumed to be fixed and to reveal behavioral patterns that account for different outcomes. But "culture" is a construction or invention. More important to Steinberg is history and the socioeconomic power structure that provide causal evidence for certain outcomes. The success of Asians and Jews in the United States has more to do with their previous socioeconomic class origins rather than their cultural values. Oppressive, institutional, power structures decide who can succeed and who will not, thereby producing inequalities. Those who argue from this "class analysis" perspective tend to deny that individuals adopt and choose among different values within a culture or within a multicultural environment. The class analysts inject their own rigidity and determinism, which they then often proclaim can be overcome only dramatically or violently by some sort of revolutionary upheaval.

Do classes and institutions clearly define who people are, or are they arbitrary and loose concepts? Is "oppression" and domination so clearly an across-the-board, total phenomenon leaving no room for freedom and opportunity? Can we just see humans as socioeconomic creatures (a possibly crude and lowly picture) lacking in personal and group responsibility? Do not ethnic and cultural characteristics generate uplifting, positive contributions inspiring individuals and highlighting societies as a whole? Is not the fullness of individual identity achieved vis-a-vis a cultural, ethnic background (maybe even multicultural) rather than just an act of individual will or some subjection to material-economic factors?

The underlying justification for this multicultural dialogue is that cultural/moral incentives are grounds for individuals to overcome socioeconomic barriers and to direct their society in better ways. Culture and ethnicity are intervening factors between our socioeconomic environment including our natural endowments and the results we can eventually achieve. Ethnicity and culture are not myths in the negative sense of falsehoods and illusions. Instead they provide meaning and identity to individuals in their socioeconomic contexts leading to the existence of defined communities. On this account, communities are not just the sum of individual contingencies, nor the mere product of economic-material forces. From these communities, where individuals experience a sense of belonging and togetherness, come strivings, achievements, goals, and ideals without which most of us would not be motivated to take on our world.

THE DIALOGUE

WASP: Too often social scientists and historians are overly fascinated with the institutions of political power (statism) and/or the market economy as the key forces explaining all else. These systems, be they economic or political, are held to be the God-like, independent variables, or the God-like oppressors. What more could you expect when politics is based on the impersonal and coercive factors of power, and economics is the endless acquisitive pursuit of self-interests?! Is there anything more than this reductionist analysis of such interests, urges, and drives?

To the rescue, if there can be any rescue, comes civil society, the community of communities, the health of which can elevate and save us from will-to-power politics and self-serving economic interests. Perhaps the foremost reflection on democracy in America occurred when Alexis de Tocqueville took his historical bearings from our civil society and our political culture. Does not Tocqueville provide an insightful source regarding our Anglo-American commitment to individualism, energy, equality, rights, public-spiritedness, and progress?   And did not Tocqueville have some quite insightful and poignant observations about the status of Native and African-Americans?

Within our civil society today the most striking characteristic is the questionableness of the melting pot, assimilationist model. A tossed salad model seems more empirically and spiritually accurate since many unblended colors and ingredients can all be found in the same American bowl. Many of us may have melted via the process of Americanization, but many more of us are unmelted and perhaps unmeltable by choice. Statistically, the white population in the 1990 census constitutes 71% of all Americans, but the birth rate among whites is under 5%. For African-Americans the birth rate is 13%, for Hispanic-Americans 18%, and for Asian-Americans and others 38%. If these birth rates persist, by the year 2056 the white population will be in the minority (under 50% of the total population). Already seventeen of our major cities have "minority majority" populations. Right now the African-American population is 12% of all Americans, while Hispanics are 9%, Asians 3%, and Native Americans 1%. In the 1980s, compared to the 1970s, the minority population had a twofold increase. A great proportion of legal immigration, 80%, is non-European. In addition, in the 1990 census 199 million Americans trace their origin to foreign countries compared to those 12 million Americans who just say they are "American". Among all Americans there has been an increase in ethnic consciousness and identity. Americans are asking, "What are my roots?" Genealogy is a serious avocation for many Americans.

With all the change and searching going on, it would be wrong to have a static, unidirectional model of what it means to being or becoming an American. Nevertheless, if we are all American by being in the same salad bowl, there must be some common characteristics to this Americanness. There are commonalities, such as our long-standing constitutional form of government, our English language, our primarily capitalistic economy, our generally religious orientation (over 90% of Americans believe in God and identify with an established religion), and the fact that we do come together patriotically in times of military crisis (e.g., the Persian Gulf War got an over 80% approval rating in public opinion polls). We all have in common (probably this is the most important and strongest sense of our union) that each individual should determine his or her own fate without arbitrary interference from government, and irrespective of socioeconomic background and cultural heritage. In this respect we all uphold and honor freedom, equality of opportunity, and change.

AFRICAN-AMERICAN: As one representative of a group in America distinctive for never having originally, freely chosen to come to America, and as a consequence of having viewed Anglo-American society from the vantage point of slavery for 244 years, my immediate reaction to our WASP interlocutor is how persistently Anglo-American his perspective is (along with a Tocquevillian frame of reference) despite his being critical of a status quo of hegemonic, assimilationist oppression. However, the slave in the slave-master relationship gets to be a much more knowledgeable observer of the master than the master can ever be of the slave, since it is the master who alone reveals himself/herself when he/she makes demands of the slave. The slave as an instrument and a piece of property has to be mastered but cannot be known since there is no arena for self-expression and self-revelation in this dehumanizing condition. The master never really knows the slave humanly, while the slave only knows too much about the master who acts out his or her humanity or inhumanity. Today, the price of slavery still continues to be paid: experiences of degradation and inferiority; and a segregated and bifurcated American society still refusing "to let my people go" even more than 130 years after emancipation. Yet as modes of self-expression open up, much can be learned from the special vantage point of former slave persons.

The slave person (as well as the post-slave person) is an invisible, ghostly, substanceless nothing. (See Ralph Ellison's novel, *The Invisible Man*.) Even though on the skin surface the slave person is always seen, there is nothing more than this dark, threatening skin color. No wonder minorities including blacks are always treated by Anglos as statistics that strike fear and terror, rather than as communities with thriving cultures. It is surprising that you did not mention, out of some liberal pseudosympathy, all the "pathological statistics" that supposedly define black people—violent crime rates, hard core poverty, single-parent households, illegitimacy, school dropouts, unemployment, drug use, welfare dependency, etc. These statistics propagate stereotypes that oppress even further the oppressed. Kick the victims while she and he are down and out.

If such abstract, lifeless, pseudo-objectifications called statistics are not enough, then the other alternative is to reduce nonwhites to mere individuals with a psychocultural makeup no different from anyone else who has had whatever similar experiences. And if we are all the same (equal) as individuals, then why do not nonwhite minorities perform as well as others? Then we are either discounted, or the guilt-ridden, WASP stereotype of "the victim" offers a convenient escape to explain individual shortcomings. No matter, we bear the added burden of being the "problem minority".

None of this will do for us soul sisters and brothers. Our souls are not in any statistics or individualistic treatments; our souls are in our community and what we have in common. We need to identify with the stories of our people, not data. (See Albert Murray's *Omni Americans*.) The crucial question is: What has come out of this African-American community story that amounts to our distinctive contributions to American society? In one word, according to the African-American playwright August Wilson, it is *music*. Starting from the Negro spirituals and gospel music, to the soulful rhythm and blues, to rapping, to the creative improvisational genius of jazz, and to the most recent, popular, rock-and-roll, African-Americans have dominated and defined American music. That is why when August Wilson begins to do research for his plays to cover a specific decade in African-American experience he starts with the black music of that period. Music speaks to and touches the souls of people, be it spiritual or secular music.

Most Americans participate in the Judaic-Christian religious tradition, a tradition that raises up the lowly and appeals to the long suffering. Through religion there is solace, tapping hidden sources of strength and confidence, renewal, and, most important of all, a coming together. Religion, unlike positivistic social science, avoids statistical victimization. African-American religion and culture is outgoing, gregarious, participatory, and communal. The neighborhood is the black family. High visibility is the core of African-American culture, utterly unlike the enclaves of privacy in lily-white suburbs or in urban, high-rise apartment buildings. We are not surprised that it took an African-American law professor, Stephen Carter, to point out that the United States has enacted a political and legal culture that forces religious devotion into a sphere of irrelevant privacy.

Furthermore, black culture is oral, not written. Free-wheeling rhetoric offered as a challenge to spar is frequently misunderstood by Anglos who take words all too literally and therefore cannot deal with the confrontational style of African-American culture. Provocative language is mistaken as uppity and personally threatening. There is a greater sense of dynamic play and color with words in black culture that is quite contrary to the abstract, formal, dead, fixed classifications so often characterizing the language of white "sciences" and modes of explanation. Giving voice, and the call and response of voices, are central features and legacies of our black community. As Frederick Douglass called it in 1849: the "live, calm, grave, clear, pointed, warm, sweet, melodious, and powerful human voice."

All kinds of recent secular, individualistic trends threaten to repress or defeat these spiritual forces of African-American culture. Social breakdown is characteristic of American society at large (crime, family dissolution, drugs, violence, etc.), but black folks are most vulnerable and most blamed in the media. Yet, in fact, black people do far more harm to and among themselves as they live in a world not primarily of their own making. Such is the long legacy of slavery and segregation that does not just vanish because of some court rulings and some laws enacted. Freedom alone for individuals is not enough; there is no promised land without "a people" or a community. Can the barren, hollow character of white, middle class, suburban society be the goal for black achievers? We need a bourgeois cultural transformation and renovation rediscovering community, along with a socioeconomic revolution providing jobs for upward mobility.

Just as Americans are optimistic since they are believers in progress and change, so are African-Americans proponents of change and improvisation (jazz), avoiding a disposition towards withdrawal and despair. There is no fixed melting pot model to fit all people into. Regimentation and depersonalization are antithetical to African-American culture. There is no common culture without the inclusion of other ethnic voices. Much could be gained in white America if there were a cultural cross-fertilization of black soulfulness and Anglo-American individualism.

Today, we are overwhelmed by popular culture on radio and television carrying out a cultural amalgamation, although it is not clear how conscious and how promising this form of electronic integration is. Mixing (but not melting) promises a better future and a new sense of American unity. White Americans would be happier if they rediscovered community on a rich, cross-cultural, multicultural foundation.

JEWISH-AMERICAN: The historical pattern for advancement in the United States has been individuals exercising their rights, potentialities, and opportunities to achieve the best they can. The American Dream states a promise that if you work hard you will succeed and enjoy the better things in life. Individualism has served most Americans very well, and for the black community we need to remove discrimination and disadvantages in order to promote individual development. To put too much emphasis on one's own community, rather than on individual will power to succeed in the world, would be to lose out socioeconomically in the United States, namely, in the competitive marketplace of individuals. There are certain middle class, entrepreneurial virtues individuals must have in order to get ahead; they are frugality, discipline, energy, perseverance, a readiness to learn what an Anglo-Saxon culture prizes, managerial skills, and self-reliance. Individuals need to devote most of their energies to the serious enterprise of work, rather than diversions such as play, entertainment, and sports.

People have a public sphere of activity and a private area of activity. In the public sphere you "do as the Romans do" in order to succeed when you are in Rome. In the private sphere you carry out your own distinctive, cultural-religious activities, you revitalize and strengthen yourself, and you establish (like a rock if necessary) your identity. To confuse these two spheres or to impose private conditions on public activities is to presume that you can be the dominant force in society. In a pluralistic and individualistic society, we need to keep these two spheres out of the way of each other for the most part. Perhaps the analogy can be made to being multilingual. You need to know which language (sphere of activity) is now appropriate at a given time and place and have workable facility in different languages. There is a time for street language, a time for family language, and a time for formal, proper, English. Of course, your heart and soul may most likely remain for reasons of personal well-being in the private sphere of your ethnicity where your own firm identity is. It should be surprising to no one that Jewish people are most likely to bring court cases to maintain a high and solid wall between church and state. A minority religion and culture best preserves itself in its private sphere, and this requires that the public sphere be kept utterly neutral, which is to say fair and equal, because of all our irreconcilable differences.

Why should not African-Americans follow the path of the first major, ethnic, minority, immigrant group, the Irish? There are so many parallels between the condition of the Irish and the condition of African-Americans. For example, 20% of the Irish in the second half of the 1800s died in miserable transatlantic crossings. Many Irish were indentured servants on arrival in the United States, and even by 1890 40% of the Irish in America worked as servants. Broken families, violence, alcohol abuse, short life-span rates, wretched ghetto living conditions, and societal prejudices such as claiming the Irish never could be assimilated (the Know Nothing Movement in the 1850s flatly believed this) characterized the lowliness of the Irish. But the Irish developed their "gift of gab" skills to good use in politics, unions, government jobs, sports, journalism, and entertainment. The Irish did not have the intellectual traditions and inklings of other groups (not for nothing do we use kindergarten, a German term, for our earliest formal education), and they were not as entrepreneurial as other immigrants. Yet the Irish made it; by 1970, average income among the Irish was 5% above the national average for all Americans.

AFRICAN-AMERICAN: The historical model of upward mobility you would impose on nonwhite Americans (frequently labeled the "American Dream") has left out key factors and is not respectful of those cultures fundamentally different from Anglo-Saxon culture. Crucial factors benefiting lowly whites you ignore. Take the many philanthropic community groups and associations such as revolving loan associations, mutual benefit societies, political patronage, etc. that were set up to help voluntary immigrants. In other words, the success of German, Irish,

Italian, Jewish, and Asian immigrant groups is more related to the communities they entered upon arrival in America rather than their purely individual aspirations. It is common for white European people to take for granted and ignore all of their assets such as positive community and family factors promoting their own success. Also, many of these immigrants came to the United States with relatively high socioeconomic backgrounds and origins and were quite prepared to function in white, Anglo society.

The history of African- and Native-American peoples is radically different. Neither of these people was left alone to progress. Just the reverse; both were degraded: slavery for blacks and reservations for Indians. African- and Native Americans became peons and dependents of American governments and their political, legal, and welfare bureaucracies. This dependency was never "chosen" by these oppressed peoples, nor is it characteristic of their cultures. African-Americans and Native Americans have had to rediscover themselves and locate their identity in an alien (to say the least) world. The white immigrant groups that have become Americanized chose to both identify with and fit into the dominant Anglo-Saxon society. Many immigrants were free to come and go and even planned to return to their European native lands once they achieved their dreams of fortune here.

Nonwhite Americans are not desperate victims needing the sympathy of white Americans. All that we nonwhite Americans ask is to be able to make our own contributions to the mosaic of American society, which will mean both a long journey and a new receptivity to adding diverse elements to our already (descriptively, but not yet spiritually) multiethnic society. Only in a society respecting comprehensive cultural pluralism and group self-determination, as well as a society willing to forego some preordained, fixed unity will we be able to find ourselves and flourish.

While the Irish were lowly in nineteenth-century America, they did not have the even worse disadvantage of being marked by the color of their skin and by the bondage of slavery. American public opinion did not really begin to acknowledge the real presence of African-Americans until after World War II. A much heavier price has been paid for all of the external factors that have obstructed us over and over again, for a long period of history (more than 300 years), stymieing any advances in the black community. Very often the only blacks who could advance were "Uncle Tom" type blacks, which is to say, blacks who performed the way whites wanted. Only recently have blacks started to explore their own identity on their own terms, thus the preference for a self-defined name, be it black (the pride of our colorful culture) or African-American (the duality of our heritage).

Every immigrant and/or ethnic group in America has to find their own distinctive way—that is truly what freedom and equality of opportunity are, not aping the way of others, not fitting some other culture's mold, unless that is your own chosen way. Perhaps German, Irish, Slavic, and Scandinavian immigrants have blended beyond any remaining, distinctive, recognition. Intermarriage fosters this as well as the growth of a common culture. But African-Americans do not want, for the most part, to dissolve. Nor will African-Americans accept a split personality, sharply divided between public and private persons. African-American culture is of a different sort than Jewish-American culture. African-American culture is inclusive, gregarious, liberating, and outward; whereas, Jewish-American culture is exclusive, tight, controlled, and inward. The public/private, secular/religious duality that Jewish-Americans adamantly uphold is diametrically opposite what African-Americans have experienced and resisted: the divided identity. Thus, W.E.B. DuBois' challenge: "One ever feels his two-ness—an American, a Negro; two souls, two thoughts, two unreconciled strivings; two warring ideals in one dark body, whose dogged strength alone keeps it from being torn asunder. The history of the American Negro is the history of this strife, this longing to attain self-conscious manhood, to merge his double self into a better and truer self. In this merging he wishes neither of the older selves to be lost. He would not Africanize America, for America has too much to teach the world and Africa. He would not bleach his Negro soul in a flood of white Americanism, for he knows that Negro blood has a message for the world. He simple wishes to make it possible for a man to be both a Negro and an American, without being cursed and spit upon by his fellows, without having the doors of Opportunity closed roughly in his face."

Perhaps this distinction between black and Jewish cultures goes a long way toward explaining the uproar at CUNY over the statements by Dr. Leonard Jeffries and Dr. Michael Levin. Jeffries believes that melanin, the substance that makes for black skin color, endows physical and mental superiority to blacks over the white-skinned race. Levin contends that IQ statistics prove that blacks are inferior in intelligence to whites. If we were to be extraordinarily generous, we would interpret their positions in terms of the most prominent characteristics of their different cultures.

Levin represents a caricature of narrow, "scientific" intellectualism, as if there were some sole or decisive, determinate characteristic, such as intelligence, that could be isolated from all other factors. Levin's single-minded logocentrism plays into the hands of Jeffries' attack on whites as being cold, clinical-analytical, oppressive, and destructive. For Jeffries, blacks are warm, peaceful, outgoing, beneficent, cooperative folk: Sun people, not Ice people, as white people can be labeled.

Given black culture, let us make some rhetorical allowances and not take Jeffries literally. Black people are just not dry, cold, intellectual fundamentalists. They love the rhetorical play of language (rapping), especially in order to be provocative and confrontational, not to be final and definitive. It is true that many cultures (other than black culture) pursue an individualistic, exclusivistic, deal-with-me-on-my-terms-or-not-at-all, style. But black culture is inclusive, participatory, boundary-breaking, spiritual, and communal. As long as we do not get too dogmatic, it rings true to say metaphorically that black and Hispanic cultures are both warmer compared to cooler white cultures (Anglo, German, Jewish, and Asian). Do we really want an American, WASPish, public culture that is so obsessed with work that we cannot avoid the rat race, ulcers, a population that feeds on over-the-counter drugs, back-stabbing, career-ladder climbing, and so on? Why should not leisure time play also be an important part of our public culture?

HISPANIC-AMERICAN: We agree with the African-American spokesman that Anglo-Americans do not respect basically different cultures. Hispanic or Latin culture is communalistic not individualistic. Family ties are more important than individual self-assertion. Alternative models of educational and economic development will have to be found for the Hispanic community to overcome the statistics of high drop-out rates and unemployment related to unskilled labor. The statistics do not pick up on the discrimination and mistreatment we face on the basis of our appearance and language. To take our language from us is to rob us of our culture and community, preventing us from being productive members of American civil society. Statistics do not reveal how uprooted, alienated, and ghettoized Hispanic-Americans are today. We are the migrating immigrants who were never wanted and were never expected to accomplish anything. How could we establish our roots/communities? Therefore, the cold, hard statistics that show Hispanic-Americans having very low voter turnout and weak (if not nonexistent) coalitions with other disadvantaged groups are only surface phenomena. Anglos frequently throw up their hands in despair when the disadvantaged do not behave as "they ought to". Yet the underlying explanation, the real personal narratives of disadvantaged people, detail their experiences so we can understand why they are prevented from living up to the norms of white civil society. Of course, they were not supposed to for hundreds of years. We need to listen to the many voices of personal experience from outcast ethnic groups so that we can refashion the American Dream (if it is not to be a nightmare).

WASP: The reliance on statistics as a measure for insight and policy making is always hazardous if unqualified, yet statistics do give some empirical, objective basis for arriving at conclusions. Statistics do not simply speak for themselves; they require interpretations and valuational qualifications. I guess we have to run both cold (scientific objectivity) and hot (storied intersubjectivity). There are different ways of talking about people. The scientific way, separating facts from values, can lead to atrocities—such as the parade of body counts during the Vietnam war, which supposedly meant victory but failed to take into account another culture (the Vietnamese culture) that sought the goal of victory nonstatistically. Statistics (including IQ and standardized test scores) may reveal a educational/cultural dilemma showing that African-American people are not succeeding on WASP American terms. What do we do?

Perhaps what we really need is a multicultural critique whereby each culture engages in its own process of self-examination. As a result we could have a pluralism of high quality. Maybe public schools with a high dosage of African-American cultural content will improve the education of African-Americans. Experimenting with different educational approaches is desirable, but the central educational goals have to be the common basic skills and abilities that prepare all of us for productive participation in our common world. To be diverted from this goal by divisive cultural and religious therapies will be to perpetuate real socio-economic disadvantages.

The most serious matter is not the domination of Anglo-American culture but our exploitative popular culture—the big money industries of sports, entertainment, and ubiquitous advertising. The White Anglo-Saxon Protestant (WASP) culture of the work ethic, individual rights, limited government, self-reliance, pragmatism as the test of value, and the energy and optimism found in our go-getting entrepreneurial spirit has been radically altered and damaged by commercial, popular, countercultural trends since the 1960s. These trends have not qualitatively benefitted any members of our society since they have discouraged responsibility towards others (see Jean Bethke Elshtain's *Democracy on Trial*). However, the more advantaged members of our civil society often have been more able to afford such countercultural excesses since they have someone (suburban mom and dad) or something (a good bank roll) to fall back on.

Popular culture, spread by the ubiquitous mass media, is the great solvent force today, rather than social and educational Americanization. Besides breaking down socioeconomic barriers between people, popular culture has lowered standards, diverted energies wastefully, and ravaged those most vulnerable to "letting it all hang out." One reason we have a *kulturkampf* today is the backlash from conservative religious groups who feel they are losing their children to the mass media's Sodom and Gomorrah. There is not only too much violence in popular culture, there is also too much violating of traditional moral and religious norms.

Commercialization, even when it parades itself multiculturally, is the great common foe we all have if we are concerned about the care of civil society and our souls. Some African-American groups and leaders have demonstrated against the alcohol and cigarette ads targeting black people. African-American communities are pillaged by these enticements. Instead of African-American communities pooling their limited resources (Anglo-Americans have on average six times the net worth assets of African-Americans), there are these wasteful expenditures on immediate gratifications, which of course is a very white American thing to do. Why cannot we all come together, across ethnic boundaries, and unite in a moral revival of our civil society? Service to others, responsibility for our neighborhoods, and concrete community-building activities could overcome the despair and hostility so prevalent among all the disadvantaged members of our civil society.

NATIVE AMERICAN: At last it is time for Native Americans to speak—the forgotten natives, the most alienated and most destroyed (by genocide) of all people "discovered" by European settlers. No other group knows how the dominance of Anglo-Saxon culture obstructed, if it did not destroy, the only indigenous tribal cultures in the Western hemisphere. Immigrant groups tend to believe in the myth that America is the land of opportunity, if only individuals apply themselves. Thus the test is one of adaptation, another way of imposing surrender on Native Americans. That

America is the asylum for oppressed peoples from elsewhere is only an ideological rationalization for conquering and owning our native people's territory. How odd it is that those who flee persecution so quickly forget the evil forces of persecution when it comes to another people that stands in their conquering way. Yet socioeconomic structures of power in a capitalistic society are quite discriminatory. Some groups are welcome; others are unfit. Survival of the fittest! Social Darwinianism! We are the endlessly "alienated minority," what is left of us.

"Human capital" theory holds that if an ethnic group has the right cultural traits—effort, energy, thrift, enterprise, confidence, ambition—then socioeconomic barriers will fall. If only it were a matter of human behavior and not structures, institutions, and systems of oppression. There are enough members of ethnic groups who have tried to succeed and have not been permitted. Native Americans, Hispanic-Americans, and African-Americans share in this multicultural suffering. The rules are against them ethnically, not because of their own supposedly deficient cultural traits. Powerful structural prejudices exist, working against different ethnic groups succeeding on their own terms and offering their own insights and contributions.

Today there are over 400 recognized tribes in the United States. Native Americans receive $3.5 billion in federal grants, albeit the cost of the Bureau of Indian Affairs (the BIA bureaucracy) is $1 billion, and only 11% of these federal grants reach Native Americans. Clearly, Native Americans do not accept this dependency and the corresponding oppressive reservation status (which is really a child, ward status). Consequently, some tribes are leading the way toward becoming self-determination success stories. The Siletz tribe in Oregon, which was officially abolished in the 1980s when the U.S. government had a policy known as "termination," now is rebuilding its tribe to partake of the best of both worlds—Anglo and tribal. The goal is for the Siletz to be economically self-sufficient by starting enterprises and investing all profits in a community trust.

Fortunately, Congress has passed recent legislation decentralizing the BIA to allow for local tribal control of federal government programs. Seven other tribes are experimenting in self-government by negotiating with the U.S. government as sovereign nations. They now set their own budgets, run their own programs, and negotiate for federal services. Previously, those functions were performed by the Bureau of Indian Affairs, a not very honored federal bureaucracy. [Likewise, on a smaller scale, low-income women in housing projects have taken over their buildings and worked with Housing and Urban Development (HUD) to gain control, ownership, and self-determination in their neighborhoods.] Twenty more Native-American tribes are ready to take part in this self-government project.

Native Americans, the original peoples of this continent, along with African-Americans, have had the lowly opportunity to watch palefaces and their ways. It just seems that Anglos do not have some of the essential cultural ingredients to solve their own self-created problems. From our Native-American perspective, white America is just as lost as Christopher Columbus was in 1492. For example, look at what the dominant white American society has done to the environment. The pollution, contamination, and destruction of the environment in the name of relentless agrichemical and industrial projects have upset the balance within Nature. Did white America ever have a proper attunement to Nature? White America could learn a lot from Native-American culture, which is matrilinear (tracing descent from the mother) and more in harmony with Mother Earth. A caring, warm, and nurturing relationship with Nature (which could be called distinctively feminine) can be found in Native-American tribes because the land has always been held to be sacred and not just raw material to be exploited.

Native-American culture accordingly brings a spiritual dimension similar to the music of African-Americans. An entirely different sense of time pervades the Native-American consciousness. Time is a peaceful, cyclical flow in accord with the changing seasons of nature. Time is not money, hyperactivity to meet deadlines, productivity on the assembly line, or a mechanical ticking clock. Materialistic, white culture lacks a spiritual sense of freedom. Those of you who have had the opportunity to listen to Native-American music know of its immediate therapeutic value in bringing calm and harmony to restless souls.

Native Americans also have a highly personal and communal sense of memory, tradition, and history that gives them their strong tribal identity. This is more important than being chained to the wheel of individual progress. Not only are women given more respect in the slow-paced environment of motherly-spiritual Native-American tribes, but the elderly are also respected more because they represent teachers transmitting the traditions of the past without which we are nothing. Do Anglo-Americans have a time-honored, living past that is recognized and celebrated and that has not been fundamentally altered by their uprooted "New World" experiences? Anglos seem to favor the use of the bulldozer regarding the past, tearing down the old and ever-constructing something anew.

The Iroquois Confederacy was shaped by the decision-making power of women. In fact, there was a feminist rebellion in the Iroquois tribe in 1600 when women demanded control over warfare conducted by men or otherwise they would not bear children. The women won. You now know why the stereotype of the squaw as beast of burden is a terrible anti–Native-American slur. Modern day feminists could learn much from Native-American traditions based on connectedness with a tribe or community including men, rather than some Protestant sort of rugged individualism that alienates women and men and advises that women are to succeed on men's singular terms if they are to succeed at all.

Other characteristics of Native-American culture that have made a contribution to American civil society and need to be considered in bettering American society are: stories that dramatize one's inter-relationship with other people and the environment; fierce pride, courage, and endurance; raucous laughter at the absurdities of life; sharing goods and possessions rather than accumulating and hoarding one's own; and politically, the fashioning of pluralistic and federalistic forms of government that accommodate diverse groupings of people (the Iroquois federal system of government was studied by Benjamin Franklin).

It would have been easy for me, a Native American, to tell the victim's story about how Anglo-Americans practiced genocide against Native-American tribes. A terrible cultural clash occurred in the 1700s and 1800s as Anglo-Americans entered into fraudulent treaties with Native-American tribes (about 400 treaties from 1787 to 1867) punctuated by the "Trail of Tears" expulsion of Native Americans to barren lands west of the Mississippi and to miserable reservations (America's official concentration camps). Only since the 1970s have Native Americans begun to recover land, water, and fishing/hunting rights through the courts, paralleling the court successes of African-Americans originating in the civil rights movement of the 1950s. But the victim's approach to the circumstances of Native Americans (as well as to African-Americans) is offensive to our pride and independence. Native Americans do not seek sympathy. Beyond victimization is respect for the unique contributions of Native Americans and then our acceptance and inclusion in a multicultural national community.

There are five phases that Professor Peggy McIntosh explores to describe the travails of the feminist movement. These same phases could be equally applied to Native Americans, Black Americans, and other ethnic minorities.

(1) Exclusion, domination, and invisibility mark the minority groups that are treated as outcasts (the cigar store Injun).

(2) Exceptional, great minorities stand out and are recognized, but not any others, least of all, "ordinary" minorities (the Pocahontas legend).

(3) A minority becomes a problem and an issue; statistical negatives are recited; victimization and suffering are emphasized (Little Big Man).

(4) Respect is found for the positive contributions that minorities bring and a period of diversity and pluralism flourishes.

(5) Inclusion and connectiveness is accomplished in an all-embracing, multicultural community. Only a civil society that respects multicultural diversity would be a civil society that Native Americans felt they belonged to. Multicultural diversity means acknowledging, accepting, and enjoying non-Anglo cultural norms.

Let us hope we are (and, if not, are preparing for) entering phase (4) on the way to phase (5).

ASIAN-AMERICAN: I suppose the Asian-American community, which is quite diverse in and of itself including Chinese, Japanese, Vietnamese, Filipinos, Koreans, Thai, Cambodians, et alii, would be more comparable to Jewish-American community experiences. Asian-Americans put a lot of emphasis on the exclusivity of family and clan identity, yet also take on the outside world where we are skillful businesspersons or just extremely hard and durable workers who build up our capital resources within a generation or two as all family hands pitch in.

An Asian-American motto that all Americans understand as the "gung ho" spirit, is "if it is easy, it is not worth doing." Asian-Americans quickly "learn the ropes" regarding what is required of them to progress and succeed. They take very seriously (almost religiously) the importance of learning. They have "neng kan," the ability to put their minds totally to a task. Privately, their tight-knit communities are enclaves of security and identity as they maintain their own culture and traditions. Some of this isolation was forced on Chinese-Americans, who faced racial persecution, negative stereotypes, segregation, degrading jobs, and denial of citizenship until 1924. Asian-Americans know well the ghetto of alienation that Jews, blacks, and Native Americans also experienced, albeit in different ways.

On the other hand, certain vices have been internal to the Chinese community: secret societies, Mafioso-type groups, gambling, drugs and prostitution, and sweatshop slave labor have afflicted the Chinese. No culture is without its negative side and its severe obstacles, internal and external. Asians are very distinctive in appearance and clothing, and our language accent and assigned job tasks promoted the belief that we could not be fully certifiable Americans. Melting into a common pot, as the variety of European immigrants did, was not imaginable. Ghettoization was a necessary condition until white Americans accepted and respected what Asian-Americans could achieve. Many Asian-Americans saw themselves as sojourner immigrants. In other words, we had no permanent place in America, and we would return to our native lands once we had earned a sufficient amount of money. By the 1940s this sojourner status changed as Chinese-Americans became established—our industry, self-reliance, and productivity in the American community could not be denied. We fit the standards of the WASP model; we proved our status as "model minorities." In capitalistic America, money talks and opens doors. Nevertheless, we have been more satisfied and content not having a big public and political profile.

Of course, Asian-Americans greatly benefitted from strong families in which everyone had jobs and also from a set of mutual aid societies that provided economic incentives. Today immigrants are more dependent on government bureaucracies for assistance. We will have to see what recent Asian immigrants do for themselves in this new environment. The Chinese (like the Jews) were denied access to employment opportunities reserved for white Europeans, so they found their own niche in the expanding American society and economy. Many who are now successful are very grateful for having found fields of opportunity. Will the new Asian immigrants also find their niche? Chinese- and Japanese-Americans tended not to use or need public relief programs and thereby avoided dependency. They also came to the United States with considerable economic and psychological skills. Therefore, it would not be appropriate to say to other ethnic groups that they too can overcome prejudice and persecution by simply following the model Asian-American example.

Asian-Americans are more amenable to the dominant WASP culture and its criteria for behavior and success. Asian-Americans keep their own thoughts to themselves and never give up hope (read Amy Tan's *Joy Luck Club*). And the Asian-American community is better situated to overcome obstructions and discriminations. Joining up with the American Dream did not necessarily mean the loss of cultural identity and strength among Asian-Americans. Asian-Americans are less likely to fall victim to the anarchic ravages of individualism where there would be family and moral breakdown. A strong sense of duty, honor, and responsibility toward one's parents and one's community (called "shou") creates internal norms (called "chu ming") that limit unproductive, alienating behavior.

The internment of Japanese-Americans in California during World War II was especially damaging to the integrity of Japanese-Americans who were firmly loyal (there were no contrary, treasonous examples) to the United States. Millions of dollars of property were lost when Japanese-Americans were put in internment camps, and the basic rights of these American citizens were grossly violated. Perhaps Americans have learned since then that an ethnic group can retain its culture very adamantly, but still be staunchly loyal to the United States.

Today the reverse burden is placed on Asian-Americans: we are "the model minority," expected to be so exemplary in whatever we do. Now Asian-Americans are not allowed to fall short. Always having to perform in a superior manner puts terrible psychological pressures on Asian-Americans. In mathematics, computer science, and the natural sciences, Asian-Americans are always supposed to be at the top of their class (thereby raising the grading curve for all other students).

Even positive stereotypes can hurt. Consequently, some Asian-Americans fear (along with Jews) the affirmative action quota limits now being imposed by universities, governments, and private employers are limiting the numbers of successful ethnic groups. How ironical that these successful minority groups can become discriminated against by reason of their success!

HISPANIC-AMERICAN: The Hispanic-American community likewise is not monolithic but also is internally diverse: Mexicans, Cubans, Spanish from Spain, Puerto Ricans, Jamaicans, and other Latinos from Latin American countries can be found in the United States. Hispanic-Americans constitute the last of the major immigrant groups and have such a high birth rate that our numbers may surpass African-Americans in a decade or two. In the 1930s and in 1947, there were mass expulsions of millions of Mexican-Americans from the United States. Only recently in the 1960s have Mexican-Americans been allowed to stay in the United States as opposed to being treated as only sojourners—doing farm, stoop-labor jobs that other Americans would not do. Yet we cannot forget the migrant laborers still going as far north as New York and Michigan to harvest a variety of crops. Unbelievably miserable, exploitive working conditions exist for these Mexican migrant workers. They are given pitiful wages as if they were North America's peasant class. America's nonfeudal society was not supposed to know about and have such a caste of workers. Such a migrant lifestyle imposes severe health care problems and educational deprivation on these families with special impact on their children.

It is amazing the degree to which so many American immigrant groups are uprooted wanderers and pioneers in their own distinctive ways (the Jewish peddlers, the Chinese railroad workers, the Mexican migrant workers, the forced marches of Native Americans westward, and the black worker migration from the South to the North). Such are the trials and tribulations of peoples who have no firm ground in which to take root. In general, high rates of mobility (frequently changing addresses among young Americans) are quite commonly American. Yet to settle down and establish roots is a necessary precondition for accumulating the resources to progress both materially and psychologically. Everyone should realize that only recently have Hispanic-Americans been assured of a secure place (if they so choose) in American society. In Texas there was even a recent attempt to deny education to alien Mexican children, until the U.S. Supreme Court overruled this latest form of exclusion and discrimination. California now is trying to implement discriminatory laws and practices against Latinos. We rely on the courts (similar to the experiences of African-Americans and Native Americans), not majoritarian public opinion and referenda, to safeguard our human rights.

Acculturation has been slow because of the back-and-forth movement of Mexicans, the deep alienation of Puerto Ricans herded into inner city ghettoes, and the language barrier confronting Latinos. Retention of Spanish and bilingualism perhaps has been more pronounced among Hispanic-Americans because Hispanics (like blacks) are so distinctively outgoing, gregarious, inclusive peoples, unlike Asian- and Jewish-Americans, who draw a sharper definition between their public and private lives. We (along with African-Americans) cannot live a schizoid, double life going back and forth between separate public and private spheres. Consequently, Hispanic-Americans (especially our children) try hard to learn English, and they do succeed in order to participate more fully in American society.

Hispanic-Americans have also had higher rates of high school dropouts (even higher than Black Americans) and one of the lowest rates of political involvement. Voter turnout among Hispanics is second lowest of all ethnic groups. Hispanics account for less than 1% of all elected officials. There is less labor force participation among Hispanic women than black women, and this, of course, keeps overall family income low. Yet there exists strong family and strong community solidarity. The exception is the Puerto Rican community mostly on the East Coast, especially in New York City, which has had considerable family breakups and high rates of crime and violence. Puerto Ricans are more alienated than other Hispanic-Americans. Among all Hispanic-Americans (like Black Americans) there has been considerable dependence on the welfare bureaucracy rather than the self-help and mutual aid societies that earlier immigrants benefitted from. It is wrong-headed to blame Hispanics and blacks for this dependence when these two groups are more vulnerable to the forms of breakdown and dependency that have plagued American society as a whole over the past 30 years.

Today, American popular culture emphasizes immediate gratification (consumerism) over saving and self-sacrifice and has an array of countervailing tendencies: the decline of the work ethic and values associated with it; a more sophisticated, skill-requiring, white collar employment market with fewer unskilled, blue collar jobs; a premium on education and literacy while the electronic media dumbs people down; a decline in public manners, public spiritedness, and public responsibility; liberated teenage behavior and the rise of teenage pregnancies and female-headed households; and dangerous, deadly addictions such as drugs and alcohol. No ethnic group can be scapegoated (contra David Duke) for all these general societal trends. In fact, the best within all American ethnic groups is antithetical to these popular culture trends.

A sort of youthful, 1960s-based, irresponsibility and rebellion linked to a new, go-it-alone individualism threatens the best within all our traditional ethnic cultures. Nevertheless, while there are problems with American popular culture, it, more importantly, has been the one place where African-Americans and Hispanic-Americans have been able to be included in a participatory way. Popular culture is open, liberating, youthful, and dissenting—therefore, promoting change. Does our WASP interlocutor want to take us back to the 1950s where all cultural representations were flat, white, moralizing, conforming models of dominant Anglo culture?

The strengths of the Hispanic-American community are its warmth, solidarity and togetherness, energy, and hard, physical labor efforts. Cuban-Americans have proven how entrepreneurial and middle class Latinos can be. Anglos could learn much from our togetherness and strong family values. Not every American needs to join the entrepreneurial rat race and contract ulcers to be certified as an American. The Latina way of life is slower paced ("manana" is fine) and closer to the natural, biological rhythms of life. A greater inclusion of Hispanic-, African-, and Native American life practices would make for more healthy and wholesome Americans. All Americans would benefit from having another language in their possession, just as many Europeans are ordinarily bi- or multilingual. Certainly knowing the Spanish language will have pragmatic economic advantages as American businesses seek growing markets in Mexico and Spain and the developing countries of Central and Latin America.

WASP: You are correct that all Americans, especially white Americans, need to understand and adapt themselves to the important contributions of its ethnic groups—the music of African-Americans, the spirituality of Native Americans, the linguistic and communal richness of Hispanic-Americans, the dutiful, diligent, dogged drives of Asian- and Jewish-Americans. All American immigrants (including Native Americans, who are not immigrants) have a sense of being wanderers or sojourners, yet they are expected to settle down and be productive citizens. Therefore, since the beginning of the United States, in ideals and in principles, there have been a civil society and republican government established for *all* peoples. The particular cultural roots of our country are Anglo-Saxon, but the ideals and the principles of republican government and society are universal and culturally neutral for everyone. Republicanism is built on universal, natural, human rights, limited government based on popular consent and participation, and the practice of self-government whereby people determine for themselves their own government.

We call this "empowerment" today. Yet we all agree this should be an empowerment of community, not just individuals. In some cases of multicultural politics there has been a tendency to provoke unnecessary conflict, rather than to find the ties that bind. America was not only an asylum for oppressed refugees, but also an opportunity for them to determine their own fate. In their civic life experience (politics and society) diverse Americans can come together and find consensus without letting their ethnic, religious, or economic differences foment turmoil and disunity.

Would it not be more beneficial to concentrate on the unity that civic allegiance can forge, rather than the divisiveness and conflict that ethnic and religious allegiances tend to excite? A vibrant, middle-class culture characterized by common beliefs and aspirations and relatively equal economic opportunities should be our primary objective. Liberal democracy is mostly based on content neutrality because our social agreement requires burying those particularistic interests and beliefs that we can never reach agreement on. Americans have great freedom to express and develop their own interests and beliefs, but legally and politically we have to find a less parochial and more neutral common ground.

Pennsylvania, the Quaker state, was the model of true Americanization. No political or religious tests were applied to differing groups of people. Quakers even at the beginning of our country recognized the freedom of black people and their right to vote. According to republican principles, citizenship was given to all who participated freely. Other states such as Massachusetts had different models in which religious and political tests were applied, especially toward those ethnic groups that came from nondemocratic cultures. The Federalists perhaps were the first to have WASPish fears, and the Alien and Sedition Acts were a legislative product of such fears of newcomers from different cultures. So we did, in fact, terribly discriminate against, abuse, and even kill some of those whom we thought were unassimilable. But our principles and ideals were not at fault, even though our practices were, which is to say we failed to be true to our own ideals in practice. Basically, Dr. Martin Luther King, Jr. exhorted us to achieve this in his "I Have a Dream" message: America needs to reenact its own cherished principles and ideals (colloquially called "myths" and "dreams"). Frederick Douglass and Langston Hughes were also Americanists; the latter wrote, "I, too, sing America"; "Its dream lies deep in the heart of me."

If we have no common core of beliefs and principles, then we will be at terrible odds with each other, unable to negotiate a peaceful, integrated, united society. We need to be full participants in our body politic and to find spiritual/cultural connections with others who are like and unlike us. Otherwise we will have in the United States the type of separatist ethnic strife that we see burgeoning today in Canada, India, the former Soviet

Union, and the former Yugoslavia.

AFRICAN-AMERICAN: Before there can be some reality to this communitarianism you so prize, there will have to be greater appreciation and respect for ethnic pluralistic differences. From these differences, *e pluribus*, some unity, *unum*, may eventually be created. However, your WASPish position would impose a WASPish universality on the variety of American ethnic communities. The universality being imposed, ironically enough, is individualistic, not communal at all; it is too procedural, not substantive (i.e., ethnic) enough, and therefore would fragment and isolate Americans. Everyone would be locked securely in their suburban bungalows watching television and soaking in their jacuzzis.

The principles of republican government and civil society are not universal and neutral historically. Were they ever intended for all people? Even if they were so intended, gross socioeconomic inequalities makes participation very unequal; and the procedures of such a government are majoritarian, which naturally keeps minorities without power. You expect us to compromise politically, as if we could do so, being in the minority, without loss of our ethnic identity? Limited government means assuring that great socioeconomic inequalities are justified, because does not everyone equally have individual rights? But having individual rights such as are included in the First Amendment (free speech, free press, and free exercise of religion) does not mean much in practice if you have few economic resources.

The traditions of African-, Hispanic-, and Native Americans are communal, tribal, and associational. In WASP America, the African-, Hispanic-, and Native-American cultures experience dissolution, and they have had to rebuild themselves in support groups, networks, and community development efforts which rugged, individualistic white America cares not about and does not understand. Until out-groups know and establish who they are, they cannot expect real functioning equality in white America. How can there be equality and harmony when we have such deep cultural splits between individualism and communalism, entrepreneurship and solidarity, economic acquisition and spiritual fulfillment, competition and cooperation, intellectual resourcefulness and prideful task mastery, and modernizing development/change and environmental nurturing? Within one country we are many peoples with many ways of behaving. Mere words about consensus will not bridge the gaps between these divisions.

JEWISH-AMERICAN: There are ominous signs today on our university campuses related to your advocacy of diversity. We now see a new tribalism and racial conflict at our northern, liberal campuses, the resegregation of students and student activities on the basis of race, the conversion of education curricula away from the core values in Western civilization, backlash hostility as the result of affirmative action policies, and *in loco parentis* student conduct codes that threaten the First Amendment's freedom of speech rights. We seem to have lost a firm consensus in our society and politics (we used to be bipartisan in foreign policy and Republicans more or less accepted New Deal legislation).

Young people have gone libertarian with an "I-can-do-as-I-please" notion of liberty without a social concern of commitment to others less fortunate. A new meanness has arisen against those on welfare, those who have committed a crime, and those who have not succeeded on white middle class terms. Our politics is riddled with the pluralism of special interest group pleadings and privileges. The liberation movements of the 1960s undermined the very social values and norms that enabled Americans to work together. We need a revival and reinvigoration of American civil society, perhaps by way of a National Public Service Corps that would put culturally diverse young people to work productively and patriotically. If we find concrete and practical ways of working together to strengthen our public/civil society, then we will not have to worry about all the diverse and conflicting strands of culture and ethnicity in the United States.

HISPANIC-AMERICAN: The breakdown in American society is not related to the ethnic reaffirmation that is occurring as minorities seek to find meaning and purpose in American society. WASPs are too individualistic and libertarian on their own and have pushed themselves to extremes. The money and power behind exploitive popular culture is WASPish. What ethnic minorities want is to rediscover their identities. Culture is a conversation among many diverse voices. If there is going to be a common core culture in the United States, it has to include non-Western traditions, and it cannot be just dead, white, male voices. A vibrant and common culture for a diversity of Americans is yet to be established but will have to be accommodatingly colorful and open to change. Multiculturalism is especially important in education to instill pride and hope and then to rebuild a broad, common American culture.

Feminist, Afrocentric, and bilingual approaches in education offer the opportunity to include those who otherwise would be excluded. Your general and supposedly universal principles and ideals of the "American way of life" need to be refurbished and their content, focus, and application need to recognize ethnicity and gender. This is no threat to dominant white males if they truly are not seeking to preserve some oppressive power structure of their own making.

ASIAN-AMERICAN: What is so amazing is that many multiculturalists and Afrocentrists do not acknowledge that Western civilization alone is tolerant of diversity and change and is more self-critical of its own faults than other cultures the multiculturalists and Afrocentrists favor and want us to emulate. The politicalization of education with ideologies which themselves are exclusivistic and intolerant is not very promising. Should not knowledge be based on facts, objectivity, and critical distance rather than psychological sensitivities, ideological reconstructions, and passionate interests? Will education become personal conversion therapy and sensitivity sessions? Is loyalty to a particular ethnic group the most important form of human expression? Can we ever have a politics of ethnic identities that gets beyond division, misunderstanding, hostility, and breakdown? Once a particular ethnic group gets governmentally defined, have not new boundaries been established, bureaucratically cutting people off from one another? A healthy civil society allows individuals to choose freely their own kind of ethnic participation without using social pressures and governmental decisions to provide special forums and benefits for ethnic groups.

NATIVE AMERICAN: Multiculturalism will permit ethnic minorities to have the time and space to pursue their own community self-development. For Native Americans the community is the tribe. The majority, advantaged population should not be fearful of other people having their own opportunities. Much of our history and our ways of teaching about this history need to be revised and reconstructed. A more credible Asian-American, Ronald Takaki, has begun this rewriting of history to include the stories of minorities in his *A Different Mirror: A History of Multicultural America*. When disadvantaged ethnic groups are included in the history books, then we can appreciate their differences and recognize their different potentials. It is false to assume that there is some totally agreed-upon, already-known-and-achieved social unity that everyone should just fit into.

Prevailing inequalities regarding African-Americans, Hispanic-Americans, and Native Americans require that government provide equality through favorable civil rights laws, nationally recognized ethnic celebrations, the financing of ethnic education, seed programs for economic development, and proportional political representation. A neutral government and a laissez-faire politics only give advantage to those who have already succeeded. There is no such thing as real neutrality in fact because there is no such thing as full equality in practice. A politics of group rights and benefits is necessary to compensate and correct for the ravages of American individualism. Minority groups would have no power without group organization. Our sense of distributive social justice refuses to accept the unjust status quo.

It may be fine for Western European ethnic groups to adopt the motto "I am my own person; I do my own thing." For disadvantaged persons such individualism perpetuates their disadvantaged status and is culturally destructive of the basis for community togetherness. Only group social action, group economic development, and group political representation will equalize outcomes for disadvantaged people. Majority Americans have nothing to fear from stronger representation of disadvantaged ethnic peoples. We need to abandon zero-sum, all-or-nothing attitudes, i.e., if I, a disadvantaged Native American, win, you, the advantaged WASP, necessarily loses. Instead we must start believing that we all advance together. As economists say, "a rising tide of economic growth and development lifts all boats." We are all in this together. As minorities advance they become less dependent on government social programs, and they contribute more to national prosperity. The difference is that a community path of development, rather than the acquisitive, individualistic path of upward mobility, is true to the inherent ethnic character of the cultures of Native Americans, African-Americans, and Hispanic-Americans. Specifically, we need to experiment more with workers' cooperatives and profit-sharing organizations.

Anglos do not appreciate the unique and fundamental characteristics of Native-American tribes—we are by definition set apart, our ceremonies are necessarily secret and not for outsiders, only for adherents. We resent the trend of nonnatives (or only fractional natives) to try to capitalize on the Native-American heritage, and we have had enough of logos, mascots, stereotypes, slurs, and misrepresentations. Even if you do not mean

"Redskins" as a slur term, it has been and still is a slur against Native Americans. We are not overly sensitive; we just want recognition and respect. We have a serious task ahead of reconstituting ourselves and only we can do that. You can be a friend (albeit always an outsider), but you cannot convert. The only individual "ethnic choice" for Native Americans is to deny our own Native-American heritage!

Because the Anglo-American capitalistic heritage is so powerful, one of the greatest dangers is commercialization and commodification of our heritage and people. We are not for sale. Yes, the presentation of Native-American crafts and celebrations will help outsiders understand that we too have our skills and genius. But no country, no people, sells its heritage, its artifacts, its memories, and its core meaning. Such an expropriation would be the final slaughter of our souls.

ASIAN-AMERICAN: There is a sense of irretrievable loss as we watch the younger generation grow up Americanized and much less cognizant of their language, stories, and ethnic ways. Contemporary Americanization can be a vulgar process. It consumes peoples' lives because the distractions of generic popular culture overwhelm most individuals. Peer pressures make it almost impossible for young people to retain their unique ethnic identities without peer ridicule. Valuable cultural characteristics become old-fashioned, parental, and at best quaint. American-born minds seem closed to the traditional and ancient.

It does not appear that American circumstances of opportunity blend well with Asian (Chinese and Japanese) thinking. American circumstances mean that you are not stuck in the stratum in which you are born. Asian thinking means reference to the traditional stories that teach how not to reveal yourself, how to obey and revere your parents, how to swallow your shortcomings, and how always to have the energy that springs from hope. Somehow we must find the balanced, inner harmony of the mind's thoughts and the body's desires. There is a whole art to achieving such inner power, but what does this have to do with being a materialistically successful American? We need to concentrate more on a renovated, multicultural civil society and put to the side the individualistic market and the collectivistic state.

WASP: I just cannot understand why we are unable to acknowledge our common humanity and our respective individualities. Why do we have to accentuate ethnicity, which excites parochial differences and loyalties?

The centrifugal forces in our society are ethnicity, religion, economics (class), interest groups, educational status, residential segregation, family breakdown, media violence, and many characteristics of popular culture. All these differences and inequalities keep us on edge and divided. Why not reenliven the centripetal forces such as teamwork in the workplace and in sports, coalition building in political parties, the public school mission, marriage and the extended family, and community spirit? All these factors tend to bind us together in larger, integrated wholes. They are mediating and connecting structures elevating self-interested, isolated individuals to a sense of the greater public good. Perhaps we have also lost sight of mediating persons, public intellectuals, who give life to mediating agencies. We need a call by our intermediating associations to reestablish a civic culture dedicated to quality of life concerns.

Certainly American exceptionalism means a diversity of peoples establishing a common history, a common identity, a "new nationality" and a new future model for all people to live in peace with each other, accommodating not stifling diversity. Yet, is there not a meaningful common core, an American political culture, that distinguishes us from other countries and unites us? Acculturation does not necessitate assimilation. Our common acculturation is our political, constitutional union regarding law and order, due process, fundamental human rights, limits on governmental power, and debate about what constitutes the "general welfare" (a high quality of life and "the pursuit of happiness") for Americans. Without being steeped in the best of our traditions we will not have orderly change. It is frightfully precarious to propose some tabula rasa.

AFRICAN-AMERICAN: The problem with your position is that it is too beholden to traditional Eurocentric norms without including cultures that have a different perspective, such as the cultures of African-Americans, Hispanic-Americans, and Native Americans. Our traditions have a different flavor and rhythm. Consequently, a radically new unity (not the old unity) needs to be created because in the past we three groups were excluded, and in the present we need to stand on our own terms for any proper accommodation to occur.

Cornell West in his essay "Malcolm X and Black Rage" recommends that we "use the term 'jazz' here not so much as a term for a musical art form, as for a mode of being in the world, an improvisational mode of protean, fluid, and flexible dispositions toward reality suspicious of 'either/or' viewpoints, dogmatic pronouncements, or supremacist ideologies. To be a jazz freedom fighter is to attempt to galvanize and energize world-weary people into forms of organization with accountable leadership that promotes critical exchange and broad reflection. The interplay of individuality and unity is not one of uniformity and unanimity imposed from above but rather of conflict among diverse groupings that reach a dynamic consensus subject to questioning and criticism. As with a soloist in a jazz quartet, quintet or band, individuality is promoted in order to sustain and increase the creative tension with the group—a tension that yields higher levels of performance to achieve the aim of the collective project. This kind of critical and democratic sensibility flies in the face of any policing of borders and boundaries of 'blackness', 'maleness', 'femaleness', or 'whiteness'." West offers to us a dynamic model for interrelating our differences, not some given "American" framework that we need to fit into.

In general, there are positive contributions that African-Americans, Hispanic-Americans, and Native Americans can make to improve American society. The goals are not special privileges or the power to dictate over others. However, dramatic socioeconomic change will have to occur. Your bourgeois standpoint does not address those who are not comfortably middle class and perhaps never want to be. The defeat of Lani Guinier as assistant attorney general for civil rights and the firing of Jocelyn Elders as Surgeon General are symbolic examples of the white power structure unable to accept different perspectives. The hallowed status quo is unacceptable to us. A lot more variation and diversity will have to be tolerated and respected before we can have a new American unity. Anglo society's individualism needs to be beneficially tempered by more communal experiences; rootlessness and impersonal behavior can be modified by a sense of service and obligation to others; and the pace of society can be slowed so that we all smell the multiflowered bouquet.

JEWISH-AMERICAN: Frequently, minorities and the disadvantaged automatically look to big government to work big socioeconomic changes. Such a response is the consequence of their personal powerlessness and frustration, and their analytical critique that stresses systematic institutional racism and structural oppression. A big problem requires a big solution. Libertarian conservatives go to the other extreme relying on individuals to succeed in a so-called free marketplace of opportunities. An individual is expected to pull himself or herself up by his/her bootstraps (an ugly cliche). Perhaps the truth is in between these extremes. Why not attend to civil society and develop mediating associations between powerless, isolated individuals and the impersonal, coercive state? Such associations would mediate our differences and would have a community development function. We then could build solidarity across ethnic lines of division among those who have common socioeconomic difficulties (health, employment, education, crime, etc.). Most activists at the grass roots know it is necessary to enlist and organize people in a holistic manner, since their life difficulties are intertwined and not really treatable separately. Fortunately, recent reforms of the Job Training Partnership Act (JTPA) are heading in this holistic direction. Individuals alone or a distant bureaucratic state are both recipes for failure.

To preserve our identity we must follow Thomas Jefferson and insist on a high and solid wall between church and state, which means in this context that it is a mistake, only inviting unresolvable conflict, to advocate that culture and ethnicity mix with politics and economics. Secularism and the enlightened liberal democratic model are the best remedies for diverse people to live together harmoniously. Deliberative reasoning in politics and a calculating reason in economics provide the common ground for individuals to compete so that meritorious results occur. Likewise, we should have a tragic sense of life and avoid utopianism by recognizing that there are limits to improving the human condition. There will always be injustices to fight against; there is no final, transformational solution.

HISPANIC-AMERICAN: The immediate basis for effectively building solidarity is the particular culture, religion, and ethnicity of a people. You cannot deal with people as discrete individuals or abstract groupings such as civil society. The strongest thing going for disadvantaged groups is their personal ethnicity. It is not clear that socioeconomic-political factors alone cutting across ethnic identifications will unite diverse people sufficiently. In any case there is considerable de facto, ethnic and racial segregation in the United States. Therefore, organizing people where they now are will require a lot more attention to specific ethnic and cultural characteristics. Perhaps, African-American, Hispanic-American, and Native-American cultures are less capitalistic and respond more to cooperative models of economic organization. Proposals to redistribute wealth through a more steeply progressive income tax are unavoidable if jobs are to be created, educational reform to be achieved, health care delivered, and our inner cities rebuilt. Will Americans in positions of power and wealth and Americans in the self-satisfied middle class accept and promote such a radical project of change?

JEWISH-AMERICAN: My people have been scattered throughout the world, yet in the United States we have been able to flourish in our own private sphere as well as in the greater public sphere of civil society and government. Jewish people have a long history in the United States questioning the WASP model. Yet we chose a more cosmopolitan perspective of inclusion, rather than a particularistic focus fostering separation. Many second-generation Jewish people sought considerable emancipation from the ghetto of their narrow, Old World, immigrant forebears. Such an awakening is occurring among many young African-Americans, Latinos, and Asian-Americans and they too will find their identity, but will it be parochial or cosmopolitan?

The Judaic-Christian imagery of the covenant comprising one body (politic) with many members (ethnicities) in our civil society is an appropriate model for reconciling the one (we are all Americans) and the many (we are all ethnically various). Our differences alone, if overemphasized, lead to breakdown and anarchy. Already we have people claiming on the basis of their race, ethnicity, and gender that those outside their exclusive ethnic category can never hope to comprehend them and communicate with them meaningfully. Blacks think black, and whites think white. Women think female, and men think male. However, the truth is that who we are, our identity, is only knowable through a dialogue with others that reveals what we share and do not share with others. Have we lost the art of rational deliberation? You cannot find yourself when cut off and alone. Has private, ethnic identity become a badge more important than a public identity that would enable us to achieve working coalitions among groups? Is there enough trust and good will just to begin?

NATIVE AMERICAN: We too have experienced a diaspora. But we do not agree (at least at this time) with the transcultural range of community that you propose. Perhaps our lowly socioeconomic situation and the immediacy of the suffering of our people (note how in the United States swastikas are prohibited but not Indian logos) prevent us from entering into a greater community before we have shored up, strengthened, and flourished in our own civil societies. For example, it took a quarter of a century for the general public and historians to acknowledge that 400

Navajo code talker soldiers in World War II prevented the Japanese from breaking our military code communications in the Pacific. The Navajo language has no roots in any other language, and thus served as an indecipherable military language. We need to find our own common goods and public identities as Native Americans, Hispanic-Americans, African-Americans before entering into discussions, negotiations, and mediations with others. Otherwise, we will persistently be disadvantaged and any compromises or agreements will be at our expense.

We are not sure, given the legacy of our dealings with Anglo society and government, that we can get a "fair shake." That is why we do not "buy into" this greater unity you proclaim so assuredly. Most likely, as tests of good faith, we, the disadvantaged minorities, would seek programmatic commitments (e.g., investment seed money, government-funded childcare, educational resources, heritage preservation) that address our needs yet preserve our independence and do not make us dependent clients of government. We too believe in the need for an educational and moral revival (young people know so little of their own ethnic traditions), but we see this as subject to the control of leaders in the various ethnic communities, not at all a matter we can entrust to American civil society and government in general.

In fact, one of the big dangers of multiculturalism in the hands of well-intentioned white liberals is that it will become so diffuse that it forgets the serious problems and the great fights we still have to undertake against racism and sexism. For example, there are court cases now concerning Native-American children adopted by non–Native-American parents who are being legally enjoined to return these children (under the Indian Child Welfare Act of 1978) to their original Native-American tribes. This is a battle between abstract custody rights and substantive cultural heritage claims. Many people do not know that in the past Native-American children were removed from their tribal families in order to undergo compulsory assimilation. The talk of the Jewish-American and the WASP is too abstract and not grounded in the very survival of specific, real, ethnic communities. While there may be intellectual meaning in abstract concepts (e.g., civil society, democracy, morality, individual rights, oneness, common good), how can we (most of us who are not professional intellectuals) get there unless meaning is more rooted in particular ways of life?

WASP: It appears that our Native-American, African-American, and

Hispanic-American spokespersons would elevate their private particulars (ethnicity and culture) over our public universals (citizenship and common humanity). This choice is fraught with difficulties, if not turmoil.

BIBLIOGRAPHY

Albanese, Catherine. *Sons of the Fathers: The Civil Religion and the American Revolution.* Philadelphia: Temple University Press, 1976.

Asante, Molefi Kete. *Afrocentricity.* Trenton: Africa World Press, 1988.

Asante, Molefi Kete. "Multiculturalism: An Exchange." In Berman, Paul. *Debating P. C.* New York: Dell, 1992.

"Asian-Americans in Politics? Rarely." *New York Times* (June 3, 1993).

Barber, Benjamin. *The Conquest of Politics.* Princeton: Princeton University Press, 1988.

Bellah, Robert. *Habits of the Heart.* New York: Harper and Row, 1985.

Bender, Thomas. "Negotiating Public Culture." *Liberal Education* 78 (March/April 1992): 10-15.

Blanchard, Kenneth. "Ethnicity and the Problem of Equality." *Interpretation* 20.3 (Spring 1993): 309-324.

Blum, Laurence. "Philosophy and the Values of a Multicultural Community." *Teaching Philosophy* 14.2 (June 1991): 127-134.

Bourne, Randolph. "Transnational America." *Atlantic* (1916): 86-97.

Brooks, R. L. *Rethinking the American Race Problem.* Chicago: University of Chicago Press, 1990.

Charles, Nick. "Black Troops Feel Tie and Tension in Somalia." *Grand Rapids Press* (January 10, 1993): A16.

Chavez, Linda. *Out of the Barrios.* New York: Basic Books, 1991.

Coughlin, Ellen. "Sociologists Examine the Complexities of Racial and Ethnic Identity in America." *Chronicle of Higher Education* (March 24, 1993): A7-A8.

Cornell, Stephen. *The Return of the Native.* New York: Oxford University Press, 1988.

Cruse, Harold. *Plural But Equal.* New York: Morrow, 1987.

Deloria, Vine, Jr. and Lytle, Clifford M. *American Indians and American Justice.* Austin: University of Texas Press, 1983.

Dippie, Brian W. *The Vanishing American: White Attitudes and U.S. Indian Policy.* Middletown: Wesleyan University Press, 1982.

Dorris, Michael A. "The Grass Still Grows, The Rivers Still Flow, Contemporary Native America." *Daedalus* (Spring 1981): 43-69.

Du Bois, W.E.B. *The Souls of Black Folk.* New York: Random,1903.

Eastland, Terry and Bennett, William J. *Counting By Race: Equality from the Founding Fathers to Bakke and Weber.* New York: Basic Books, 1979.

Egan, Timothy. "Back From Oblivion, A Tribe Forges a Future." *New York Times* (November 20, 1991): Al, Al0.

____. "Indian Tribes Seeking End to Shackles of Dependency." *New York Times* (January 9, 1991): A1, A11.

Ellison, Ralph. *The Invisible Man.* New York: Vintage, 1947.

Eoyang, Eugene. *Coat of Many Colors.* Boston: Beacon, 1995.

Franklin, John Hope. *From Slavery to Freedom.* New York: Knopf, 1964.

Elshtain, Jean Bethke. *Democracy on Trial.* New York: Basic Books, 1995.

Fuchs, Lawrence. *American Kaleidoscope.* Hanover: University Press of New England, 1990.

Gambino, Richard. "From the One, Many: The Multicultural Threat." *Freedom Review* (September-October 1992): 34-36.

Gates, Henry Louis. *Loose Canons.* New York: Oxford University Press, 1992.

Glazer, Nathan. *Ethnic Dilemmas.* Cambridge: Harvard University Press, 1983.

Glazer, Nathan and Moynihan, Daniel P. *Beyond The Melting Pot.*

Cambridge, MIT Press, 1963.

_____ eds. *Ethnicity: Theory and Experience*. Cambridge: Harvard University Press, 1975.

Gleason, Philip. "American Identity and Americanization." In *Harvard Encyclopedia of American Ethnic Groups*. Cambridge: Harvard University Press, 1980.

_____. "Assimilation in America: Theory and Reality." *Daedalus* (1961): 163-185.

Gordon, M.M. "Assimilation in America: Theory and Reality." *Daedalus* (1961): 263-285.

_____. *Assimilation in American Life: The Role of Race, Religions, and National Origins*. New York: Oxford University Press, 1964.

_____. "Models of Pluralism: The New American Dilemma." *Annals* 454 (1981): 178-188.

Greeley, Andrew. *Ethnicity in the United States*. New York: Wiley, 1974.

Higham, John. *Strangers in the Land: Patterns of American Nativism, 1860-1925*. New York: Atheneum, 1963.

Howe, Irving. *World of our Fathers*. New York: Schocken, 1976.

Huntington, Samuel. *American Politics: The Promise of Disharmony*. Cambridge: Belknap Press, 1981.

Hymowitz, Kay. "Multiculturalism is Anti-Culture." *New York Times* (March 25, 1993): editorial page.

Isaacs, Harold. *Idols of the Tribe*. Cambridge: Harvard University Press, 1980.

_____. "The One and the Many: What Are the Social and Political Implications of the New Ethnic Revival?" *American Educator* 2 (Spring 1978): 13-14.

Jen, Gish. *Typical Americans*. Boston: Houghton Mifflin, 1991.

Kallen, Horace. "Democracy versus the Melting Pot." *Nation* 100 (February 18 and 24, 1915): 190-194, 209-212.

Kelly, G. A. *Political and Religious Consciousness in America*. New Brunswick: Transaction Books, 1984.

Kermode, Frank. "Whose History Is Bunk?" *New York Times Book Review* (February 23, 1992): 3, 33.

Landry, B. *The New Black Middle Class*. Chicago: University of Chicago Press, 1987.

Lemann, Nicolas. "Black Nationalism on Campus." *Atlantic Monthly* (January 1993): 31-34, 43-47.

Litt, Edgar. *Ethnic Politics in America*. Glenview: Scott Foresman, 1970.

Lovin Robin. "Must We Disown Our Past?" *Liberal Education* 78 (March/April 1992): 2-9.

Lyman, Stanford. "The Assimilationism-Pluralism Debate: Towards a Postmodern Resolution of the American Ethnoracial Dilemma." *International Journal of Politics, Culture, and Society* 6.2 (1992): 181-207.

Martin, Joel W. "New Perspectives of Native Americans." *Chronicle of Higher of Education* (October 23, 1991): B1-B2.

McIntosh, Peggy. "Interactive Phases of Curricular Re-Vision: A Feminist Perspective." *Working Paper #104*. Wellesley College, 1983.

Moyers, Bill. *A World of Ideas*. New York: Doubleday, 1990. See the interview with August Wilson.

Naispaul, V.S. "Our Universal Civilization." *New York Review of Books* (January 31, 1991): 22-25.

Nelson, Dale C. "Ethnicity and Socioeconomic Status as Sources of Participation." *APSR* 73 (1979) 1024-1038.

Njeri, Itabari. "Changes in Culture, Population Pushes Aside Old Ideal of Melting Pot." *Grand Rapids Press* (February 10, 1991).

Patterson, Nerys and Patterson, Orlando. "St. Patrick Was A Slave." *New York Times* (March 15, 1993): A11.

Patrick, Michelle. "An American Voice." (An August Wilson Interview) *Philip Morris Magazine* (March-April 1989): 40-43.

Platt, Anthony. "Defenders of the Canon: What's Behind the Attack on Multiculturalism." *Social Justice* 19.2 (1992): 122-137.

Portes, A. "The Rise of Ethnicity." *American Sociological Review* 24 (1993): 47-60.

Quade, Quentin. "Pluralism versus Diversity." *Freedom Review* 22.2 (1992): 16-19.

Ravitch, Diane. "Multiculturalism: E Pluribus Plures." In Berman, Paul. *Debating P.C.* New York: Dell, 1992.

Rodriguez, Richard. *Days of Obligation: An Argument With My Mexican Father*. New York: Viking, 1992.

Roy, Donald. "Multiculturalism and the Public Good: The Guidance of Alexis de Tocqueville." Unpublished paper delivered at the 1991 Michigan Conference of Political Scientists.

Safire, William. "The Wigwam Casino." *New York Times* (June 30, 1991): A15.

Schlesinger, Arthur. *The Disuniting of America.* New York: Norton, 1991.

____. "Reply to Gambino." *Freedom Review* (November-December 1992): 5.

Scott, Joan. "The Campaign Against Political Correctness." *Change* (November-December 1991): 30-43.

____. "Liberal Historians: A Unitary Vision." *Chronicle of Higher Education* (September 11, 1991): B 1-B2.

Shanker, Albert. "Courting Ethnic Strife." *New Republic* (February 23, 1992): 16-19.

Simonson, Rick and Walker, Scott, eds. *The Graywolf Annual Five: Multicultural Literature.* St. Paul: Graywolf Press, 1988.

Skerry, Peter. *The Mexicans.* New York: Free Press, 1993.

Sollors, Werner. *The Invention of Ethnicity.* New York: Oxford University Press, 1989.

____. *Beyond Ethnicity.* New York: Oxford University Press, 1986.

Sowell, Thomas. *Ethnic America.* New York: Basic Books, 1981.

Spindler, George and Louise. *The American Cultural Dialogue and Its Transmission.* New York: Taylor and Francis, 1990.

Steinberg, Stephen. *The Ethnic Myth.* Boston: Beacon Press, 1989.

Szulc, Tad. "The Greatest Danger We Face." *Parade Magazine* (July 25, 1993): 4-5, 7.

Tan, Amy. *The Joy Luck Club.* New York: Ballantine Books, 1989.

Takaki, Ronald, ed. *From Different Shores.* New York: Oxford University Press, 1987.

____. *A Different Mirror: A History of Multicultural America.* Boston: Little, Brown, 1993.

Taylor, Charles. *Multiculturalism and The Politics of Recognition.* Princeton: Princeton University Press, 1992.

Thomas, R. Roosevelt, Jr. "From Affirmative Action to Affirming Diversity." *Harvard Business Review* (March-April 1990): 107-117.

Tocqueville, Alexis de. *Democracy in America.* New York: Shocken Books, reprint 1964.

Walzer, Michael. "The New Tribalism." *Dissent* (Spring 1992): 164-171.

____. *The Politics of Ethnicity.* Cambridge: Harvard University Press 1980.

Wang, L. Ling-chi. "Roots and Changing Identity of Chinese in U.S." *Daedalus* 120 (Spring 1991): 181-206.

West, Cornel. *Race Matters*. Boston: Beacon, 1993.

White, Robert. "Indians' New Harvest." *New York Times* (November 22, 1990): editorial page.

Wilson, James Q. *Character*. Washington, D.C.: AEI Press, 1991.

Wilson, William Julius. *The Declining Significance of Race*. Chicago: University of Chicago Press, 1980.

____. *The Truly Disadvantaged*. Chicago: University of Chicago Press, 1987.

Wortham, Anne. "Errors of Afrocentrists." *Academic Questions* (Fall 1992): 36-50.

Wurzel, Jaime. *Towards Multiculturalism*. Yarmouth, Maine: Intercultural Press, 1988.

Zangwill, Israel. *The Melting Pot: Drama in Four Acts*. New York: Macmillan, 1922.

EIGHT

SPEECH'S PARAMETERS:

CIVILITY OR POLITICAL CORRECTNESS?

At one and the same time public opinion polls show a significant increase in tolerance of minorities and ethnic groups among the majority, white/Anglo population, and yet there also is a rise in racist/ discriminatory incidents against these same minorities. How explain this discrepancy? Are many Americans concealing their true opinions because there now are social penalties for openly admitting their prejudices? Or are we failing to differentiate Americans in polls, thereby submerging the perhaps more prejudiced lower middle class and poorer Americans who feel threatened, insecure, and neglected? Do we have a backlash in the younger, rising generation against their parents' sponsorship of liberal entitlement programs now seen as special preferences and advantages for minorities? Why are we experiencing racist incidents on *Northern liberal* college campuses such as the University of Wisconsin, the University of Michigan, the University of Connecticut, and the University of Pennsylvania? Or is this another case of now recording what previously we ignored?

Whatever the causes and characteristics of our heated multicultural environment, we have to deal with the parameters of free speech when it comes to offensive, abusive, racist, sexist, hate speech. How far do we stretch freedom of speech in the First Amendment clause? Is freedom of speech an absolute right? Do we have to protect people from words alone, or are some words (language) inextricably linked to deeds characterizing who we are and the society we live in? Why cannot people just be *civil* with one another? Do we know what civility is, and do we agree on what civility is? Or is it that any defining of civility results in "political correctness," which is to say, some kind of bureaucratically-regulated, unfree speech?

THE DIALOGUE

LIBERATION: During the past sixty or so years just about every time the U.S. Government or a state government has attempted to clamp down on individual rights the U.S. Supreme Court has responded by broadening such individual rights. For example, freedom of expression in the form of symbolic, protest expression has been extended as far as allowing "F... the Draft" on a T-shirt (see *Cohen v. California*, 1971) and burning the U.S. flag (see *Texas v. Johnson*, 1991). Likewise, we are guaranteed freedom of the press (no prior restraint), freedom of association (a legal Communist Party), freedom from unreasonable search and seizure ("probable cause" and the exclusionary rule), the right to privacy (legalized abortion), etc. As a society we are better off when individuals and associations have untrammeled liberty to "do their own thing" within the laws that protect the rights of others likewise to "do their own thing."

The First Amendment's freedom of expression clause is the basis for a full airing of opinions. We have nothing to fear from a free market of competition among ideas, interests, viewpoints, and standpoints. Taking *offense* at remarks alone is never a sufficient basis for restricting or otherwise interfering with a person's free speech. Yes, words can offend deeply, but to counter such words with alternative, better words or with dead, cold silence—that is the kind of respect that succeeds in a free society.

EQUALITY: Abstractly, your position sounds quite reasonable. Everyone at some time in his/her life is subject to offensive words, and we go on by putting behind us these unpleasant moments. The assumption is that everyone experiences this offense simply as individuals, and that such offenses or insults are equal in emotional consequences. However, this presumed harmless equality (dealing at the level of a child's pain-avoidance retort: "sticks and stones may break my bones, but words will never hurt me") evades the very real harm and debilitation that occurs when a whole *class* of people is verbally accosted. Racism and sexism are such attacks. Consequently, there are some types of speech and words that are inherently contradictory to a free society since such words denigrate and enslave the targeted class of persons.

Such words do not contribute to any meaningful discourse. That is why your analogical reference to a free, competitive marketplace of ideas and opinions is misleading. First of all, we know well the tendency of a free, competitive market of *goods* to result in a monopolistic outcome. Likewise with racist and sexist hate/abuse speech; they thrive on and perpetuate a monopoly position of power and gross inequality. There is no fairness in such a society analogous to a truly free marketplace. Therefore, we need antitrust and monopoly-busting laws also in the area of free speech. In 1991, in 32 states 4,558 hate crimes were committed, and 60% of these were racially motivated. Klanwatch has identified 230 organized hate groups in the United States. We are not debating some abstract, academic question.

LIBERATION: Agreed, sexist and racist speech is hateful, abusive, and harmful to those victimized. However, there are all kinds of other speech that are equally harmful to those affected as individuals or as classes of individuals. What about the class of teenagers with acne that are ridiculed? Or the class of short people who are looked down upon? Why should we protect some and not others? And what would happen to free speech if we attempted to protect everyone from hurtful words? Certainly handicapped people who are slurred because of their handicap and rich people who are verbally assaulted because they wear animal furs can be personally and emotionally devastated as a result. Psychological harm and injury cannot be an adequate legal basis for restricting certain kinds of speech when so many kinds of speech can cause psychological harm and injury. (Of course, everyone has recourse to libel and slander suits *after* the fact of free expression in order to recover for harm and damage to reputation.) The courts have tried appropriately and adequately to draw a line between words and actions. Actions that harm and cause injury are punishable. But words alone are protected under the First Amendment freedom of expression clause because once we start to ban some words on the grounds that they are injurious, we would not know where to stop.

In addition, words that incite illegal behavior, and words that create an imminent danger (threats, intimidation and terror) can be regulated and punished. The classic example is that "you can't yell fire in a crowded theater" (*Schenck v. U.S.*, 1919) for the very reason that such words directly cause danger and harm to others. *Schenck* has been updated by *U.S. v. Lee* (1993), which ruled that a "clear and present danger" must be imminent, and the effect must not be just a verbal effect on an individual, but an imminent behavioral incitement such that speech and deed are conjoined.

There is no attempt by me to deny the special severity of the pain caused by racist and sexist speech. However, we have to protect all beliefs and the consciences of persons, even those we despise. If we do not, then we signal to people that our society is not based on an open, freewheeling expression of all opinions, but rather is based on who has the political power to suppress others. Those attacked need to fight back *verbally*. Many people are sitting on the fence watching and wondering whether racist and sexist speech might have some sense in a situation. The contest goes on. You succeed with these uncommitted persons when you offer a civil alternative to mean-spirited speech.

A college or university campus is precisely the special place where we want to encourage a verbal free-for-all, since this is what real education is all about. To put up a wall of restrictions because there is harsh and offensive language characteristic of the real world of people is no preparation for young people going out into that world. Actually you ought to feel provoked in the best sense of learning what other people are all about. Face up to the slings and arrows of the real world, perhaps for the first time away from the womb of home and neighborhood. Too much psychological, educational gobblygook has defensively stressed a too precious self-esteem, putting the cart before the horse. Does not self-esteem truly occur *after* a hard effort and a job well done?

EQUALITY: You are naive to believe that words are not a form of action and that our society as it is now constituted does not disfavor and suppress types of speech depending on who has political power. Because words are not just the *rights* of free expression but rather betray the *interests* of those who express such words, we have to look at power relationships. Consequently, rights and liberties have to be balanced by considerations of power and inequality. Racism and sexism are defined precisely in power terms, namely, those who have it and those who do not. You are naive to believe that there is some level playing field on which we all equally utilize our rights of free expression. When matters of inequality are honestly faced, then we discern how those who are unequal and disadvantaged suffer and are victimized by racist and sexist language. Those in positions of power and security do not readily understand and feel this personal diminishment. They lack sensitivity and awareness, since such abuse is outside their personal experience.

Is it too much to ask that we have rules and regulations that do not perpetuate and promote inequality? How can a disadvantaged and victimized person possibly respond forcefully when verbally dominated?

Sexist and racist words are not just words, but are trademarks of institutions and the whole system of repression. Therefore, unlimited rights of freedom of expression only provide unlimited liberty to dominate. Attention to the norms of equality and the Fourteenth Amendment's "equal protection of the laws" will put speech on the right, qualified footing. Equal protection will mean equal personhood. Speech that degrades and humiliates will not be admitted and given protection in civil discourse.

LIBERATION: It is a simple and clear distinction: words that cause offense, make others feel uncomfortable, and "victimize" (whatever that means) are protected, while words that immediately cause violence or civil disturbances (a breach of peace) are not protected under the First Amendment. Human beings have a billion different sensitivities; we cannot possibly legislate and regulate for all of them. It is the whole *art* of human living that we choose our friends and shun our enemies, that we pick and distinguish and in the process *informally self-regulate* our affairs. To use authorities, be they university/college administrators, faculty/ student boards of review, magistrates, or whomever to devise codes and regulations is to threaten both academic freedom and personal freedom by way of an authoritarian regime of political correctness.

Another boundary between the private and the public has lost its meaning and distinction by your argument. You would raise most speech to the level of public discourse with legal parameters. What is behind all of this is the self-designated mission (more characteristic of college administrators than faculty) to rehabilitate and reeducate a troop of young people whose primary education emanates from all the crudity and rock'em–sock'em of popular media culture. No doubt we would all be better off if the level of common basic civility were raised in our contemporary society. But authoritarian legislation will only inspire acts of rebellion and defiance against such externally-imposed conformity. This is not the route of persuasion, internalization, and consensus. The heavy hand is no sure, quick fix. Mandates and dictates have only caused people to see college administrators as the new oppressors.

A better way to discredit the discreditable has to be found. Victimization status hardly uplifts persons and gives them the strength to handle difficult situations. Is there not also evidence that the very minorities you seek to protect by hate/abuse speech codes are those more likely to be charged with violating these regulations? How can Louis

Farrakhan and representatives of the Nation of Islam speak on campuses uttering their anti-Semitic ideology? What about Two Live Crew and Ice-T, both of whom use hate words of attack on women, police, and whites?

We need to have more open and broad (covering all groups) discussion of racist and sexist ideologies to remove the barriers, to alleviate the fears, and to release the pent-up energies people have on these issues. If we concentrate on the norms and rules that make for propitious civil discourse (minus the urge to regulate, codify, and punish), then we can be living exemplars of beneficial human dialogue. Indeed, we in the academic community have a responsibility to educate students regarding the better and proper ways to respond to racial and sexual discrimination. Destroying 19,000 copies of the University of Pennsylvania student newspaper, which black students proudly took responsibility for, is hardly a constructive and responsible way to deal with what offends most of us.

EQUALITY: Actually you offer no cure or remedy at all because you persist in believing that all of this is an individual matter rather than a community or society problem. Colleges and universities exist as special communities within a larger society. They are special because they can be so constituted as agents of reform, change, and improvement for society at large. What you propose is a minimal, informal, haphazard, individualistic response. Glory be, were it only enough! The status quo is much more resilient than you comprehend.

Colleges and universities clearly must adopt policies regarding *harassment*. You use words such as "uncomfortable" and "offensive" as if this truly captured the nature of the hate/abuse we experience. Terms such as "lacerating" and "assaultive" more accurately hit the mark. Under the rubric of *harassment*, codes for the unequal can be established and properly enforced via due process. Otherwise colleges and universities will not be able to ensure an atmosphere where higher learning can progress. We have competing models of what a university is. You would let it all hang out, and in the hullabaloo students would learn from this all-out freedom of expression, whereas we choose to model the university after a community of relative equals who learn from and with each other. Universities exist to lead the way regarding corrective and remedial action to be applied to society at-large. Your model of the university is more a reflection of society than a critique.

The minority students at the University of Pennsylvania who

destroyed copies of the majority's student newspaper were only responding out of frustration and alienation. Yes, they should have found other alternatives since the same "take and destroy" activity could be applied to their own newspaper, but you ignore how unequal the alternatives are for minorities as well as the severe, secondary consequences of published or uttered derogatory opinions. You have to live day-after-day with situations of abusive discrimination because of your obvious group affiliation to understand why printed material becomes the last straw.

Since you are so enamored with distinctions, there is a very important distinction that has to be made between a Nation of Islam event and popular music entertainment and on the other hand a *personal*, verbal, sexist or racist attack. The former does not target a person directly and is meant to raise issues and problems in the case of the Nation of Islam, or to entertain and parody behavior in the case of Two Live Crew and Ice-T. There is value and learning that can come from such events, whereas a direct, personal, verbal blow renders the targeted person a helpless victim. The verbal blow is meant to incapacitate and reduce the victim to nothing. Hardly can it be said that a Nation of Islam event or a Two Live Crew concert are incidents of personal harassment.

Perhaps now is the time to resurrect the *Chaplinsky* case (1942). The U.S. Supreme Court made an important distinction about a type of unprotected speech, namely, "fighting words." Words that immediately cause a fight, words that incite not just anger but blows are not within the jurisdiction of First Amendment protection. When a person utters certain words directly at another person to elicit a response and to wound, then we have speech that constitutes an action and no longer has discussion value. You have no protected First Amendment rights to intimidate, terrorize, assault, and inflict pain directly and intentionally *at* a person. Your freedom of thought, belief, and conscience are fully protected when they are directed at no one—thrown to the breeze as it were.

LIBERATION: All of a sudden you are abandoning your previous argument of an atmosphere of hate. For Jewish people, a Nation of Islam event creates a very hostile environment and may encourage individuals to personal attacks using anti-Semitic words and actions. Also, Two Live Crew, by popularizing in music sexist slurs, gives legitimacy to this mode of expression, so you would argue if you were consistent. Would you countenance the KKK Grand Dragon speaking at a university? If you admit one, you must admit the other, if your real interest is to apply equality to freedom of expression.

As for the important distinction of "fighting words" made in the *Chaplinsky* case, this distinction has never been so important for the U.S. Supreme Court to ever revisit and uphold again. Most constitutional lawyers find the "fighting words" exception to be a dead distinction. Of course, the reasons for this are clear. *When* someone resorts to blows because of words is a highly subjective matter, more likely to be a male than female response, and depends on certain cultural variations (some cultures are more prone to fighting, others more prone to passivity); that make it tricky, to say the least, to know what counts as "fighting words." So much for equality of application under the rubric of "fighting words."

Again it is not words but actions that must be regulated and punished if injurious. By putting so much emphasis on words, might not any words cause a fight, if the *tone* in which words are expressed is also considered? Again: At the University of Pennsylvania an Israeli student yelled out in Hebrew the epithet "water buffaloes" to some black female students who were causing noise late at night when he was trying to write a paper. The black students felt this was derisive, and the university made a big deal of the incident. Is this the kind of incident we are going to belabor? Are you not asking for a fight by collapsing the distinction between words and actions? Are not we unnecessarily raising the stakes of "just words" to some level of aggression and counteraggression? Let's calm down and back off.

What you are proposing is precisely what a Wisconsin federal court struck down as unconstitutional. The University of Wisconsin had a "hate speech" regulation that banned speech that created a hostile learning environment by demeaning a person's race, sex, religion, color, creed, disability, sexual orientation, or ancestry. The problem with such regulations is that they are "overly broad" regarding the First Amendment; i.e., they cover too many speech possibilities, especially including protest speech that is protected despite being offensive and instigating anger. Ironically such regulations are overly narrow as well, privileging a certain class of people to the exclusion of others who also could be similarly "harmed". Consequently, these regulations can not pass the test of impartiality and neutrality, both of which count for legal equality. Content restrictions are inherently dangerous because they tread on freedom of belief, thought, and conscience no matter where your beliefs, thoughts, and conscience may take you, short of conduct that *violates* others. Such violations must mean a real harm or injury. Too many universities that have constructed speech codes are hell-bent on a crusade to stifle expression rather than to examine the root causes of uncivil speech.

EQUALITY: You entirely miss the point of my defense of equality. Those who are already in power and dominate in American society have their viewpoints widely expressed. Precisely for this reason we should admit all kinds of minority and disadvantaged voices even if they offend (but do not harass). While it is true that the KKK does not now rule the roost as it once did in segregationist times, there still linger considerable residues of racism in the legacy of slavery and segregation. As a result, a university environment should be overly tolerant of the voices of the disadvantaged to equalize what it is that students get to hear and learn about. As for Louis Farrakhan and minority pop singers, their negative message is only a small part of their overall empowerment message. As for the *Chaplinsky* case, it was referred to and upheld in the recent St. Paul case, *if all* such "fighting words" were banned and prosecuted rather than specific kinds of "fighting words." While I disagree with the court's divided majority (a slim five person majority of the unanimous court made the distinction between all and some "fighting words"), nevertheless the overall constitutional validity of the distinction "fighting words" was acknowledged, confirming its judgment that some words at least are action-loaded. The analogy Justice Scalia made to a sound truck being limited as an example of acceptable content neutrality makes an absurdity out of clearly different kinds of speech such as threats based on race and sex. Certainly we can make a content distinction between race and sex on one hand and height and skin condition (acne) on the other hand. Have a whole group of short people and acne-ridden people been relegated to second-class citizenship? Has not sexual and racial discrimination been far more egregious in practice than height or skin condition?

Let us return to what we are going to *do* about persons who exercise their First Amendment freedoms short of legally punishable action. We need to consult some actual cases. Examine this realistic scenario. A female student, staff member, or faculty member is subject to catcalls and whistles almost regularly when she passes a certain dorm on her way to her class or office. Add further that there have been increasing incidents of rape in this vicinity after dark. An atmosphere of threat and fear exists for women, who can no longer assume that this college campus affords them equal protection. Note that the federal government is now requiring colleges and universities to collect and report data on crime on campuses. How can a college or university protect its reputation? Imagine that these catcalls occur when prospective students and their families are visiting this campus. Some means have to be found to stop systematic, as opposed to just random, acts of sexism. Many women living in major cities now report they are increasingly subject to sexual slurs on streets and in public transportation. Some reversal of these trends is required. Without some stiff fines, censures, and punishments, why will things ever change?

In the *Wisconsin v. Mitchell* case in 1993, the Supreme Court rose to the challenge (after the disappointing *RAV v. St. Paul* case in 1991). The court was unanimous in favor of the Wisconsin penalty-enhancement law for hate crimes. Thirty-eight states now have similar penalty-enhancement laws. Harsher penalties are directed at conduct, not just expression, since courts can take into account *motivations* behind conduct. Penalty enhancement also acts as a deterrent and educates the public as well as law enforcement officials. The University of Texas and Pennsylvania State University have devised hate/abuse speech codes for their campuses which stress the importance of content (sexism and racism) when illegal conduct occurs.

LIBERATION: The scenario example you use falls under what I would call "proprietary responsibility," not the First Amendment and a court case. Universities, construction companies, and any other businesses or organizations have an obligation to control their personnel. It is not always easy to decide what constitutes "harassment." Do pinups in a male locker room (which females do not enter) constitute harassment? Does a work of art with a prominent nude woman exhibited in a university building hallway constitute a "threat" to women? Those who think they are being subjected to harassment need to file complaints and bring pressure. Making a public issue and debate of such a problem is the proper route of education and reform. Those who want to abridge the First Amendment and punish violators are looking for a quick fix much like those who think crime will go away if we just build more prisons and have harsher, mandatory sentences.

The problem with penalty-enhancement laws is that this intrudes on the inner workings and motivations in the minds of individuals, which results in attempted regulation of their thoughts and beliefs. People should only be punished for their wrongful conduct, not their wrongful thoughts and beliefs. The reign of political correctness on our universities and college campuses is the result of trying to regulate certain kinds of speech. Is it racist speech to criticize affirmative action programs? Is it sexist to oppose women's studies programs? Is it discrimination to argue against the practice of homosexuality? The answer to all three questions unfortunately is "Yes" on many college campuses. You will become a candidate for mandatory sensitivity training sessions if you speak against these cherished liberal causes.

Why are some epithets punishable when directed at women and African-Americans, but other odious epithets such as "redneck" and "guinea" are not? Are not slurs against someone's clothing or mannerisms just as assaultive and injurious as slurs of a racist and sexist nature? There are all kinds of jeers. Just go to a sporting event. Could we ever regulate all of them? As Oliver Wendell Holmes said, "Every idea is an incitement to somebody." The First Amendment protects your right to be a jerk and your right to offend. From offense comes the challenge to get motivated to make things different, if you so choose. As Professor Eugene Genovese wrote, "Thus I submit the First Law of College Teaching: Any professor who, subject to the restraints of common sense and common decency, does not seize every opportunity to offend the sensibilities of his students is insulting and cheating them, and is no college professor at all."

EQUALITY: We are proposing nothing new. The courts have always distinguished between different types of speech. Commercial speech (with all the possibilities of fraud) is less protected. Obscenity and libel are not protected by the First Amendment. In fact, a strong analogy can be made between hate/abuse speech and libel (defamation) and obscenity (an assault on dignity and self-respect). It is intriguing how the *Chaplinsky* case uses language that the Supreme Court would similarly use in the *Miller* obscenity case in 1966: language "likely to provoke the *average person* to retaliation" is similar to what the average person in a community would find obscene now, used as the basis for obscenity restriction ordinances. In addition, we do punish those who make abusive phone calls when this constitutes harassment.

Naturally, we are not talking about private language but public language. Public language that is sexist and racist is personal vilification, stigmatizes, assaults, and is corrosive of the fundamental purpose of the First Amendment, an exchange of views. The First Amendment traditionally has sought to support a free and broad exchange of political views in public. We make no challenge to this noble, democratic objective. However, the logic of our position is simply this: how can we extend a right to certain people, such as freedom of expression, when these very same people would use this right and freedom to negate the rights and freedoms of all others? Hate/abuse speech is a preemptive strike that forecloses speech or any kind of rational exchange. A true dialogue occurs among relative equals who share norms of civility. The First Amendment was meant to foster and liberate speech; hate/abuse speech oppresses its targets and renders them powerless.

We need to avoid a theoretical and abstract, above-it-all definition of the First Amendment, as if the First Amendment were some mantra. Hate/abuse speech is a real and present abridgment of the rights of others. It is persecution and aggression, as critical race theorists contend. That is why there is a compelling state and university interest that sometimes overrides the right and freedom of speech. Rights and freedoms are means, not ends in themselves. Justices White and Stevens in the recent *St. Paul* case made it clear that there can be special rules for special risks and harms. First Amendment values cannot give legitimacy to expressions of intimidation. Hate speech is a social evil.

LIBERATION: The real chilling effect comes from your support for restricting speech. Already many people on campuses are afraid to speak openly about certain volatile topics.

EQUALITY: Since 1970 Canada has had a hate speech law that prohibits advocacy of genocide, the willful provocation of hatred, and public incitement of hatred. The Netherlands, France, the United Kingdom, Austria, Germany, Sweden, Norway, Australia, and New Zealand all have similar laws about stirring up hatred. These countries recognize the social harm of hate speech. Such an atmosphere in society at large, at the workplace, or in a university community chills and toxifies such that individuals who seek to develop themselves are instead subjugated.

LIBERATION: We doubt that there is a sufficient compelling need for authorities to supersede the fundamental right of freedom of expression, especially when a left-wing ideology of political correctness is determining the decision. The courts have always instructed authorities to seek the "least possible means" of interfering with our fundamental rights in the

First Amendment. Authoritarian repression of offensive speech is a counterproductive, false remedy.

BIBLIOGRAPHY

Adler, Jerry. "Taking Offense." *Newsweek* (December 24, 1990): 48-54.

Anti-Defamation League. *Hate Crime Laws: A Comprehensive Guide.* New York, 1994.

Brooks, Thomas. "First Amendment: Penalty Enhancement for Hate Crimes." *Journal of Criminal Law and Criminology* 84 (1994): 703-742.

Brown, Steve. "Free Speech Undermined, Racism Left Untouched." *Civil Liberties* (Spring/Summer 1991): 1, 4.

Butterfield, Fox. "Parody Puts Harvard Law Faculty in Sexism Battle." *New York Times* (April 27, 1992): A8, A10.

Congressional Quarterly Research. "Are Longer Sentences for Hate Crimes Constitutional?" (January 8, 1993).

Delgado, Richard and Stefancic, Jean. "Overcoming Legal Barriers to Regulating Hate Speech on Campuses." *Chronicle of Higher Education.* (August 1, 1993): B1-B3.

Delgado, Richard. "Regulation of Hate Speech May be Necessary to Guarantee Equal Protection for All Citizens." *Chronicle of Higher Education* (September 18, 1991): B1-B2.

Finn, Charles E. "The Campus: An Island of Repression in a Sea of Freedom." *Commentary* (September 1989): 17-23.

Fish, Stanley. *There Is No Such Thing As Free Speech, And It's A Good Thing Too.* New York: Oxford University Press, 1993.

Gale, Ellen. "Curbing Racist Speech." *Responsive Community* (Winter 1990/1991).

Gates, Henry Louis. "Let Them Talk." *New Republic* (September 20/27, 1993): 37-49.

Goldstein, Richard. "Hate Speech, Free Speech, and the Unspoken." *Tikkun* 7 (May/June 1992): 53-56.

Grano, Joseph. "Free Speech v. The University of Michigan." *Academic Questions* (Spring 1990): 7-22.

Greenawalt, Kent. "Free Speech in the United States and Canada." *Law and Contemporary Problems*. (Winter 1992): 5-33.

Greenhouse, Linda. "High Court Voids Law Singling Out Crimes of Hatred." *New York Times* (June 23, 1992): A1, A11.

_____. "Justices Uphold Stiffer Sentences for Hate Crimes." *New York Times* (June 12, 1993): A1, A8.

_____. "Two Versions of Free Speech," *New York Times* (June 24, 1992): A1, A11.

Hentoff, Nat. *Free Speech for Me, But Not for Thee*. New York: Harper Collins, 1992.

Lawrence, Charles R. "If He Hollers Let Him Go: Regulating Racist Speech on Campus." *Duke Law Review* (June 1990): 431-483.

Levin, Jack and McDevitt, Jack. *Hate Crimes*. New York: Plenum Press, 1993.

MacKinnnon, Catherine. *Only Words*. Cambridge: Harvard University Press, 1993.

Mahoney, Kathleen. "The Canadian Constitutional Approach to Freedom of Expression in Hate Propaganda and Pornography." *Law and Contemporary Problems* 55 (1992): 77-105.

Matsuda, Mari, Lawrence, Charles R. III, Delgado, Richard, and Crenshaw, Kimberle W. *Words That Wound: Critical Race Theory, Assaultive Speech and the First Amendment*. Boulder: Westview, 1993.

Melville, Keith. *The Boundaries of Free Speech*. New York: McGraw Hill, 1992.

Smolla, Ronald. *Free Speech in an Open Society*. New York: Knopf, 1992.

Strossen, Nadine. "Regulating Racist Speech on Campus: A Modest Proposal?" *Duke Law Review* (June 1990): 484-573.

Sullivan, Kathleen. "The First Amendment Wars." *New Republic* (September 28, 1992): 35-40.

Sunstein, Cass. *Democracy and The Problem of Free Speech*. New York: Free Press, 1993.

NINE

SYMBOLS AND HERITAGES:

MUCH ADO ABOUT NOTHING

OR SOMETHING?

Recently, minority ethnic groups have publicly expressed, as well as organized, their opposition to certain images of themselves perpetuated as stereotypes in our powerful, mass-media transmission of cultural representations. Many nonminority Americans have reacted with disbelief that fairly common images—logos, mascots, symbols, the Confederate flag, etc.—have come under such severe attack. Those identifying with these symbols rarely consider themselves bigots or racists. They cannot understand why these symbols cannot be just "left alone" in the same way that evocative minority ethnic symbols are more or less given free reign in our popular culture. On the other hand, minority ethnic groups find these stereotypes to be a sensitivity test of the majority culture's commitment to rejecting ethnic prejudice.

Certainly the majority culture has demonstrated its own enhanced emotional concerns about how the United States flag is displayed. Never should it be said that symbols are not important to people. They are rallying points of identification, freighted with emotional firepower, and capable of bringing us together or driving us apart. In a multicultural society, how do we deal with varying symbols reminding us of diverse meanings and heritages? Do common American symbols still have the same psychological "pull"? If they did, would it matter as much (ironically) if we also had diverse, particularistic, ethnic symbols?

THE DIALOGUE

MINORITY VIEW: Today we have the opportunity to redeem the past. Certain logos, names, and symbols of Native Americans, blacks, Hispanics, and Jews amount to stereotypes that are derogatory and intimidating. They have no place being represented in American society. People of good will should voluntarily agree to cleanse our society of such demeaning representations. When necessary, laws and regulations need to be enacted to ban the swastika, the Confederate flag, and depictions of Native Americans as savages. All of these symbols are the same as obscenities, which we do not permit on public display.

In principle, ethnic groups need to be empowered to control the representations of themselves since they are the best judges in their own case of what is proper and fitting. Television programs that ridicule and downgrade minorities (e.g., "Amos and Andy", the "Cisco Kid" and Pancho, the "Untouchables" and Italians, the "Lone Ranger" and Tonto) need to be exposed for what they are and replaced. We have already come a long way, even though there still is a problem with newscasts that consistently portray Black Americans as the only criminals and drug-users in America and only show Arab-Americans as rock-throwing demonstrators and terrorists. Stereotyping a whole people does not help solve the serious problems in our society.

MAJORITY VIEW: You make it all sound so simple and easy as if we could all agree in this matter of ethnic sensitivity. Take the examples of the old television programs that you mention. Was Tonto such a bad depiction of Native Americans? He certainly was loyal, trustworthy, honest, and as much a fighter for good against evil as the Lone Ranger. Did he not save the Lone Ranger's life over and over again? Yes his pidgin English speech and his sidekick status make him subject to jests, but did he not have his own shrewdness and independent pride, both of which are admirable Native-American attributes? "The Lone Ranger" television program is a dated program, and certainly we can do better today. In fact, there is a very healthy debate going on in the movie industry regarding the films "The Last of the Mohicans," "Dances with Wolves," and "Black Robe." I would stress that there is no one norm or standard or even sets of norms and standards that can be applied as if we all agreed. That is why a free marketplace of possibilities and many opportunities for critical voices (pluralism and diversity) are the best recommendations for the controversy over ethnic representations.

As for a television program such as "Amos and Andy," we are dealing here with another genre, humor and the boundaries of humor. During its time, the "Amos and Andy" program may have helped dissolve differences of race since humor does have that function. They were lovable characters you could identify with, since they had very human propensities. Yet we can see now that "Amos and Andy" was not just lighthearted fun, but a mockery and gross exaggeration of supposedly Negro characteristics that actually belittle black persons. However, the contemporary television program "Living Color" also portrays blacks in grossly exaggerated, self-demeaning roles, all for the sake of laughter. And do not the most overdrawn statements, postures, and behaviors of blacks in contemporary sit-coms get the biggest laughs?

How are people laughing, *with* or *at* the expense of blacks? Do not these contemporary television shows also perpetuate stereotypes even while mocking them? Do these minority programs promote role models and standards of behavior that will encourage respect and reward in our society? There is no simple and easy way to determine the intentions behind humor and especially the consequences of humor among diverse audiences. The best intentions can fail miserably, and consequences may be fairly unpredictable.

MINORITY VIEW: You fail to see my key point (perhaps purposely) because you are in the empowered majority and feel comfortable with just letting the so-called "free marketplace" determine outcomes. Television programs such as "The Lone Ranger" and "Amos and Andy" were written and directed by those in the majority white power structure who explicitly or implicitly sought to keep Native Americans and blacks in their subordinate place. What is at stake here is who has power. "Living Color" is controlled by African-Americans who then can bear the responsibility for the consequences.

The point of humor and especially black humor is to disarm and expose. If there are people out there who have their antiblack racism fed by "Living Color," then that serves the purpose of drawing out what needs to be exposed to the light of day. While African-American sit-coms may use some stereotypes, the purpose is to overcome and redeem these stereotypes, not to present them as what black people are finally reduced to by the majority power system.

There is a fundamental distinction that is missing in your treatment of movies and television programs. There is the primary matter of being true and fair to reality, be it history or the humanity of an ethnic people. On the other hand, there is propaganda, scapegoating, self-serving white supremacy, and all the manipulations that characterize bias and *libido dominandi* relationships. The only way to start to factor out the latter distortions and menaces is to let many minority ethnic voices be heard so that they have the power to correct their own portrayal. Is it necessary and healthy for the white power majority to dominate? Are not we better off when movies and television programs reflect the given diversity of American society?

MAJORITY VIEW: Yes it is better that our movies (e.g., recently "Robin Hood," "Peter Pan," "Pocohantas,") and advertisements on television reflect our diverse, multicultural society. And minorities should have power at least proportionate to their share of the population, albeit not limited to this proportion. However, can we be so sure that just because minorities are writing television programs that there will be the avoidance of terrible stereotypes? There is too much in popular culture that is so degrading and harmful even when minorities (such as in the popular music industry) have decisive power.

Your emphasis on power (especially the political power to dominate) implies that there was and is a conscious effort (perhaps a conspiracy?) to perpetuate the power of the white majority. A better explanation takes into account powerful, impersonal, technological forces that impact minorities and majorities alike. There is a general problem with mass media technology that you have not discerned. Inherent in the very reproduction of images and sounds (radio, television, and newspapers) there is unavoidable stereotyping and bias.

First of all, all these media have time and space limitations, so there is only so much that they can cover. Some editor makes decisions as to time and space based on capturing the audience's attention. In most cases, economic profitability and survivability are at stake. So what sells drives out what does not sell. Brilliant, objective documentaries that are learning experiences may have no chance up against cheap, vulgar entertainment. Numbers are everything; majority tastes cutting across ethnic lines win out.

Secondly, there is the tremendous power of images in newspaper photos and, of course, on television. The indoctrination effect occurs whereby your mind is programmed to see people in certain expectable characteristics (stereotypes) even when you know this is unrepresentative and distorting. It is natural and economic for everyone's mind to harbor a few sets of simple images since complicated, diverse images unsettle the mind and cause dissonance. Most people crave the expectable, predictable, set, defined situation, all of which constitutes their desired normality. Stereotypes are unavoidable and inherent in both the mass media and the working of the human mind. The general public seeks to be made comfortable and reassured, and the mass media comply by serving up immediately recognizable stereotypes. Try watching people who watch television, and then see what they readily tune into.

MINORITY VIEW: Your analysis of the mass media, for all its merits, leads to a passivity and fatalism, not an activism for change, in the omnipresence of the technology of the mass media. This is unacceptable. We need to find ways to take charge, to take ownership responsibility. There is such a thing as better and worse representations, which is why we need to empower minority ethnic voices as advisors, producers, and directors. I do not think people are as dumb as you suggest in their reliance on and need for stereotypes. People succumb to stereotypes because they have never been given choices, which is to say, power.

MAJORITY VIEW: Even if we go in the empowerment direction that you recommend (and I believe we are going in this direction already), it does not solve the problem of conflict over publicly accepted images. For example, there is quite a business in objects and replicas depicting blacks as slaves and servants. Perhaps you have seen these figures on lawns, i.e., private property. I hope you are not suggesting laws and regulations that would intrude on private property and privacy. I find these relics deeply offensive, but in a free society in the private sphere we *tolerate* even what is offensive as long as it does not cause real, objective harm to others. For example, a public school teacher could possess privately all kinds of slavery memorabilia depicting the utter abjection of African peoples in the South, but to bring this to his/her public school classroom and use it as a resource to demean black people would be unacceptable and illegal.

Then there is the great controversy over the use of the Confederate flag. To a great majority of Southerners the Confederate flag represents what it truly means to be a Southerner, to have fought and died for the

Southern cause. It is a memorial to the dead and to states' rights which remains an alternative, and a not-entirely-dead understanding of our nation. The Confederate flag is not any kind of immediate threat to black Americans and is not reducible simply to a symbol of slavery. Black people do not have to wave the Confederate flag. They may be offended by it, but where is the serious harm? Perhaps the most common use of the Confederate flag is at football games of Southern high schools and universities. This flag demonstrates school pride and affiliation. It is a tradition with a lot of emotional resonance. In a world depleted of symbols and allegiances, a naked public square so to speak, people yearn for something they can identify with that gives them some psychological uplift.

If we are going down the road of sensitivity, then sensitivity cuts both ways. We have to be sensitive about each others' sensitivities. There is a T-shirt in the South with one side having the Confederate flag and the other side the Malcolm X symbol. The wording on the Malcolm X side is "You wear your X," and on the other side of the T-shirt are the words "We have our flag." Why not merge the songs "Dixie" and "The Battle Hymn of the Republic"? Is not this true multicultural diversity?

MINORITY VIEW: There are countries such as Canada that have passed laws banning the use of hate symbols such as the swastika. Why cannot we have laws and regulations that ban all symbols that represent genocide and slavery, not just for Jews but for Native Americans and blacks as well?!

Yes, I will accept regrettably your public/private distinction for the sake of limiting the power of government when it comes to individual freedom, but I doubt if, in reality, this distinction holds. The public school teacher trafficking in racist relics is not likely to keep his/her views private, and this person's dealings with children could more than likely witness and promote racism in subtle ways. So public school authorities are going to have to screen their teachers and then reprimand, if not fire, those who deny any person's humanity. We are talking about a very basic, foundational principle, without which there can be no tolerable human society. Consequently, we cannot mix symbols of freedom and oppression. It is simply ludicrous to merge "Dixie" and "The Battle Hymn of the Republic."

As for the Confederate flag, you are not facing up to what is at stake in the use of that flag since the defeat of the Confederacy. This flag represents the Confederacy and its states' rights defense of slavery, which is a major part of, albeit not the whole of, what it means to be "Southern." Since the end of the Civil War, this flag has been revived for use precisely during those moments when certain white Americans have wanted to continue the oppression of black people. For example, the first known revival of the Confederate flag was in the 1890s when many states were enacting Jim Crow laws to keep in their place that new generation of African-Americans that never experienced slavery. The next time the Confederate flag took on some public meaning was during World War II when soldiers from the South wanted to distinguish their bravery from that of northern soldiers. Did such militancy have wartime value only?

The next time Confederate flags became prominent was in 1948, when Southern Democrats broke away from the Democratic Party and formed the Dixiecrat Party in opposition to the civil rights platform of the Democratic Party. And in 1956 after the Supreme Court's *Brown* decision, Confederate flags appeared in defense of segregation, waved in the faces of civil rights marchers to make it clear that the Ol' South was not about to change its ways. We are not just dealing here with a sense of pride and identity, a benign tradition. The Confederacy was a renegade, secessionist government, never legitimate. This government lost not only the basis for its system of slavery, but also its justification for a confederation conception of government that goes by the shorthand term "states' rights." Clearly, we the people of the United States did not form a loose league or alliance of independent, sovereign states; rather we the people of the United States formed and ordained a *union* under a strong and energetic national government with some rights and responsibilities reserved to the states. But there was no right of secession, and Congress was empowered to regulate interstate commerce, which would include slavery.

Certainly you must be aware that hate groups such as the KKK, Nazis, and skinheads proudly use and display the Confederate flag as part of their racist message. The Confederate flag sends out a clear signal to African-Americans. This flag is meant to intimidate, to arouse fear, and to repress. Why cannot there be some sensitivity regarding the terrible injustices of slavery? Is it asking too much for Southerners to deny themselves the horrible part of their tradition of the Confederacy and to resurrect what is best in the Southern tradition (e.g., literature, food, the slower pace of life, manners and kindness)?

MAJORITY VIEW: You are making too much of a piece of cloth, and
for all your sensitivity concerns you show too little sensitivity for those
who identify with the Stars and Bars of St. Andrews Cross. If we were
to adopt your mode of reasoning, then we would have to bar the U.S.
flag, which U.S. soldiers displayed in battle when wiping out American
Indians. On your terms, both flags are equally tainted with blood and
horrifying injustice. But the fact is that there are no pure symbols. Even
though hate groups use (actually misuse) the Confederate flag, that cannot
be the test of the worth and value of the Confederate flag.

Unfortunately, in a free country any symbol can be appropriated for
its emotional value. What about violent minorities using the Malcolm X
symbol, or rap singers using the traditional black mode of signifying to
vent their violent rage in popular music? We have to rely on the good
sense of most Americans to reject being manipulated by the perverse use
of symbols, rather than passing all kinds of restrictive laws, regulations,
and rules. Once we start down the legal road, where will it stop? Are not
we heading in the direction of government censorship? Will we end up
removing monuments to the Confederacy on public property?

To prove that I am not being unduly alarmist, recently the U.S. Senate
refused to extend a century-old patent to the United Daughters of the
Confederacy. That patent was for a rebel flag surrounded by a wreath.
The United Daughters of the Confederacy has a long history of opposing
the use of the Confederate flag by racist groups. We are today embroiled
in the scourge of "political correctness," which makes no distinctions as
it tarnishes anyone who does not obey the latest, arbitrary emotional
pleadings of an ethnic group. ˙ This is a very divisive promotion of
"culture wars" that prevent us from uniting to solve real, socioeconomic
problems.

Years ago, the black mayor of Atlanta, Andrew Young, made it clear
that he was not interested in conflict over symbols on pieces of cloth. He
wanted economic opportunities for those who have socioeconomic
disadvantages.   The most virulent forms of racism come out of
socioeconomic deprivation. Why are we not discussing practical issues
such as job growth, welfare dependency, crime as a way of life, early
childhood education, community building, etc.?

MINORITY VIEW: I would understand, in the light of our awful history,
if Native Americans could never pledge allegiance to the U.S. flag despite
being good U.S. citizens. In fact, we have given tribal sovereignty to

Native Americans, and we are recognizing their rights to property, water, and mineral resources under treaties made with them but never properly observed. Perhaps all peoples, especially minority ethnic peoples, have great burdens of the past to bear. We ask that tolerance be shown to those who cannot pledge allegiance (Jehovah Witnesses, Native Americans, and other dissenters) as well as cleansing the *public, official* sphere of derogatory, demeaning symbols. We are heartened by decisions in Alabama and Georgia to not use the Confederate flag as the state flag. We are referring to only a recent, since the 1950s, revival of the use of this flag to resist segregation. The University of Mississippi also will not officially use the Confederate flag. Certainly we hope all others will voluntarily, once educated, abandon a deeply offensive symbol such as the Confederate flag. Sadly, we probably will have to wait a generation or two.

What is occurring is not some test of "political correctness," which is a term bandied about to make people appear to be members of a gang of "thought police." What is at stake is political community sensitivity. Do you respect the very real pain that ethnic minorities feel when confronted with symbols that arouse memories of a horrifying past?

Perhaps the most vulnerable and alienated of all Americans are Native Americans, who still have to endure the cigar store Indian, the mascots, the cowboy-Indian westerns in film and on television, and the romanticization and mystification of the Indian. Non-Indians can reap economic profits by the expropriation of Indian artifacts for sale to white Anglo society. Yet why is it too much for white society to abandon the Braves and the tomahawk chop, the Indians and the goofy smiling Indian caricature, the Redskins, the Miami University chieftain's head that is placed on their basketball floor for everyone to run up and down on, and Chief Illiniwek of the University of Illinois who does absurd Indian dances? To their credit, some universities of higher example such as Stanford, Dartmouth, and Syracuse have made such redeeming changes.

This is not simply a matter of two groups *equally* wanting what they think is appropriate. How more unequal could Native Americans be to the white majority? Out of a sense of respect and fellow feeling, as an act of good will and remission, why not drop such symbols? Can it really hurt as badly to drop these symbols as it hurts Native Americans to be treated on the level of savage animal mascots? You have buffaloes, lions, dolphins, bears, cardinals, rams, and then you have redskins! And when Chief Illiniwek does his Indian dance, this ridicules everything sacred about Native-American ceremonial dances. Imagine a sports team (let's call them the "Papists") mimicking a priest performing the rite of communion! We need to find symbols that bring us all together. And symbols are very important. Notice that the majority of Americans are deeply disturbed by the so-called constitutional right to burn the American flag. It is more than a piece of cloth; it is a representation of a people's way of life and a people's fundamental affections and loyalties.

MAJORITY VIEW: Rather than an emotional "burden of the past to bear," I think and prefer that we concentrate on "burdens of proof." I see no proof (beyond the powerful force of emotion) that our country suffers from allegiances to prejudicial symbols. This attachment to symbols is a consequence, not a cause, of our failure to build a better society in which people can live together in mutual respect and peace. Too many people feel there is uncontrollable change discarding their traditions and values.

Allowing oneself and others to adopt a victim's psychology will get you nowhere. It is just plain self-defeating. Making an issue of Confederate flags, mascots, etc. only incites people and engenders more racism since you are attacking other people's attachments at a time when people feel they are losing meaning in their lives. Most people do not see and feel the bigotry that you attach to these symbols. Ironically, some of these people feel justified in being bigoted when symbols they identify with are challenged and banned. Would not it be better to follow that practice of Supreme Court Justice Clarence Thomas, who has a small replica of the Confederate Georgia flag on his desk to remind him every day to fight with all he has to disprove what that flag represents to black persons? As a personal, individual matter, we need to convert the negative to the positive.

MINORITY VIEW: You operate from a false and unreal framework, namely, that we are all just self-defining individuals and it does not matter much what symbols characterize our community as long as individuals have freedom of choice for whatever symbols warm their private hearts. However, people do not just normally reach deep down inside themselves to find what it takes to succeed. The social/cultural environment of people has a big effect on their motivations and values. The resort to and the clinging to discredited symbols is a form of resistance to progressive change that would *include* ethnic minorities in the benefits of our society. Symbols are neither innocuous nor dispensable. With all due respect for people's privacy, there is the public sphere (including the mass media) that needs to establish certain norms based on our common humanity and our need to live and work together harmoniously. That is why the mass media must be ever so careful about simply presenting Arab people as terrorists.

We applaud those 100 reporters in Super Bowl 1994 who walked out when the national anthem was played, since the Confederate flag of Georgia was hoisted along with the American flag. We applaud the Portland *Oregonian* for refusing to publish any sports teams names demeaning to Native Americans despite loss of subscriptions and fifteen to one reader opposition in their mail. These are small but significant steps forward in socially responsible journalism.

MAJORITY VIEW: Not only do I put your position in the context of a power ploy to impose minority ethnic "political correctness" on the majority, but I also see this as a delegitimating attack on what has held American society together in the past. When we moved from uncivilized to civilized conditions and defeated far-away tyrannical government in favor of local democratic government responsible to the people, there was a great American achievement which now you question and deny. The governor of Alabama cannot publicly say what is a historically true description of Americans, that we are a white, Christian nation. To make any kind of overarching statement is taken as a threat to anyone who is left out. In the end, we will have nothing left that defines us and does not exclude others, if we desymbolize, neutralize, and deracinate the American public realm. All that will be left is a chaotic carnival of voices and behaviors. Can this multicultural dream be a good thing?

MINORITY VIEW: We are only asking for respect, the basis on which all of us can be included in a common, multicultural society. Asking for empathy is not adopting victim status. If the American majority could put itself in the place of ethnic minorities, then there would be less of an effort to ignore and sidestep these issues. You would think we are asking for economic reparations, taking money right out of the pockets of non-Native Americans! Our requests are quite minimal and moderate. Without understanding the perspectives of minority ethnic groups, there can be no new American community.

BIBLIOGRAPHY

Aleiss, Angela. "A Race Divided: The Indian Westerns of John Ford." *American Indian Culture and Research* (Spring 1994): 167-186.

Appleford, Robert. "Coming Out from Behind the Rocks." *American Indian Culture and Research* (Winter 1995): 97-118.

Coltelli, Laura, ed. *Winged Words, American Indian Writers Speak.* Omaha: University of Nebraska Press, 1992.

Cunningham, Richard. "Racy Nicknames." *Quill* (May 1992): 10.

Davis, Mark. "Looking into a Broken Mirror." *Newsweek* (August 7, 1993): 10.

Eaton, Maynard. "It Never Flags." *Black Enterprise* (June 1988): 44.

Editorial. "The Hurons are Better Off." *Grand Rapids Press* (May 29, 1991): A10.

Fitzgerald, Mark. "SuperBowl Walkout." *Editors and Publishers* (February 5, 1994): 24.

"Flag in a Flap," *Economist* (February 13, 1993): A28.

Gassaway, Bob. "The New Storytellers." *Quill* (May 1991): 32-33.

Giago, Tim. "I Hope the Redskins Lose." *Newsweek* (1-27-92): 8.

Halton, Mark. "Time to Furl the Confederate Flag." *Christian Century* (May 18, 1988): 494-496.

Hill, Richard. "The Non-Vanishing American Indian." *Quill* (May 1992): 35-37.

Horn, Miriam. "Passions that Stir in the Breeze." *U.S. News & World Report* (May 29, 1989): 54, 57.

Kincaid, James. "Who Gets to Tell Their Stories." *New York Times Book Review* (May 3, 1992): 1, 24-29.

Lederman, Douglas. "Old Times Not Forgotten." *Chronicle of Higher Education* (October 20, 1993): A51-A52.

Letters to the Editor. *Chronicle of Higher Education* (December 3, 1993).

Lidz, Frank. "Not a Very Sporting Symbol." *Sports Illustrated* (September 17, 1990): 10.

Mieder, Wolfgang. "The Only Good Indian Is a Dead Indian." *Journal of American Folklore* (Winter 1993): 38-60.

"A Rebel Tamed?" *Economist* (June 11, 1994): A23.

Springer, Chris. "The Troubled Resurgence of the Confederate Flag." *History Today* (June 1993): 7-9.

Stewart, Nikita. "Confederate Flag is Banned From Trinity Campus." *Louisville Courier Journal* (August 30, 1995): B1.

TEN

LANGUAGE POLICY: COMMONALITY

OR DIVERSITY?

THE POLITICS OF SYMBOLS

One manifestation of the controversy that has been swirling around the topic of multiculturalism is the appearance of the Official English Language and English Only movements. Both seek to preserve and protect our English language, fearing the loss of its dominance as a result of the increased prevalence of Spanish and Asian foreign language usage in the United States. On the other side of this dispute, there are those who believe in language rights. They perceive this English hegemony movement as a threat to the freedom of expression of non–English-language Americans. In counterresponse, they have formed an English Plus movement recognizing the value of non-English languages in our public life. Consequently, one side believes that language is crucial to national unity while the other side finds a diversity of languages to be an enrichment factor in our multiethnic nation.

Being a country of multifarious immigrants, "Americans" have always been confronted with the problem of how to deal with "the Other." Should we encourage or make the Other to be like us, the same for the Other's own good, in order to be accepted as one of us? But why not just allow the Other to be Other, different and various? Does not the Other have rights too, which may lead to another common ground more diversitarian since it partakes of Others on their terms as well? Is not a particular language an essential part of a particular culture, without which language that culture would not survive? Historical, national, public policy issues involving assimilation and pluralism, the public and the private spheres, and Americanness and ethnicity are the issues grounding and focusing this debate.

THE DIALOGUE

OFFICIAL ENGLISH: Already English is the informally accepted, predominant language of public usage in the United States. We propose a law of Congress and/or a constitutional amendment to formalize (i.e., make official) what already is the case. What is the big deal? English is the dominant language in the world; three-fourths of all world publications are produced in English. English is the *lingua franca* of the world. The world is technologically coming closer and closer together, given the media communications revolution. Only those who develop the highest proficiency in English will be able to partake socially and economically in the twenty-first century.

Today, Americans are threatened by non-English language movements that would require the use of their non-English language in the public arena of government and business. An unprecedented number of people in the United States operate exclusively in a non-English language. In California and Florida you can go to public school and never learn or use English. We only ask that Americans stand up and defend their own language, the bedrock of our unique culture. What is at stake is our constitutional integrity, namely, "We the People . . . in order to form a more perfect Union. . ." as defined by our own language.

LANGUAGE RIGHTS: Your position is motivated by a nonexistent threat and irrational fear which you indirectly self-refute: English already is well entrenched and dominating informally. So why cause a ruckus? Around seventy-five percent of Hispanics speak English daily. A poll of Hispanics in Los Angeles revealed that ninety-five percent believed that it was essential for their children to learn to write and speak English well. Only 10% of Americans speak a non-English language at home and only 20% report that their mother tongue is not English. In fact, in many cities there are more adults wanting courses in English language instruction than there are openings. An estimated one million adults need and want these English language instruction courses. Hardly is this the kind of evidence of a country reluctant to learn and use English.

It is understandable that non–English-speaking parents want to preserve and protect their own native language because their language is crucial to their own personal identity and their traditional cultural heritage. The real fear in the United States today is the loss of such nondominant languages, and along with their language the loss of their identity and cultural heritage, which frequently occurs in the thoroughgoing American assimilation process. Actually modern mass communication (the omnipresence of television) in the area of popular culture produces a tremendous pressure for conformity, namely an English monolingualism. As a result, European countries (especially the French) have taken action to resist "Americanisms" in their language.

As for us, we favor a national language policy that recognizes the full participation of all languages in our multicultural, multilingual nation. English certainly is the language of wide and common communication. The preamble of the U.S. Constitution that you quote makes no mention of the English language as the only official language. The framers of our government had no such restriction in mind, and a diversity of languages was spoken back then. In addition, the Fourteenth Amendment to the U.S. Constitution provides the right to equal protection of the laws. Parents who want to raise bilingual children should have every opportunity and be given support. Therefore, non-English languages have rights, and they need to be acknowledged when it comes to legal services, education, and social services. Linguistic differences, or being in the language minority, should not mean the denial of one's civil rights.

To repeat, there is nothing to fear. Hispanic-Americans and Asian-Americans know full well the need to learn English and they are not putting up any resistance. By the second or third generation the English language is completely acquired. At the same time Latinos and Asians do not want to lose their own heritage and only ask all Americans to recognize and respect their language, as much as they enjoy their distinctive, ethnic fast food.

OFFICIAL ENGLISH: We too favor the full achievement of all rights for all Americans. That is precisely why we advocate the highest proficiency in English in order for everyone to enjoy U.S. citizenship and to advance socioeconomically. English language training, Asian-Americans know, has always been a part of our naturalization, citizenship process. We fear, justifiably, the possibility that Hispanic people may refuse to speak English, especially when motivated by language rights extremists. This refusal to communicate in a common language has already occurred in Quebec, Canada. Also, English as a language of proficiency has always been strongly required in K–12 and college education. Your emphasis on multilingualism will have the consequences of establishing linguistic ghettoes and isolating young Americans from paths of economic upward mobility. People who do not become proficient in English become a burden to American society, an underclass, ending up on welfare or resorting to a life of crime. Our Constitution does not give specific language rights as do the constitutions and laws of other countries such as India, Belgium, Sri Lanka, and South Africa, where there is considerable ethnic conflict.

The formation of the U.S. English organization and movement in the 1980s was meant to "maintain the blessings of a common language" and to "reverse the spread of foreign language usage in the nation's official life." Specifically, U.S. English advocates the repeal of laws mandating multilinguistic ballots and voting materials and mandatory, exclusive (no other alternatives) bilingual education programs. Most of these bilingual education programs are driven by foreign language maintenance rather than transition to English language proficiency. Very prominent persons have joined U.S. English: Walter Cronkite, Saul Bellow, Linda Chavez, Walter Annenberg, Arnold Schwarzenegger, Sidney Hook, Alistair Cooke, Jacques Barzun, Bruno Bettelheim, S.I. Hayakawa. In California our organization succeeded in getting Proposition 63 passed in 1986, and by 1991 eighteen states (Alabama, California, Florida, Georgia, Indiana, Kentucky, Mississippi, Missouri, Nebraska, North Carolina, North Dakota, South Carolina, Tennessee, and Virginia) had official English language constitutional amendments or statutes.

LANGUAGE RIGHTS: Yes, you have had some victories but another twenty-eight states blocked and refused to pass such laws or to entertain such state constitutional amendments. In fact, an important counter-organization called English Plus has appeared. In four states, New Mexico, Hawaii, Oregon, and Washington, there are now English Plus laws recognizing the importance of other languages besides English and protecting the rights and opportunities that exist for all languages.

Since 1990 the Official English movement has been stopped in its tracks. There are two reasons for this: (1) the exposure of the racism and discriminatory consequences of this movement, which really goes beyond English as our official language to English-only restrictions; and (2) the realization by most Americans who strongly support English as our official language that this is meant primarily for symbolic value, not for the purpose of coercing people to use only English. Maybe more Americans desire to wear a badge of Americanism, but not at the expense of mistreating and coercing other Americans.

Let me explain both of these developments. In 1990, a 1988 memo surfaced written by the founder of U.S. English, John Tanton, a Michigan ophthalmologist. The memo had the following statements characterizing Hispanics:

". . . the tradition of the *mordida* (bribe), the lack of involvement in public affairs, Roman Catholicism, with its potential to 'pitch out the separation of church and state', low 'educability', and high school dropout rates, failures to use birth control, limited concern for the environment, and of course, divisions."

"Will the present majority personally hand over its power to a group that is simply more fertile?"

"As Whites see their power and control over their lives declining, will they simply go quietly in the night?"

"On the demographic point: perhaps this is the first instance in which those with their pants up are going to get caught by those with their pants down."

The author of this memo, John Tanton, went on to found FAIR (Federation of Americans for Immigration Reform), an anti-immigration movement that received $370,000 of funding from the notorious Pioneer Fund, an organization that promotes racial betterment via eugenics. In many ways the English-only crowd have gone on to attacking immigration and, in general, insinuating that aliens are polluting our country's American-First bloodstream.

The second development is that Americans never believed and understood that the symbolic act of formally acknowledging English as our official language could eventuate in denying non-English speakers their language rights. Most Americans do not want immigrants to be denied access to emergency services because they do not speak English. Also non–English-speaking people should not be prohibited from using their language in the workplace as long as this does not interfere with reasonable business needs. At the same time most Americans want non–English-speaking persons to learn English, and they realize that by the second or third generation this is an accomplished fact without having to resort to any kind of government coercion.

OFFICIAL LANGUAGE: Your description of U.S. English and your rendition of what has happened to the Official English Language movement is erroneous. John Tanton did not represent what the leaders of U.S. English stood for, and both Cronkite and Chavez immediately resigned once his memo (which they originally knew nothing about) was made public. All political-social movements attract extremists or generate extremists that do not fairly represent a decent movement's goals.

You are wrong to tarnish the Official English Language movement as some sort of racist, exclusionary English-only movement. This movement has correctly observed that there is a general decline in "citizenship" attributes, especially the tremendous decline in voter turnout as well as public cynicism and negativism about politics in general. Non–English-speaking Americans such as Latino and Asian ethnic groups have the lowest voter turnouts and the weakest political representation. We are not blaming them for this; if anything we blame their own unrepresentative and malrepresentative elite activists who have spread anti-American propaganda. They claim the United States is a racist and ethnocentric society. Thus, minorities should "circle their wagons" and huddle in their own separate enclaves. On the contrary, to give ethnic groups more access to politics and more economic opportunities we favor the enforcement of English as our official language. Therefore, there will be no ballots printed in any language but English, although obviously there still can be foreign language communication and courses covering American politics. It is just obvious and natural that when Hispanics and Asians learn English they will be more motivated to engage in mainstream political participation.

Economically, it is even more important that non–English-speaking ethnic groups attain the highest level of English proficiency to become employed, to advance in a career, and to benefit economically from our expanding economy. Certainly another language besides English will be very valuable in our globally interdependent world economy. But English is the gateway language in the United States. In no way do we propose to deny non-English speakers their language rights as regards social services and emergency services. At the workplace, the courts have properly ruled that employers must demonstrate the business necessity of English usage to require English usage. We would never support the firing of a waitress for translating a menu, or the imposition of English only when workers are talking among themselves, as long as this is not disruptive of business requirements. We leave the issue of bilingual signs to local ordinances.

The only question involves the *public* arena of politics and government where English predominance is important as a spur to full integration and participation. Actually, we believe that those who push language rights to the extreme of celebrating diversity without a common unity are the ones engendering a new segregation by language and increasing hostility in communications among ethnic groups.

LANGUAGE RIGHTS: Your very use of the term "anti-American propaganda" conjures up all the fanaticism and ridiculousness of McCarthyism in the 1950s. Your sense of unity in the United States requires monolingualism, thus denying the rights of those with different native languages. You talk about not favoring certain discriminatory consequences, but it is no more than talk because these incidents have already begun happening at your instigation. Your position of forced assimilation and Americanization has been recurrent in American history when there has been an economic crisis, or war, or a so-called flood of immigrants.

A whole train of recent laws based on the First and Fourteenth Amendments counter this intolerance. In 1968, Congress passed the Bilingual Education Act providing funds to local educational agencies to develop and carry out programs to meet the special education needs of children from low-income families with limited English speaking abilities. In 1974, the *Lau* case upheld public school instruction in a person's own native language as essential to equal opportunities in education. In 1974, the Equal Educational Opportunities Act allowed educational agencies to overcome language barriers and provide equal educational participation by having instructional programs suited to the needs of non–English-speaking students. These laws and decisions recognize a policy of language rights affirming ethnicity and multilingualism.

What is frightening about the Official English Language movement is its strong potential for English-only consequences. For example, the proposed English Language Amendment to the U.S. Constitution would leave it entirely within the powers of Congress to legislate the details that determine whether English is mandatory. Note also that the California law (Proposition 63) gives Californians the power to sue if they believe that the English language is not being publicly observed. And the Arizona law that was passed was so prohibitive that it was declared unconstitutional by a federal district court judge in February 1990 on the grounds that it violated the guaranteed right of free speech. Communicating in one's own language is a fundamental right of free speech and should not be subject to legislative regulations.

OFFICIAL ENGLISH: We have considerable Hispanic and Asian support from their own leaders and their own general population. The proper place for a secondary language is in the private sphere—the home, church, neighborhood, and club.   The central issue between us concerns mandatory bilingual education in public schools. The research shows that bilingual education does not rapidly enough advance children toward English proficiency. Bilingual program students, in one New York City study, tested out at a rate of 51% in three years, whereas students in an English as a Second Language (ESL) program tested out 79% after three years. New York City spends $300 million a year for ten, different-from-English, language programs. Students who are in bilingual programs, which really tend to be foreign language *maintenance* programs, rather than language *shift* programs, are not as academically well prepared as other students.

  A recent op-ed article in the *New York Times* by Barbara Mujica, a Latina, complained about an all-Spanish high school in Florida that communicated with students only in broken English and accordingly prevented her niece from attending an academically better college because of her weak English-speaking skills. Frequently, parents who want their children to learn English rapidly and at the highest proficiency have encountered a bilingual education bureaucracy denying other alternatives (such as ESL or structured English immersion classes). Sixteen states have mandatory bilingual-education-only programs. Yet alternatives to bilingual education in Berkeley, California, El Paso, Texas, and Dade Country, Florida have been quite successful. Only in 1988 was it possible (not without a big fight) to change the Bilingual Education Act of 1968 to include alternatives to the monolithic bilingual education approach. After Congress looked at the research evidence, 25% of the appropriations were set aside for alternatives to bilingual education. Bilingual education encourages separatism and alienation, rather than integration and assimilation into the education mainstream.

LANGUAGE RIGHTS: You have distorted the research findings regarding bilingual education. More recent, high-quality research reveals the positive consequences of bilingual education. The Government Accounting Office (GAO) conducted an investigation that supports bilingual education. Apparently you would return to the days when we threw non–English-speaking children into all-English classrooms to swim or to sink.

The whole point of bilingual education is to provide a psychologically sound basis for learning English. The research shows that when a young person develops proficiency in his/her own non-English native language, then he/she can more easily proceed to full proficiency in English. The emotional, self-esteem, and confidence factors cannot be ignored in favor of just achieving a cognitive outcome. Emotions and cognition go together. The facts are that 90% of all bilingual programs are transitional not maintaining, and the time period is from two to four years depending on the age of the child. The older the child, the longer the process. Speed and haste are *not* the answer. The National Association for Bilingual Education has found that bilingual education improves achievement test scores, reduces dropout rates, reduces school absenteeism, and increases self-esteem and cross-cultural communication efforts.

There is no reason why more Americans cannot become masterfully bilingual or mulitlingual, as are many Europeans. Practically and economically, this will have many advantages as we become more closely intertwined with economic developments in Mexico and Latin America. Learning another language improves one's own native language skills and broadens the mind. Also it is a fact that the English language is not some static, fixed vocabulary. Another language enriches and expands the English language as new words and ways of saying things and capturing feelings and thoughts improve our overall communication skills. It is reactionary and backward to have phobias about language change and what is different. We are quite capable of accommodating what is other. Fostering linguistic pluralism is a great plus.

OFFICIAL ENGLISH: In no way are we advocating some return to the sink or swim practices of the past. We care about the psychological state of young children, and we care even more than you do that they overcome the alienation of having inadequate English communication skills. Our attack on bilingual education is that it is too slow a transition, in many cases taking six years. In some cases no transition occurs at all because the main objective of its practitioners is maintaining native languages. The whole effort of foreign language maintenance (the culture and heritage of non-English speakers) should occur in the home and neighborhood (the private sector) and not be funded by the general public.

What is the National Association for Bilingual Education (certainly a self-promotional body) comparing the success of bilingual education to? Nothing? Today the dropout rate for Hispanics is 40%, the highest of any group. The number of Hispanics who go on to college is 3%, one of the lowest for any ethnic group. When you compare bilingual education to ESL or structured English immersion alternatives, there is no special advantage or success rate for bilingual education. However, we maintain that a non-English language is best nurtured at home while the public schools need to achieve the highest proficiency and excellence in English so that young people can take advantage of all the opportunities available to them. Our much more sophisticated economy today puts a greater burden on all young people to not just be able to use English but to be able to master and attain excellence in English communication skills. Too many bilingual education programs only aim at a low level of English usage, and thus we have the socioeconomic ghetto outcome.

LANGUAGE RIGHTS: Many of the shortcomings of bilingual education revealed in research studies are related to the fact there are not enough excellent bilingual education programs. Bilingual education is even conceived as "special education" in the Bilingual Education Act of 1968. As a result, non–English-speaking children are treated alongside the mentally deficient and the emotionally disturbed. However, any bilingual education program whatsoever is better than the catastrophe of the old fashioned fend-for-yourself, sink-or-swim programs, as if Hispanic children have cognitive deficits as opposed to a majority language deficit.

We do not favor classroom segregation by language, but we recognize the need to have many academic courses in Spanish to build up Spanish proficiency while at the same time heading in the direction of English proficiency. The problem of ESL and immersion programs is that they force English on young people without due consideration for their emotional needs, such as identity with their parents' heritage. With language comes a culture and a source of identity. Forcing English on non-English peoples contributes to breakdown of the family and is analogous to the consequences of youth rebellion, which presumably threatens the American values you hold so dear.

The proponents of Official English and English Only make a very serious mistake in contending that English exclusively is the language of political unity and democracy. This virulent ethnocentrism, a kind of hegemonic passion, ignores the foundation of political unity in democratic values of individual rights, tolerance, equality, participation, consent, and a whole field of opportunities for everyone irrespective of race, gender, and national origin. One's particular language is not some overriding determinant. A language is a relative, contingent attribute. There is no essence of a language such as English that is inherently democratic. Why do you not acknowledge the fact that there are many Englishes, which is to say, many dialects of English presently being used and being developed?

OFFICIAL ENGLISH: Now we do get to the heart of our dispute. Your position is a veritable Tower of Babel where any lingo goes. You eschew any standards of excellence in your all-out relativism, as if any kind of English is acceptable. There is such a thing as standard, formal English, which, to the degree it is mastered, there will be success, be it the success of the entrepreneur or the poet. Leading English language authorities such as Edwin Newman, William Safire, John Ciardi, and S. I. Hayakawa believe we have a language crisis in the United States today. The misuse and abuse of the English language, the failure of the public schools to teach good grammar, and the consequent serious decline in high levels of literacy are the problem. While our less sophisticated economy in the past may have given many opportunities to the less literate, no longer is this so. Expertise and mastery are more in demand as the complications of a sophisticated economy materialize. Abandoning standards in favor of accommodating street language dialects is a criminal (because irresponsible) dumbing-down of public education. Black English, for example, may be fascinating to explore, to use, and to research, but only an educated linguistic elite can market this diversionary form of language play. The promotion of Black English is the relegation of persons to a linguistic socioeconomic ghetto of underachievement that is comparable to what racism and discrimination did to African-Americans.

It is not assumed that English and democracy are inherently united to the exclusion of all other languages. We offer no language determinism; the English language did not make democracy, although democracy and individual rights historically have been an original development among English-speaking people. English culture has been less susceptible to on-going authoritarianism. In one sense the English tradition of individual rights going back to the Magna Carta of 1215 has made it more likely for peace to occur among different religious and ethnic groups. The reason for this is concentration on individual rights rather than group rights. Multiculturalists such as you who push language rights, in effect favor group rights on the basis of language and ethnicity. Consequently, we have a society divided into groups. Yet the prospects for harmony and peace are much more favorable if people submerge their religious and ethnic identities into a private sphere and recognize the significance of individual rights and equality in their public sphere. The public sphere cannot afford differentiating and conflicting religious and ethnic claims that tend to be separatist. Such is the modern, liberal, democratic, Enlightenment tradition that offers the best prospects for the recognition of our common humanity.

English is the *lingua franca, via media*, of the United States, and the failure to attain the highest excellence in standard English will mean not partaking to the fullest in American democracy. Too many multilingual language rights proponents attack American democracy for discrimination and intolerance. They should rather be helping remove language barriers, instead of calling on government and taxpayers' money to support non–English-speaking services. Ethnic groups can maintain their own cultures, languages, and religions without government support. That is the American tradition of the separation of church and state, which extends to the separation of ethnicity and government. We should not become a country that needs interpreters to do everyday business.

Language is a bond and glue that supports civic unity. Right to our north we see in Canada how language rights' battles can threaten political cohesion and stability. From Benjamin Franklin (his concern over German language separatism) to Teddy Roosevelt (we are not a polyglot boarding house) to S.I. Hayakawa (proponent of an English Language Amendment) we have had outspoken leaders supporting the English language as our necessarily dominant language of communication.

LANGUAGE RIGHTS: There is so much intolerance and prejudice in your claim to make English the predominant language in the United States. We have had a whole history of non-English languages being used and maintained while at the same time respecting English as the common language of communication. Your rejection of a multilingual, pluralistic society is antidemocratic and uses the guise of national unity and patriotism to conceal xenophobia and racism. We are, and should be, an open, diversitarian society because this is the type of society that progresses rather than stagnates. There is no reason why other languages cannot be respected and incorporated if the goal is such democratic values as tolerance, equality and diversity, and a multicultural identity.

Because of intermarriage, most Americans are not one ethnic identity, and most Americans are highly conscious of their multicultural roots being the source of their personal identity. Such multiculturalism is the proper basis for integration and national unity, not some coercive homogenization according to one fixed mold. The Balkanization of the United States is much more likely to happen if an intolerant oneness is forced on a diverse, multicultural people.

The problem with relegating a nonmajority language to the private realm is that this makes the language mostly irrelevant, like a hobby. Furthermore, you are dealing with some very gregarious, outgoing cultures (e.g., Latinos). To restrict the Spanish language to private dealings goes contrary to the natural way in which Latino culture expresses itself. What is the threat if people are bilingual? Would it hurt Anglos to know a little Spanish? Your claim of achieving one humanity on the basis of modern liberal democratic individualism has historically suffered considerable setbacks. I would not relish trying to defend what the "English way" tried to achieve in India, Northern Ireland, and Canada. Clearly such individualism is too hollow since it detracts from the longing that people have for religious and ethnic substance. Give us spicy meat not flavorless, homogenized milk. The political problem is how various strands and perspectives (religious and ethnic) can be tied together and united without the loss of the cultural variations that constitute the mosaic, the tossed salad, the symphony, etc. Diversitarian factors are alive and strong and cannot be simply squelched by uniformitarian imposition.

OFFICIAL ENGLISH: For the life of me I cannot comprehend how your elitist, intellectual adoration of multicultural diversity can bring together and hold together a people in one democratic nation.

LANGUAGE RIGHTS: For the life of me I fear your appeal to anti-intellectual, nativist populism will divide Americans into those who are true red, white, and blue, and those who are alien because of their simple desire to retain their non-English language, culture, and traditions.

BIBLIOGRAPHY

Adams, Karen and Brink, Daniel T., eds. *Perspectives on Official English*. New York: Gruyter, 1990.

Anderson, Benedict. *Imagined Communities*. London: Verso, 1991.

Baron, Denis. *The English-Only Question: An Official Language for Americans?* New Haven: Yale University Press, 1990.

Castillo, John Roy. "English As An Official Language: Policy Statement and Rationale." *Michigan Civil Rights Commission*. (March 20, 1989).

Citrin, Jack. "Language Politics, and American Identity." *Public Interest*, (Spring 1990): 96-109.

Crawford, J. *Bilingual Education: History, Politics, Theory and Practice*. Trenton: Crane, 1989.

Daniels, Harvey, ed. *NOT Only English*. Urbana: NTCE, 1989.

Dillon, Sam. "Bilingual Education Effort is Flawed, Study Indicates." *New York Times* (October 20, 1994): A20.

Donahue, Thomas. "US English: Its Life and Works." *International Journal of Sociology of Language* 56 (1985): 99-112.

Gonzales, Roseann D., et al. "The English Language Amendment: Examining Myths." *English Journal* (March 1988): 24-30.

Greenbaum, Sidney, ed. *The English Language Today*. Oxford: Pergamon, 1985.

Hakuta, K. and Garcia, E.E. "Bilingualism and Education." *American Psychologist* 44 (1989): 374-379.

Hakuta, Kenji. *The Mirror of Language: The Debate on Bilingualism*. New York: Basic, 1986.

Halton, Mark. "Legislating Assimilation: The English-Only Movement." *Christian Century* (November 29, 1989): 1119-1121.

Hayakawa, S. I. "Make English Official: One Common Language Makes Our Nation Work." *The Executive Educator* 9 (1987): 36.

_____. "Why English Should Be Our Official Language." *Educational Digest* 52 (1987): 36-37.

Hays, Constance. "Immigrant's Town Divided Over Official Language Issues." *New York Times* (November 8, 1989).

Hornberger, Nancy. "Bilingual Education and English Only." *Annals* (March 1990): 12-26.

Imhoff, G. "The Position of U.S. English on Bilingual Education." *Annals* (1990): 48-61.

Judd, Elliot. "The English Language Amendment: A Case Study on Language and Politics." *TESOL Quarterly* 21 (1987): 113-133.

Marshall, David. "The Question of an Official Language." *International Journal of Sociology of Language* 60 (1986): 7-75.

Mujica, Barbara. "No Comprendo." *New York Times* (January 3, 1995): A11.

_____. "We Need a Lingua Franca." *Dallas News*, July 24, 1989.

Padillo, Amado. "The English-Only Movement." *American Psychologist* 46 (February 1991): 1201-29.

Piatt, B. *Only English: Law and Language Policy in the United States*. Albuquerque: University of New Mexico Press, 1990.

Porter, Rosalie Pedalino. "Language Choice for Latino Students." *Public Interest* (February 1991): 48-60.

Stalker, James. "Official English or English Only," *English Journal* (March 1988): 18-23.

Sundberg, Trudy. "The Case Against Bilingualism." *English Journal* (March 1988): 16-17.

Tarver, Heidi. "Language and Politics in the 1980s, The Story of US English." *Politics and Society* (June 1989): 225-245.

ELEVEN

NATIONAL STANDARDS AND

MULTICULTURAL EDUCATION:

THE WAR OVER OUR CHILDREN'S EDUCATION

American public school education has come under a hail of fire ever since the 1983 report *A Nation at Risk*, and the 1986 book of Allan Bloom, *The Closing of the American Mind*. Just about everyone (except for professional bureaucratic defenders of the status quo) finds something wrong with American education. In the 1980s billions of new money was pumped into K–12 education, yet standardized test scores dropped, when they did not remain unchanged. Recent reports of the rise of SAT scores may reflect changes made in the test, rather than real improvement. Employers routinely deplore the products of K–12 education, as they have to spend millions of their own money on basic skill courses for their future employees. And there are deep controversies over the validity of standardized tests.

School choice plans are mainly the conservative response to the problem. Won't competition break the stifling monopoly of the public school system and weed out the worst public schools? The conservative assumption is that our public schools have forsaken standards of excellence and that someone out there knows exactly what these standards are! Liberals counter by saying that the public schools have been burdened with all the social problems of broken families, drug and alcohol abuse, crime, unemployment, and a new and immobile underclass of poor. How can teachers be counselors, therapists, wardens, social workers, and parents as well as being teachers? Liberals believe we have grossly excessive expectations regarding what the public schools can achieve on their own. The liberal assumption is that the schools are a reflection of society, therefore society has to be overhauled first. Better educational performance cannot be had until socioeconomic problems are greatly alleviated.

Certainly the nature of the mission of our public schools is at the center of the debate over American education. But whose and which standards and objectives are we to follow? We do not seem to have any consensus (not the only area of American public life lacking and/or losing consensus) about what the general purpose of education is. Should we advocate national standards when our educational system is fundamentally local and decentralized? Is the situation so bad that we cannot entrust a revival of public school education in neighborhood communities? Is the public school mission today a matter of socialization, i.e., to bring together respectfully and harmoniously a whole diversity of people in order to acknowledge what they have in common and to celebrate their significant differences? What is multicultural education, and does it mesh well with improving academic performance? All these questions rock the very foundations of our public school education.

THE DIALOGUE

NATIONALIST: American public school education is in deep trouble today. Guns, drugs, violence, dismal learning environments, poor standardized test performance compared to our world competitors, neosegregation, waste, demoralization, and in some states scandalous teacher competency results all paint a horrible picture. A lot of change and innovation since the 1960s simply has not succeeded. The public is in a hostile mood, in many cases unwilling to be taxed more for schools, unwilling to sympathize with problems in the inner city, and usually ranking public schools as mediocre at best. It is true that the public tends to see other peoples' schools as much worse than their own, much like their negativity toward Congress as a whole, while rating their own congressmembers more highly. Nevertheless, just about everyone believes that something major needs to be done to turn around our public schools.

In this context, the resort to multicultural education in our schools is a sectarian diversion away from the common, national educational standards we need. The promotion ("cheerleading" contends Arthur Schlesinger) of the particularistic interests of ethnic groups denigrates the effort of common, public schools to espouse those civic values that bring us together as Americans. It is counterproductive to divert our children away from those skills and abilities that make them productive, contributing citizens in our society today. A combination of national *academic* standards and *civic character* education that brings us together as a people is the antidote for our educational troubles.

MULTICULTURALIST: Your depiction of the deplorable state of American public school education fails to take into account sharply contrary evidence that can be found in the annual Bracey Reports (see *Phi Delta Kappan*, October 1994 issue for the latest Bracey report). Bracey finds that media distortion and fabricated data widely publicized by critics of public school education are behind an insupportable parade of negatives regarding public education in the United States. In actuality, SAT scores have risen for three years in a row, graduation rates are up to 83%, and the great majority of American students finish at the top or near the top in mathematics when compared to other countries. The real problem is not the overall quality of public schools, but the difficult, particular socioeconomic environment in which some of our public schools are located. In other words, the serious problems are localized and *not* universal. (You engage in the fallacy of composition when you leap from particular problems to a broad, overall indictment.)

For whatever reason, the public schools in the United States today for the most part do not stand for anything common, and they are not significantly successful, especially when this concerns the poor—be they nonwhite minorities or not. Perhaps the mission of the public schools in the past to Americanize all kinds of immigrant and native peoples, worked fairly well. Such assimilationist aims may have been more easily acceptable because the cultures involved were primarily white European. In the case of the smaller numbers of Asians and Jews, cultural similarities regarding individualism and the work ethic may have made the Americanization transition amenable.

Today Hispanic-Americans and African-Americans do not assimilate and integrate as well when the terms are conformity to the model of WASP America and/or the model Asians. We too are concerned with the stalled socioeconomic situation of poverty-stricken Americans, but we do not believe that the *motivational* factors, especially for minority children, are present in the WASP model. Consequently, we find multiculturalism, which respects the diverse histories of minority ethnic peoples, an attention grabber and powerful motivator, building the kind of self-esteem without which there will be no impetus to master difficult, practical subjects such as mathematics and the natural sciences. In the past, some European immigrant groups had their own schools (public, private, or religious) to provide a hospitable educational stimulus for their children. The Hispanic-American, Native-American, and African-American communities do not have the status and wealth that many immigrant groups previously had to support their own private and/or religious schools.

However, imagine if they were to receive the equalized funding from local and state governments that they deserve, rather than the present, highly discriminatory funding formulas! With such better funding, minorities and low-income people could take over the public schools in their communities and refashion them along multicultural lines. This is already happening to a degree in Chicago and Detroit. Afrocentrism and bilingual education are two such "coups" that minorities are achieving.

We also propose that all public schools become more multicultural, because this is the indispensable basis for some future, new unity (beyond the old WASP conformity), thus encompassing the existing multicultural diversity of Americans. We do not believe a unity can or should be imposed from above by those (usually WASPs) who command institutional positions of power. Unity, democratically inspired, starts from the grass roots and is voluntary, flexible, shifting, and progressive. Unity is not the static, fixed model of Americanism dictated by some cultural elite of bygone days.

We are not surprised about the "failings" of American public schools when standardized tests alone are consulted. And the so-called "decline" in standardized test scores can partly be attributed to the increased number of students taking these tests and the greater number of poor and/or minority students being tested. Yet these standardized tests are biased towards white, middle-class skills and standards. They do not tap the true potential of students in the lower economic class or in different ethnic groups. That is why we strongly support multicultural education: because it provides the right psychological basis for student growth and development and encourages revision (if not abandonment) of these old standardized tests.

A sense of pride about one's ethnicity is not reducible to "fan" identification with an athletic team. Your metaphor of "cheerleading" is just plain insulting. It is easy for those who have all kinds of advantages (such as Arthur Schlesinger, a leader of the liberal establishment in America) to ignore those who lack a powerful enough sense of identity to be motivated to improve their lives. When Schlesinger wrote his landmark study, *The Age of Jackson*, he excluded treatment of African-Americans and Native Americans, despite the well-known fact of Jackson's hatred of "Indians" and Jackson's exclusion of blacks from his expansion of democracy. Nor are students just industrial slugs to be trained to acquire skills to serve the capitalist machine of profit-making. Education involves enrichment and expansion of horizons, which is the core thrust of multicultural education.

NATIONALIST: As Arthur Schlesinger and others claim, education is not a form of social or psychological "feel good" therapy designed to elevate the self-esteem of students. There is no evidence that self-esteem is the cause of poor school performance; stronger correlations exist between low-income, broken family backgrounds and poor academic performance. But neither can the public schools take on the whole task of socioeconomic change. The public schools need to dedicate themselves to a serious (and joyful) atmosphere of learning. Multiculturalism frequently degenerates into a negative attack on America's past, creating hostility, resentment, and feelings of victimization that hardly can be characterized as "motivational" in the best sense of this term.

Students today need a solid education in the basics so that they can be job-ready for multiple possibilities in our rapidly changing economy. This is the American success story, in which immigrants and the poor have been able to pull themselves up into the middle class. What does multiculturalism contribute to these very practical and beneficial aims? Too much emphasis on multiculturalism leads to particularism and divisiveness. Students experience what separates them from each other rather than what advances all of them irrespective of ethnicity, class, and gender. All kinds of heavily politicized factions representing differences (among or within) ethnic groups create conflict rather than a concerted, working consensus to achieve practical, basic results. Much of multiculturalism targets lower income, poor educational achievers, but they need a solid education, not a substitute religion of woe. A perfect example of this is the National Standards of American History (promoted by Professor Gary Nash of UCLA). Not only do these standards cater to all kinds of groups missing the unifying themes of American historical experience, but they also overemphasize the negatives about American history. Is our history really a history of false ideals and habitual oppression? Can we judge the past entirely in light of today's prevailing beliefs, even when today these beliefs are still imperfectly realized? An ideology of revision against the mainstream, debunking high ideals, and dwelling on the underside of American history characterize this National History Standards project. Young people need positive, inspiring, and uplifting examples that show a line of progress that they can identify with and join.

Your statistics of educational improvement fail to point out that more and more students (most notably low income and minority ones) are being left farther and farther behind. There has been a tremendous failure to upgrade educationally the at-risk student population. Statistics show that the differences among students within a country are much greater than between students of different countries. In fact, one study reveals that 32% of reading scores of American 17 year olds are at the 9 year old level, and 42% of science scores and 20% of math scores of 17 year olds are at the 9 year old level. Attaining basic educational achievement at one's age level in our public schools is not very promising.

MULTICULTURALIST: We do not believe that students are any more educationally incapable on average than students thirty or fifty years ago.

The demands on these students today are different. More emphasis is placed on sophisticated, symbolic skills that our parents and grandparents did not need to attain. Our economy has become more demanding of prior knowledge and paper credentials. Low-level entry jobs (blue collar jobs) have declined tremendously. Many people will need to return to school often over their lifetimes even when they have college degrees. We need to find better motivational techniques to stimulate the learning potential of our young people. We do believe our young people have untapped potential, which is thwarted by just citing quantitative data that freezes their abilities. We need to improve their family and neighborhood environment for more out-of-school learning. New methods of instruction, including multicultural approaches and multicultural content, can spark a learning revolution.

The National Standards for American History at long last removes the invisibility of African-Americans, Native Americans, Hispanic-Americans and Asian-Americans regarding their contribution to American society and the terrible injustices inflicted on them. There is nothing mandatory about these National History Standards; they are only guidelines. The key issue between us is whether a "pat," patriotic history that conceals the blemishes and deep wounds will truly motivate young people to be take charge of their lives and perhaps become progressive reformers. The kind of change we think necessary requires an activist response not a passive, memorize-those-great-dates, absorb-like-a-sponge approach to history.

What is multicultural education and why is it such an important factor to turn our schools around? Multiculturalism means at least three things: (1) the *end* of institutional racism and sexism and the *enfranchisement* of women and minorities; (2) the formation of a *new overall pluralistic culture* that includes ethnic cultures hitherto marginalized; (3) an international perspective to compare and contrast cultures (cross-cultural fertilization) and to achieve *mutual understanding* among different cultures. The hostility shown to multicultural education comes from the failure to acknowledge the endemic racism and sexism in our institutions. Normally, the response is that this problem is a thing of the past. Now only everyone's individual effort is needed, because if racism and sexism still exist it is a matter of individual failing. Of course, this position is counterfactual since it is well-documented that prejudice exists as a institutional factor in how minorities and women are treated (e.g., they cannot learn difficult subject matter; they are not creditworthy for bank loans; we cannot have too many of them in our apartment complexes and public places; they may be hireable but not promotable; etc.).

Furthermore, those in positions of power clearly see multiculturalism as a threat to their power positions. To include "others" is most likely to mean accommodating different opinions and approaches, and the loss of already set ways. Nor does there seem to be much interest among the public at large in learning about what is going on in the world. International criticism of the United States is hardly known or taken seriously by Americans, who show little interest in global affairs while they let a white, upper-class power elite carry out foreign policy. While it is true that we have cleaned up a lot of our textbooks, removing the crudest and grossest discriminatory stereotypes of women, Native Americans, blacks, and Latinos, we have done little (beyond tokenism) to emphasize the worth and relevance of those who were made invisible and are marginalized. We need a concerted effort across all the subject matter disciplines to reconstruct women and minority experiences for educational purposes.

NATIONALIST: You fail to identify the worst, most negative demands on young people today, which are the anti-intellectual, dumbing down, and immoral phenomena of popular culture. And multiculturalism is strongest and most visible in popular culture. Are multiculturalism and popular culture coordinate with one another? Most vulnerable to popular culture are low-income minorities, not the upper-income majority and minority. Young people with strong, character-building families and environments may more successfully avoid popular culture's toying with obscenity, drugs, violence, disrespect of authorities, sex, and in general, a loose and drifting attitude to life. In many ways much of popular culture legitimizes the counterproductive and disabling characteristics and conditions of being poor and oppressed. Touting dumbness and enjoying vulgar crudities (e.g., "Beavis and Butthead") hardly exemplifies a path for upward advancement. Popular culture has an immediate motivational impact on Americans of all ages and is more determinative than some sort of conspiracy theory that you hold about those WASP elites in positions of power. Cultural deficits trump racism and sexism as the cause of our educational shortcomings.

Prejudice remains a serious problem in the institutions of our country. Yet it is not so endemic as to require a political or educational transformation of our educational institutions by some power coup. Individuals need to be empowered with the skills to take on the world as we know it. Prejudice dissolves when individuals prove themselves. Multiculturalism feeds into a debilitating sense of injury, victimization, and hostility which in turn does not give impetus for positive action to correct the common world we all live in. Instead we will retire to our own ethnic enclaves and build walls. Such multicultural separatism, an oxymoron, is not the American Way. Many African-Americans, Hispanic-Americans, and Native Americans have already made it in the middle class. Most disadvantaged minorities who have not yet made it want to. Whether they choose to accentuate or not their particular ethnicity is a private matter (for home, church, and neighborhood) not a public political project, which would only cut them off and isolate them. Nobody opposes favorable representations of women and minorities in all school textbooks. The issue is whether such particularism is true to what learning's essential objectives are—to comprehend universal, transcultural truths in the natural and human sciences.

Actually, most of our "cultural troubles" are traceable to a new liberal elite that has arisen to include academics, public interest groups, journalists, mainline religious leaders, intellectuals, and television and movie directors and producers. They (unlike the American people in general) are alienated from traditional middle-class institutions and values, and they persistently call into question the bourgeois work ethic and the American Dream. They promote diversity, multiculturalism, and avant garde, shock culture to establish an "adversary culture" that has more to do with heralding the demise of Western civilization than educationally elevating tastes and sensibilities.

MULTICULTURALISM: It is the white ethnic majority that has built walled-off communities in the suburbs with their own security systems and their absolute refusal to address the problem of the central cities, even though many of these whites work there during the weekdays. The reason you mischaracterize multiculturalism as separatistic is your failure to see the two dimensions of multiculturalism. The first dimension is especially necessary and unrecognized, nay denounced, by you: the need for disadvantaged minorities to recover and consolidate their own heritages and achieve a sense of pride vis-a-vis an oppressive, exclusive majority culture. Only when disadvantaged minorities have succeeded can they then go on to the next dimension of multiculturalism, which is to explore cross-cultural interrelations and to become globally aware and connected. Because you are so confident in your own majority culture (although when you are not you demand that Americans come first and foremost), you can afford to be cosmopolitan. The real issue is whether you can be pluralistic enough to allow disadvantaged minorities "to do their own thing" and then welcome them back into the fold on their terms as well as your own.

Since you mischaracterize multiculturalism as so separatistic, it is time we put a multicultural educational agenda on the table. While multiculturalism may flow well in popular culture (MTV), what multiculturalism promotes through popular culture is change, liberation, toleration for differences, and new lifestyles. The problem of drugs, violence, sex, obscenity, etc. are integrally related to social breakdown and the perversities of consumer capitalism, not to multiculturalism, which seeks to give people an identity of their own so that they can get their lives in order. You peddle your own conspiracy theory (a la William Bennett and George Will) when you claim there is some countercultural liberal elite leading us down the road to civilizational destruction. If there is such a liberal elite, they are only reflective of the extended development of consumer capitalism.

Primarily, multiculturalism sees education in individualized terms such that personal development and growth occur in relation to a person's ethnic roots and gender. Multiculturalists reject the old style of teaching based on monologic lecturing and note-taking. Instead of one-way communication, the new style of education is participatory and experiential. Students do not deal with teachers at a distance and removed from their personal situations. This new style of education is engaging and relevant to the personal needs of young people. Multiculturalism is a positive, uplifting experience and seeks to redress the injustices of the past by advocating the equality of the sexes and ethnic groups.

The equality and justice that is at the heart of multiculturalism is based on recognition of the independent worth of each ethnicity and the need to allow each ethnic culture to propagate on its own terms. Some research is starting to show that there are different learning styles not only from individual to individual and between males and females, but also from one ethnic culture to another. Multiculturalism is in the forefront of enhancing ethnicity precisely because it is an answer to our social breakdown and goes beyond the mass consumerism of popular culture.

We are strongly opposed to people who want to exploit ethnic groups such as Native Americans by claiming to be Native Americans so they can market Native-American goods. Likewise, we staunchly resist those companies (especially beer and tobacco manufacturers) that target black and Hispanic communities. An identity politics is absolutely necessary to overcome what has been too long a historical legacy of exploitation and repression. Education is at the center of what makes for change because education at its best awakens people and creates diverse futures. In a democracy, the people decide on such matters as educational goals, and yes, if there is conflict because of differing values and interests, then we find ways to accommodate or to go our separate ways.

NATIONALIST: We believe that first and foremost the purpose of education is to impart the joy of learning, developing, and advancing in life. Secondly, skills and training are important especially for the less academic-minded students. While we recognize that schools will reflect the society around them, we do not see education advocating social change or promoting ethnic identity. It is the function of political movements, religious groups, neighborhood organizations, parents, and voluntary bodies to be so politicized and personalized. The schools need to accommodate a broad spectrum of people, which is to say that they are to be truly common, public schools. Precisely because of the pluralistic nature of American society, there is a principle of universalism that should be at work here enabling the public schools to bring together and unite a motley crew of Americans.

Contrary to your claims, multiculturalism adopts an attack mode toward the common core of being American—the middle class, Judaic-Christian heritage, and European (diverse) ancestry. Multiculturalism tends to be the celebration of minority, non-Western otherness, even though the great majority of minority people in the United States are either very Westernized (such as African-Americans) or want to be Westernized (e.g., Asians). Roger Scruton calls this multicultural elite phenomenon "oikophobia," a fear and hatred of one's home, which then leads to xenophilia or love of elsewhere. The irony, of course, is that outside the West there is little in the way of democracy, human rights, and liberation from certain long-repressive traditions and unacceptable customs. Only in the West is there acceptance of the space for thoroughgoing social and political self-criticism. A Native-American newspaperman recently found out that his critical, objective stance regarding tribal affairs on his reservation was greeted with severe hostility since he was expected to respect his people and his elders and not "air their dirty linen" in public. On the contrary, this spirit of free criticism is very American and derives from Western traditions of free speech, yet is intolerable in most traditionalistic, non-Western parts of the world.

The teaching mode of multiculturalists is scary and not at all interactional, participational, and open as you claim. Indoctrination, political correctness, and compulsory emotional togetherness characterize the educational techniques of multicultural true believers. For example, you are not to speak of the "New World" since this offends Native Americans who did not see their world as "new." You do not refer to African-Americans in the eighteenth century as "slaves" but as "slave persons," even though this is euphemistic. To not go along is to risk the charge of gross insensitivity, and there are sensitivity training sessions you may be asked or required to attend (with administrative punishments for noncompliance). Afrocentrism as it is often presented holds hard and fast positions (a dogma) that get drummed into the heads of young people (indoctrination). Frequently, the texts chosen by multiculturalism are highly political and propagandistic. Why don't we choose the best multicultural literature, Frederick Douglass and Martin Luther King? The answer is that "the best" is not radical, hostile, and polemical enough.

We actually need to return to the notion of American exceptionalism. We are a diversity of peoples to be sure, but we acknowledge an idea upon which this country of ours was founded, unlike other countries. The idea is liberal constitutional democracy based on individual rights and equality of opportunity. There is an American civil religion unrelated to ethnicity, sectarian religion, and particularistic history, and it is found in the Declaration of Independence and the U.S. Constitution. Yes, we are proud to believe that this truly is a superior way of life and government in the ideal (reality always falls short). Ideals exist to focus our aspirations and to give us goals to achieve. The Idea of America is an experiment in civic education for any person irrespective of ethnicity, gender, class, or religion.

Our notion of culture is high (idealistic), universalistic, aspirational, and inspirational, whereas your notion of culture is low (popular culture), particularistic (ethnic), and negative (anti-West). At times multiculturalism seems countercultural and deconstructionist. We do not choose to return to a state of nature (a precivilizational war of everyone against everyone), and we believe that education should resurrect our glorious patrimony, while openly scourging our sins. Multiculturalism contradicts this high cultural Idea because it doubts the value of Western achievements, finds the American Dream to be a false myth, and injects ethnicity into the equation, which inevitably separates Americans. We already fought a long battle with religious groups wanting to control public school education ("creation science" remains another such fight). We need a thriving public sphere devoted to the civic education of individual rights, the pursuit of happiness, and moral obligation to others, all of which abstracts from and transcends divisive, particularistic beliefs of one group or another.

MULTICULTURALIST: The United States is not a universal, singular nation, nor does the Idea that you trumpet have much bearing on significant numbers of minority ethnic groups. Rather than include struggling minority ethnic groups, you would dictate norms to them. Your use of the term "patrimony" gives away the "paternalistic" nature of your supposedly high cultural enterprise. In the past a policy of "educational genocide" excluded the cultures of African-Americans, Hispanic-Americans, and Native Americans. This was no accident; nor can there be a remedy under the aegis of your American universalism and exceptionalism. The gap that exists today between the white majority middle class and the nonwhite minority ethnics remains great despite civil rights laws, court decisions, and attempts at integration, liberal-WASP style. So much for your American civil religion. A new approach is needed, and one such approach is Afrocentrism.

Basically, Afrocentrism means two things: (1) the origins of humankind are traceable back to African fossil evidence; thus Africa is the cradle for all human evolution; (2) the initial, major achievements in mathematics, science, literature, and religion that Western, Indo-Europeans appropriated as their basis for the development of Western civilization originated in Egypt, an African country. In other words, humankind and Western civilization have a non-Western, African origin. White, European historians have systematically denied African origins and great African civilizations because of either an explicit racism or a latent racism. Until recently there have been no scholars such as Martin Bernal to speak out and correct this falsification of history. Therefore, today we expect that African-American scholars will attune themselves and their African-American audiences to the roots of Afrocentrism in the concrete music, art, literature, religions, and languages of Africa. We can recover the rhythmic beat of our ancestors, which is highly personalistic, whole, and filled with soul (unlike analytical Western science and technology). Afrocentrism (for African-Americans) helps overcome a spiritual alienation caused by the fragmentation of the Western, technological world. And non–African-Americans can benefit from integrating the insights of Afrocentrism.

NATIONALIST: We have a fundamental disagreement regarding the status of ethnic identity in the public political and educational arenas. The nationalist position is that such ethnicity (and religion as well) should not be overly exercised in politics and public education. In a pluralistic, liberal democratic society, we have to be fairly neutral and objective so as not to play favorites. For example, on your multicultural terms we would have to accept equally the American First curriculum of the right-wing Christian Coalition in Florida. They contend that the United States is a Christian nation and deny the importance of multiculturalism. Yet they use the same formal arguments you use to declare special public recognition of their religion (instead of an ethnic group). This is what happens when "rights" language gets expanded to include a right to religious recognition and a right to cultural recognition.

Of course, Americans have rights to religious and cultural freedom, which is to assert that Americans can just about do as they choose religiously and culturally in their private lives. This is as far as the public sector should go if we are to avoid conflict and dangerous government intrusion in private matters. Of course, in public school education acknowledgment of the contributions of different peoples and ethnic groups certainly is in order. But the objective is to highlight what is common to us all. For example, we honor Frederick Douglass not just as a black man from a slave culture, but because he fought against slavery and fought for the elevation of black people on terms equivalent to white people. Douglass was a universalist and therefore is accessible to all who are ready to learn.

Frequently, Canada is touted as a successful multicultural society, since back in 1971 legislation was passed that asserted: "Cultural pluralism is the very essence of Canadian identity and every ethnic group has the right to preserve and develop its own culture and values within a Canadian context." Recently, however, Canadians have begun to question such a "mosaic of cultures," especially over the issue of immigration. Polls report that 40% of Canadians believe there are too many visible minorities, 41% are tired of special treatment of ethnic minorities, and 72% want everyone to adapt to a Canadian value system, not a particular ethnic one. These developments in Canada demonstrate why it is important that our public schools reveal what we are as a common people first, before we go on to our differences and to other non-Western peoples. We have to know who we are before we can know who others are. And we definitely cannot go down the road that only minority, ethnic representatives can speak for and know their own ethnic group. If this were true, then there would be no basis for people connecting with each other and no common humanity. Empathy would be impossible. A universalist understanding of human nature and human rights means that we can cross ethnic, cultural, and religious boundaries.

Your defense of Afrocentrism is ironical. You have lambasted Eurocentrism for its monolithic, oppressive domination and now you exalt another "centrism" which will not be also oppressive? It is intriguing in the multicultural literature how a number of African-Americans have spoken out against multiculturalism when this would mean recognizing all kinds of other groups as equal to African-Americans. What does actually constitute a "disadvantaged minority"? Do poor hill people in Appalachia count? The plight of African-Americans, the civil rights movement, and Black Studies departments in universities would be swamped and lost in a multicultural hullabaloo of anyone-counts, anything-goes diversity. Afrocentrism keeps African-Americans center stage, more than equal, in fact, superior to all other peoples' cultures. May not Afrocentrism be committing the genetic fallacy here, that the place and pride of origin of something is more important than what developed thereafter?

It is true that African-Americans and other ethnic groups have been excluded, discriminated against, and "inferiorized" by scholars in the West and in the United States, since these scholars only wrote about the majority Western or WASP culture. That needs to be corrected and students need to learn about these past biases as well as the important contributions that minority ethnic groups made in United States history. Nevertheless, there is a serious problem of how far we can go in any one book and in any one course to include all those previously excluded. There will have to be "editing criteria" and, of course, it would be perfectly understandable that Eskimo culture be given a small part in Florida textbooks but not in textbooks in Alaska where, let's say, Cuban contributions are minimal. In any case, this kind of healthy multicultural inclusion needs to grasp some shared universal truths so that peoples of all cultures can see how their own particular ethnic culture participates and shares in the achievements of a common humanity. Pax Americana.

MULTICULTURALIST: Your example of the Christian Coalition's

American First curriculum is precisely the danger of a wrong-headed kind of multiculturalism that assumes that any and all groups are equal in reality. While such Christians may feel persecuted, they have not suffered anywhere near the injustices that African-Americans, Native Americans, and women have. They are in the majority and have irrational fears of any pluralism. Critical multiculturalism, which has other objectives than plain "diversity," will have a moral compass and will not dilute the heavy issues of racism and sexism. A person could just love all the riches of differences, but this would be a multiculturalism that accepts the status quo and is not dedicated to change. Differentials in power among groups also need to be understood when we go about devising criteria for ethnic representation in schoolbooks.

You also fail to see how biased and unneutral your idea of a common American culture and way of life is. How can such an American universalism aspire to universal human truth when it has excluded women, blacks, Amerindians, the handicapped, etc.? Your American universalism is a product of White, Anglo-Saxon Protestant history, which has limited relevance to other cultures. It is too intellectual and unrealistic to believe that people will find or see the universal in the particular. Too often those who have claimed to comprehend such a universal (e.g., Nazis and their Aryan race) have used this as a hammer to destroy those who are "other."

Also, such American ideas of justice, rights, and equality have never been fully realized and are now exemplified by a universal consumer market culture that devours individual lives. That is why multiculturalism must ignite radical change and alternatives. To enter the melting pot today would mean to adapt to an excessively individualistic and consumer-driven culture that is anticommunity, anticultural, and antiparticipatory democracy. Today's market democracy of hyperindividualism leaves us with the lonely, alienated, marginalized, and helpless, soulless self.

It is necessary that government (including public schools) respond to the historic legacy of marginalization, inequality, and injustice perpetrated on disadvantaged minority peoples. The cultural survival of such groups is at stake. Government has the resources to make amends; disadvantaged minorities do not. Simply offering "opportunities" without resources is a bad joke. Raising questions about who constitutes a "disadvantaged minority" is no more than a political move to divide and antagonize minorities to ensure majority dominance. There are plenty of statistical, economic studies that reveal what a cost and loss it is to American society to not reverse the misery and despair of significant groups of Americans—African-Americans, Native Americans, Hispanic-Americans, and yes Appalachian-Americans if they are so organized and defined as requiring government intervention.

NATIONALIST: Multiculturalism seems to be so demandingly perfectionist that we can never expect any satisfaction. Won't there always be a gap between cherished ideals and reality? Sure, we should never tire and never give up relatively improving things. But railing in an absolute way against what seems to be the imperfect structure of human existence leads to excessive hostility and divisions because there is no sense of limits and necessary human shortcomings. How can any of us ever feel complete and whole in this precarious lifeworld? Likewise multiculturalists seem to damn nonminorities no matter what. If they resist the exclusivistic demands of multiculturalism, then it is insensitivity to the needs of others, but if they are sympathetic and go along with multiculturalism, then they are guilty of an imperialist expropriation of what is not theirs.

Multiculturalism brings "race" to the forefront in the form of Afrocentrists who believe the United States is a multiracial society and one's race is determinative of who one is. At times Afrocentrism seems to be a corrective of late nineteenth century white European racism. But there is such a threat to historical objectivity from Afrocentrism. For example, most scholars do not hold that the ancient Egyptians were black Africans (and of course they were not white Europeans either). Why does the color of their skin matter so much, except to racists? Is all of humankind to be divided in binary fashion into white and black people? Afrocentrism is more myth-making, psychological propaganda to unite some black people by asserting, "Now we come first. Do not get in our way."

Molefi Kete Asante, perhaps the foremost Afrocentric proponent, characterizes Afrocentrism as the way black people can find their center and be victorious. To transform and energize people is the function of religion according to Asante, and Afrocentrism follows this pattern of life-conversion (similar to being "born again"). African-Americans are invited to relate everything in their life to African customs and ways (and what cannot be related has to be abandoned) despite the fact that Africa (as well as Europe) is a hypostatized construct within which there actually is tremendous, conflicting diversity. Who can dare speak for Africa (or for Europe) as a whole? Pan-Africanism and Afrocentrism seem very intellectually contrived, mostly a matter of willpower against the white enemy. Some of what is touted as Afrocentrism has no particular connection to Africa and sounds European. For example, from Asante there is the appeal to: "the interconnectedness of all things" and the belief that "liberation could only come from a person's active will." Many religions East and West would agree. Certainly, language, dress, art, behavior, games, and names can have African roots, but they are external to the development of some "black consciousness." Is it that Afrocentrism really is centered on the horrors of slavery, diaspora, and intermingling with whites? How independent and "other" then can Afrocentrism be?

MULTICULTURALIST: If the socioeconomic world were ready for cultural inclusion, there would be less interest in Afrocentrism. Afrocentrism is the consequence of the need to posit another center, one's own center, for African-Americans. Other Americans are asked to acknowledge the historical evidence. The seeds of Western civilization are planted in Africa, and only the whitening out of research and scholarship has prevented black Africa from coming alive today. The only "objective" kind of history is that told by ethnic peoples on behalf of their own ethnicity. There is no universal standpoint above history and one's own personal ethnic background from which to write history objectively. The whole point of multiculturalism is that there is not one, overriding, transcendent vantage point, unless it is that of the tyrant colonizer in all of us. In a democracy there are many peoples, many ethnicities, many interests, and many perspectives from which to write and understand history. There have to be many narratives to cover world history adequately. Afrocentrism is one such narrative for African-Americans to uplift their consciousness.

Yes, there are plenty of negatives that have to be dealt with; how else throw off centuries of slavery and repression? The African-American must first strip herself/himself of all foreign attributes to recover her/his lost soul. Obviously, for the sake of the spiritual health of African-American people, Afrocentrism should be taught in public schools predominantly African-American in composition. In the end, once African-Americans bring themselves up to the level of other, nonrepressed cultures, then a real debate and dialogue can occur which will query the multicultural, pluralistic basis for a common society of diverse ethnic people. You are right that a people have to start with who they are first before they can understand others, and that is all Afrocentric African-Americans are asking.

NATIONALIST: We doubt that many African-Americans are more Afrocentric than just American, although we clearly see Afrocentrism as a propagandistic/agitational effort to convince African-Americans otherwise. Not much will be left after you strip African-Americans of their affinities with white Americans. Afrocentrism rests on the flimsiest premises (not even evidence) that since Egypt preceded the Greeks in time and since there was some contact between Egypt and Greece according to the Greek historian Herodotus, then the Greeks received all their philosophy, science, and mathematical achievements from the Egyptians! Similarities between cultures do not constitute automatic borrowing, acquiring, or stealing. The differences between the Egyptians and Greeks far outweigh their similarities.

And what about the melanin theory of Cheikh Anta Diop and Dr. Leonard Jeffries? Do you believe that the black pigmentation called melanin gives blacks superiority in creative intellectual and physical activities? Do you hold that Africans are Sun People—warm, cooperative, and peaceful, while White Europeans are Ice People—cold, competitive, and militaristic? And has not Jeffries made anti-Semitic charges regarding Jews being in control of Hollywood and having the financial control to destroy black people?

In the area of science, the *Portland Baseline Essays* used in some public schools are an example of Afrocentrism making such unsupportable claims as that Egyptians were the first to discover the principles of quantum mechanics, the wave/particle nature of light, the theory of evolution, electrical batteries, and gliders. This is pseudoscience and contributes to scientific illiteracy. There is no opposition to our science curricula becoming culturally relevant by using various cultural role models, using examples of contributions from certain previously unrepresented ethnic groups, etc. But the integrity of natural science is based on a universal, transethnic method—meaning evidence, testing, facts, critical thinking, and replication of results. Simply resorting to highly subjective narrative tales may have great literary value, but fantasy is not scientific reality. Afrocentrism appears to make objective, scientific, historical statements, yet they are more psychological, literary, and religious in actuality.

MULTICULTURALIST: You do not comprehend the depths of despair and nihilism in the black community today. Young black males are literally threatened with extinction because of unemployment, gangs, drugs, and violence. Afrocentrism is an attempt to put meaning, positive energy, and pride back into the lives of young blacks so that they can take on a chaotic, life-threatening, racist world. Sure Afrocentrism may go too far sometimes because emotions are let loose; calm, rational, scientific proceedings would not exhilarate anyone. Black culture is inherently expressive, dynamic, and rhetorical. Many of the remarks of Dr. Leonard Jeffries have to be put in this context, which is not to uphold and justify the content of his remarks, but to understand the style and circumstances. Every people needs heroic memories, and consequently myths arise. Do not white people have their special myths (e.g., Horatio Alger) that are more symbolically than literally true? Why should not African-Americans have their own symbolic and metaphorical stories?

Of course, for African-Americans their stories will be emotionally charged and will have to be antidotes to counter the known legacy of racism. Consequently, you get Jeffries making white people feel the blow of racial inferiority in his melanin theory. If only white people could experience the self-destructiveness of racism now directed at them, perhaps racism would cancel itself out. There is a kind of dialectical yin and yang to Jeffries' explosive rhetoric. And why not take his colorful Sun People and Ice People imagery as primarily rhetorical and insightful? Does it not have some rhetorical, metaphorical truth? Are not African-Americans (and Hispanic-Americans) more gregarious, warm, communal, outgoing, and demonstrative than whites who are on the cold, calculating, stern, into-themselves, and dog-eat-dog, competitive side? Jeffries has hit upon some important cultural variations, and people who are involved with the black–Korean conflict in the inner city stores of New York City know exactly how such cultural variations are the basis for cultural conflict. Asian shopkeepers do not smile, do not try to develop friendly, personal contacts with black neighborhood people, and do not understand the behavioral expressions of black people. Consequently, serious tensions, misperceptions, and misunderstandings arise.

There is a growing group of minority ethnic lawyers turning to "critical race theory" to explain the failure of liberal, civil rights approaches to racism and sexism. The very culture of the American legal system, resting on neutrality, objectivity, colorblindness, rationality, and meritocracy buttresses endemic racism and sexism because this whole mind-set is a closed shop that keeps out the perspectives and experiences of nonwhites and women. Such minority and feminist lawyers want to get closer to the real world with all its imperfections and injustices, and they see traditional law camouflaging, obstructing, and distancing itself from this concrete, real-world reality. The neutrality, objectivity, and rationality of the prevailing legal system is too white to permit "other" voices to be heard and felt. To achieve change, something more psychologically grabbing and riveting is needed. As Thomas Kuhn discerns major paradigm shifts during scientific revolutions, we see critical race theorists and Afrocentrists provoking paradigm changes by impugning the old model of learning.

NATIONALIST: There is no such thing as a black or feminine "voice." In the instances of hearing such voices we actually are hearing the human voice in all its questioning, despair, joy, musing, etc. To put a label on this human voice is to make the same mistake as racists and sexists who want to single out a category of people for benefit or for harm. Yes, I know that reality is not color-blind or sex-blind, but we owe it to our highest ideals and aspirations to make the effort for this to be so. The greatest literature raises us to the level at which the voice of humanity is heard (some would add, before God who knows no such distinctions) rather than becoming the parochial propaganda of a group. In this way, we can rally together many people, cutting across race, ethnicity, gender, and class boundaries. Otherwise, the tactics of Afrocentrists and critical race theorists will only increase marginalization and irrelevance.

The central difference between us is that we want to bring about a shared public culture. There is an American political culture that can be flushed out of the political history of the United States, revealing its highest glories as well as its serious shortcomings and tragedies. Students need to reflect on what we can learn about human nature from such a political history. A moral education (enlisting parents as well as teachers) will help students make the right choices (e.g., regarding shoplifting, cheating, drugs, sex, etc.). Morality is a social, civic matter, not an isolated individual act, and consequently we need to build communities and loyalty to communities so that morality is habituated and reinforced by the examples of others. Our civic culture is hurting and too much of multiculturalism is in hostility to traditional American civic culture, having given up faith in its resourcefulness to include all Americans. In the education process students will learn to evaluate and make choices on the basis of a consideration of different viewpoints. It is not diversity that is the problem but divisiveness. Education should not mean any kind of indoctrination according to whatever some multicultural, ethnic representatives assert.

MULTICULTURALIST: The problem with your nationalist position is that you do not see how you are engaging in a form of indoctrination by holding to the orthodoxy that there is some American political culture with its universal truths about human nature. Multiculturalists are much more open to contrasting, varying viewpoints because we do not privilege *unum* (unity and oneness). As Professor Ronald Takaki implores, we seek a meeting ground, not a battleground, whereby no side claims it is right and has the final truth. You are too eager to arrive at some final end, forsaking the process of how we get anywhere. We look more to the future than to the past for some broad re-vision of America. We too stress an education whereby students learn to evaluate, criticize, and decide, but our focus would be on the injustices and inequities of American society. Then we can take action, rather than wallowing in some majoritarian self-content.

BIBLIOGRAPHY

Aparicio, Frances. "On Multiculturalism and Privilege: A Latina Perspective." *American Quarterly* (December 1994): 575-599.

Appiah, Kwame Anthony. "Beyond Race." *Sceptic* 2 (1994): 104-107.

Bassey, Magnus. "Multicultural Education." *Western Journal of Black Studies* (Winter 1993): 202-208.

Bennett, William J. *Devaluing of America*. New York: Simon and Schuster, 1992.

Berger, Joseph. "New York Joins College Debates About Diversity." *New York Times* (October 26, 1991).

Bernal, Martin. *Black Athena*. New Brunswick: Rutgers University Press, 1987.

Bernstein, Richard. *Dictatorship of Virtue*. New York: Knopf, 1994.

Bloom, Harold. *The Western Canon*. New York: Harcourt Brace, 1994.

Bracey, Gerald. "The Fourth Bracey Report on the Condition of Public Education." *Phi Delta Kappan* (October 1994): 114-127.

Chavis, Linda. "Demystifying Multiculturalism." *National Review* (February 21, 1994): 26-32.

Chira, Susan. "Rescuing Cultures from History's Footnotes." *New York Times* (July 10, 1991): A1, A13.

deMontellano, Bernard Ortiz. "Afrocentric Curriculum." *Creation/Evolution* 29 (1992): 1-8.

DeRienzo, Harold. "Beyond the Melting Pot." *National Civic Review* 9 (Winter 1995): 5-15.

Diggins, John. "Historical Blindness." *New York Times* (November 19, 1994): op-ed page.

D'Souza, Dinesh. *Illiberal Education*. New York: Random House, 1991.
_____. "The New Segregation on Campus." *American Scholar* (Winter 1991): 17-30.

Duignan, Peter. "The Dangers of Multiculturalism." *Vital Speeches* (June 1, 1995): 492-493.

Ehrenreich, Barbara. "Teach Diversity With a Smile." *Time* (April 8, 1991): 84.

Fuchs, Lawrence. "Immigration, Multiculturalism, and American History." *National Forum* (Summer 1994): 42-45.

Fullinwider, Robert. "Ethnocentrism and Education in Judgment." *Philosophy and Public Policy* (Winter/Spring 1994): 6-11.

Gates, Henry Louis. "Multiculturalism and Its Discontents." *Black*

Scholar (Winter 1994): 16-17.

Genovese, Eugene. "Heresy Yes—Sensitivity No." *New Republic* (April 15, 1991): 30-35.

Glazer, Nathan. "Is Assimilation Dead?" *Annals* (12-1993): 122-136.

_____. "School Wars." *Brookings Review* (Fall 1993): 16-19.

Gluck, Carol. "History According to Whom?" *New York Times* (November 19, 1994): op-ed page.

Graff, Gerald. *Beyond the Culture Wars*. New York: Norton, 1992.

Gross, Jane. "A City's Determination to Rewrite History Puts Its Classrooms in Chaos." *New York Times* (September 18, 1991): B7.

Haack, Susan. "Multiculturalism and Objectivity." *Partisan Review* (Summer 1995), 397-405.

Habermas, Jurgen. "Multiculturalism and the Liberal State." *Stanford Law Review* (May 1995): 849-853.

Hacker, Andrew. "Trans-National America." *New York Review of Books* (November 22, 1990): 19-24.

hooks, bell. *Yearning*. Boston: South End Press, 1990.

Honan, William. "Helping Hostile Cultures to Connect." *New York Times* (February 4, 1991): 8.

Jacoby, Russell. "The Myth of Multiculturalism." *New Left Review* (November-December 1994): 121-125.

Kim, Jaemin. "As New Head of Educational Research, Ravitch Brings Her Advocacy of Tough Standards to Reform Efforts." *Chronicle of Higher Education* (September 11, 1991): A31.

Kirp, David. "Textbooks and Tribalism in California." *Public Interest* (Summer 1991): 20-36.

Lasch, Christopher. "Politics and Culture." *Salmagundi* (Fall 1990): 25-36.

Lefkowitz, Mary. "Afrocentrism Poses a Threat to the Rational Tradition." *Chronicle of Higher Education* (May 6, 1992): A52.

_____. "Not Out of Africa." *New Republic* (February 10, 1992) 29-36.

Lind, Michael. "Are We a Nation?" *Dissent* (Summer 1995): 355-362.

Matsen, Richard. "Global Monoculture, Multiculture, and Polyculture." *Social Research* (February 1993): 493-521.

Mills, Claudia. "Multiculturalism and Authenticity." *Philosophy and Public Policy* (Winter/Spring 1994): 1-5.

Monaghan, Peter. "Critical Race Theory Questions Role of Legal Doctrines." *Chronicle of Higher Education* (6-23-1993): A7, A9.

Morgan, Eliot. "Afrocentrism Will Only Harm Black Youths." *Detroit Free Press* (September 28, 1992): ed page.

Morrow, Lance. "The Provocative Professor." *Time* (August 26, 1991): 19-20.

O'Sullivan, John. "America's Identity Crisis." *National Review* (November 21, 1994): 36-43.

Peterson, Lorna. "Multiculturalism: Affirmative or Negative Action." *Library Journal* (July 1995): 30-32.

Patterson, Orlando. "Ecumenical America: Global Culture and American Canons." *Western Policy Journal* (Summer 1994): 103-117.

Ravitch, Diane. *The Great School Wars*. New York: Basic Books, 1974.

Raz, Joseph. "Multiculturalism: A Liberal Perspective." *Dissent* (Winter 1994) 67-89.

Sato, Thelma. "Multiculturalism Is Not Halloween." *The Horn Book* (March-April 1995): 169-174.

Schlesinger, Arthur. *The Disuniting of America*. New York: Norton, 1991.

Schrag, Peter. "The New War Over the Past." *American Prospect* (Winter 1995): 56-57.

Scott, Joan. "Liberal Historians: A Unitary Vision." *Chronicle of Higher Education* (September 11, 1991): B1-B2.

Searle, John. "The Mission of the University." *Academic Questions* (Winter 1993-1994): 81-85.

Shanker, Albert. "The History Standards." *New Republic* (November 28, 1994): 65.

Singer, Alan. "Reflections on Multiculturalism." *Phi Delta Kappan* (December 1994): 285-288.

Sleeter, Christine and Grant, Carl. "An Analysis of Multicultural Education in the U.S." *Harvard Educational Review* 57 (November 1987): 421-448.

Takaki, Ronald. "Multiculturalism: Battleground or Meeting Ground?" *Annals* (November 1993): 109-121.

Vermeule, Emily. "The World Upside Down." *New York Review of Books* (March 26, 1992): 40-43.

West, Cornell. "Nihilism in Black America." *Dissent* (Spring 1991): 221-226.

Will, George. "Rewriting the Past." *Detroit News* (July 14, 1991): B3.

Wieseltier, Leon. "Against Identity." *New Republic* (November 28, 1994): 24-30.

EPILOGUE

With so much disturbance in our body politic over race, class, ethnicity, and gender, can we discern any common threads that would enable us to reunite the fabric of America? Our country's motto is *e pluribus unum* or from our plurality, some unity. Yet there may not be the trust, the agreement to go through the process, and the commitment to some common ends that allow for working through our disagreements. Each of these three preconditions needs serious attention and elaboration. We just cannot assume that the laissez-faire approach (let everything be and things will work out) and the guarantee of everyone's liberty and rights can lead us to a favorable outcome.

The recommendation that was made in the Prologue still stands: We need to find and move toward the middle ground (positions II and III in the multicultural schema) and avoid the extremes of forced assimilation and divisive separatism (respectively, positions I and IV). To put multiculturalism in perspective the following, concluding dialogue (of necessity not an overview monologue) draws into discussion the two middle-ground positions from the multicultural schema that has provided a framework for multiculturalism from the beginning of this book: position II (unity over diversity) and position III (diversity over unity). The sides are now called the Unitarian (fearful) and the Diversitarian (hopeful), respectively representing position II and position III. The Unitarian has a moderate concern for the maintenance and development of our nation's civic culture (see Lind, Schlesinger, Ravitch, Fuchs, Wieseltier, and O'Sullivan). The fear is that cultural politics, which by its very nature defies the private/public distinction, leads to unresolvable conflicts and divisiveness. On the other hand, the Diversitarian gives priority to the rights of groups to preserve and advance their own ethnic culture (see Takaki, Kymlicka, Blum, Gates, Asante, and Graff). The hope is that our nation will be more free and prosperous when it accommodates its diversity of cultures, especially since minority, disadvantaged cultures are at risk, given the demands of the majority culture.

The mood of our country circa late 1995 and early 1996 is one of growing hostility to multiculturalism. For example, Republicans are leading the charge against (and Democrats are backing off from) affirmative action, immigration, English as our official language, bilingualism, speech codes, feminism, out-of-the-mainstream lifestyles, etc. Sadly, this political combat is pushing us toward the extremes of a kind of coercive assimilation, which then foments separatism as a consequence. These two extremes have a lot in common with each other since they both have a strong sense of "mine" versus "thine." Can a dialogue bring us back to the middle ground where we have a common allegiance to what is "ours" while simultaneously being respectful of our differences? While most readers are going to choose one side or the other, nevertheless it is possible that the best practicable politics we can afford is an abiding tension between unity and diversity, each keeping the other honest, and one or the other taking the day relative to the exigencies of our all-too-human circumstances. If so, then dialoguing is the thing to keep on doing.

DIALOGUE

UNITARIAN: Unity is the aspiration and prize because what brings people together enables these same people to celebrate the achievements of their life, to plan how to overcome the shortcomings and injustices of their lives, and, in general, to experience a feeling of togetherness and oneness. We are fundamentally social beings who thrive among and with others. It is not too much to say that the greatest joys of our lives occur with others, not alone in isolation. The ties that bind should be our foremost concern today because too many developments and forces (e.g., technology, suburban living patterns, the consumer market, popular culture and entertainment) fragment us. With so much in our society pulling us apart, we need to reinvigorate the political culture that constitutes our identity as the "American people."

It would be a disaster to promote multiculturalism if that meant encouraging Americans to pursue their own separate and divisive ethnic and sexual identities. We respect plurality and diversity (of course, it is a reality), but the full development of diversity should occur in the private sphere (family, church, neighborhood) not in the public sphere (politics, government, laws). In the private sphere we can get ourselves together, figure out what drives us, satisfy basic needs and urges that are personal, and then enter the public sphere in a healthy, outgoing frame of mind and mode of behavior.

There are these two dimensions of our being, elaborated upon by Henri Bergson in his *Two Sources of Morality and Religion*. Bergson refers to these two dimensions as the closed society (private sphere) and the open society (public sphere). (Bergson made these distinctions decades before Sir Karl Popper's different, libertarian understanding of open and closed societies.) For Bergson, the closed society is the *necessary* condition for human flourishing, since it covers the necessities in life provided by the home—security and safety, nurturance, belonging, and parochial loyalties and identity. One's particular religion, culture, language, and ethnicity define a person's place. Frequently, these matters are not chosen. This is a closed society because outsiders are clearly identified and excluded. Such private security builds up a person's strength, pride, and confidence. However, if this were the only society of one's existence, there would not be the liberality and generosity that comes from open, expansive, transcending experiences. The closed society is too immanent, defensive, narrow, rooted, and turned inward upon itself.

The open society breaks through conventional boundaries and limits (that is why Socrates' questions got him into so much trouble). The open society supports cosmopolitans attracted to humanity as well as those Christians who hearken to St. Paul's pronouncement that "neither Jew nor Greek, bond nor free, male nor female, for you all are one in Christ Jesus." Whereas the closed society pulls us together, the open society draws us out. The unity of the closed society is particularistic, circumscribed, and separatist. The unity of the open society, the sufficient condition for human flourishing, requires sacrificing our self-interests (thus the demarcation of the private from the public) and fashioning the connections among people that expand our horizons. The unity of the open society is based on a certain educational adventure.

Still, there are limits to any open society or public sphere. We debate over the degree of these limitations. Respect for the public sphere of responsibility may lead to restrictions on immigration because too much immigration overburdens our society's and government's tasks. We do not deny the value of the private interests and rights of countless people in the world to receive adequate necessities (food, shelter, clothing, housing, etc.) and to have the right to freedom of movement, yet there just are limits to what one public sphere can bear. Likewise with affirmative action. While there is a great need to correct for historical injustices against minorities and women, if the public sphere alone takes on this burden by way of affirmative action, will this approach succeed? Do not minorities and women have to develop their own private resources to become competitive in the public sphere? Are there governmental/ legalistic substitutes for the family, neighborhood, and church/ synagogue/mosque in the upbringing process?

DIVERSITARIAN: We do not believe in privileging the public over the private as you do, since this relegates the private sphere (where minorities and women have been sequestered and barely allowed to develop) to meaninglessness. We oppose all hierarchies and superior/subordinate relationships. Our goal is rough equality between the private and public such that each informs the other. Where there has been a history of unjust oppression in the public sphere (e.g., sexism, racism, socioeconomic deprivation, disrespect for disabled persons, cultural imperialism, etc.), then to achieve a relative egalitarian balance we have to concentrate on the private sphere where many of our personal resources are located, albeit still in need of resurgence. Consequently, we favor the breakdown of the wall between the public sphere and the private sphere that you have so assiduously enacted. The public sphere of long-standing domination and oppression has a compensatory obligation to provide for the revived reconstruction of individuals and groups. That is why we favor the liberal public policies of affirmative action, open immigration, political redistricting to benefit minorities, disability rights, and multiculturalism in our textbooks. On the protective side, we favor hate/abuse speech laws, bans on offensive logos and symbols, no restrictive official language laws, and the prohibiting of standardized tests that invite fallacious, racist conclusions.

Our conception of the open society is the free development of all groups and orientations in an immanent (not transcendent) setting. Transcendence historically has meant the struggle to become superior and dominant (to become the "Lord of the Ring") in order to impose someone's will on all those who have not reached such self-proclaimed, transcendent heights. Immanence means tolerance and respect for differences, giving others the space to pursue their dreams. We believe that there will be various comings together and collaborations, when groups and communities find common points of intersection as they develop. There is no greater sense of solidarity than when groups of people unite on the basis of ethnicity, gender, disability, socioeconomic class interests, etc. These groups are not closed societies, because their unity is voluntary and the end product of a process of freely coming together. The unity proposed by unitarians is no real open society because it is a unity known and determined in advance and therefore acts as a Procrustean bed discriminating against the free and pluralistic development of our various communities.

A far more important "duality" has been the immediate experience of Black Americans, Native Americans, and feminists. Instead of the one-ness that you imagine and propose through some public American political culture that unites us all, these three groupings of Americans have experienced a severe form of alienation and invisibility first delineated so well by W.E.B. DuBois. You are supposed to be an American with all the rights, freedoms, and responsibilities common to all Americans, yet you are penalized and rejected for being black, indigenous, and female. That part of you is denied or suppressed, and thus made invisible, if not ridiculed, for any public presentation of these attributes.

UNITARIAN: The diversitarian is actually engaging in an intellectually-contrived type of "cult of ethnicity" (see Schlesinger). The average person of any ethnic group does not on his or her own originate and develop a particularistic ethnic consciousness. Most Americans simply consider themselves to be Americans or individuals. This is the success of Enlightenment liberalism, which secularized the public sphere and in the name of reason removed the conflict and strife (sometimes violent, hate-filled, and murderous) over ethnicity, race, sex, and religion. We are all individuals with certain endowed rights as individuals leading us to consent to a government to safeguard these individual rights. Along comes a rabble-rousing, ethnic cheerleading diversitarian who wants to inflame ethnic people and women in order to rally them to some antiestablishment cause. Do we really want to see a breaking up of the United States comparable to what is happening in Canada as Quebec leads the way to separation?

Perhaps we have come to take for granted what holds us together and what achievements we have had that correct for our past injustices. New Deal liberalism was one such unitarian success because it addressed socioeconomic matters that unite people across racial, ethnic, and gender boundaries. The great majority of Americans once were united behind corrective legislation that gave us unemployment compensation, Social Security, antitrust regulations, the GI bill, government work projects, etc. The New Deal of FDR was followed by the Great Society of LBJ to develop further our government's responsibilities in the area of poverty, health, and education. We should not take for granted the importance of government incentives (e.g., the home mortgage interest deduction on the federal income tax and college education loans). These liberal programs expanded the middle class by providing the means for more Americans to lift themselves up. The middle class shares much in common and is a very important precondition for unity. The worst threat to unity is fomenting the conflict (contempt of the poor and envy of the rich) between those who have and those who do not have.

Nevertheless, today the middle class seems to be shrinking, and we have a cycle of hard-core poverty passed on from one generation to the next. It is more common for some Americans to attack the "liberal welfare state" and demand its dismantling, even though most entitlement spending (e.g., Social Security and Medicare) benefits those who are middle class and above. Our politics has become discredited (see E. J. Dionne's *Why Americans Hate Politics*); more and more Americans are looking for some "third force" other than the Republican and Democratic parties. No one seems to have any positive and constructive set of policies to redress our political malaise. The door, therefore, is wide open for people to hunker down into their own particularistic groups because there is no inspiration and invigoration from a broad-based politics. We express our individual rights in ways that generate more conflict among each other (e.g., litigation, divorce or family breakdown, obscene speech and publication), whereas there once was a time when we heralded our individual rights to express what is great and good about our country. Energy and intellect will have to coincide to plumb the depths of the American psyche to revivify the unifying strains in our political culture.

DIVERSITARIAN: Entitlements and rights are not enough; they do not satisfy the deeper longings for substantive identity that so many Americans yearn for (see bell hooks' *Yearning*). Nor is there any fulfillment to be found in middle-class suburbs. The unitarians are dead wrong that most Americans just think of themselves as Americans and individuals, and therefore the resort to ethnicity must be some kind of cult phenomenon. Millions of Americans took seriously the television series "Roots," and public libraries all over the country serve the tremendous interest in and fascination with family genealogy. School children frequently construct their family tree as a class project. Everything from television advertisements to classic stories such as Robin Hood and Peter Pan have been revised in recent films to represent a multicultural perspective. As Nathan Glazer and Daniel Moynihan observed and understood, since the 1960s we have moved beyond the melting pot, and as Michael Novak contends we have unmeltable ethnics. Are not there many more ethnic parades and celebrations, ethnic theme merchandise, and ethnic foods all touted for the sake of cross-cultural experiences? Should we really fear ("ethnophobism") that this explosion of multicultural diversity is disuniting America instead of enriching America?

More and more Americans are identifying themselves as hyphenated Americans. The U.S. Census in 1980 and 1990 demonstrates that when Americans were asked to define their own ancestry, only 38 million or 17% classified themselves simply "American" (in 1980) and only 12.5 million or 5% did the same in 1990. In 1980, 49.6 million Americans classified themselves as English, while in 1990, 32.6 million so classified themselves. Since 1960 the government count of Native Americans has tripled, and this gain is not due to higher birth rates or lower death rates.

The increasing pride many Americans have in their own self-identification is likewise the case with Native Americans. No longer do "Indians" believe it is necessary to try to pass as "whites."

Furthermore, in 1980 one in five Americans claimed African, Asian, Hispanic, or American Indian ancestry. In 1990, the proportion became one in four. This change in ethnic makeup from 1980 to 1990 is the greatest U.S. increase in ethnic identification in the twentieth century, nearly twice as fast as in the 1970s. Demographically, only 14% of Americans can claim to be Anglo-Saxon, while the African-American heritage represents 12% and Hispanic-Americans 11% of the population. Some demographers project a minority majority population by the year 2050, given prevailing fertility rates and immigration from non-European countries.

A number of recent studies also show an increasingly positive acceptance of ethnicity. A National Opinion Research Center Survey in 1989 revealed increasing levels of tolerance for non-European ethnic groups, compared to surveys done in 1964. Another study conducted by Professor Alejandro Portes of Johns Hopkins University was based on 5,000 eighth and ninth graders in Miami and San Diego who are children of recent immigrants. Most of these children prefer English to their native language, and most believe strongly in upward social mobility by way of education. Yet while these values in the past were characterized by acquiescence to Americanization, assimilation, and the melting pot, for these children assimilation and being white is rejected. Some see the American mainstream as antagonistic; most preferred panethnic terms to characterize their own identity. Most children, especially those in California, preferred to be called Mexican-American or Mexican, rather than just American. Since these young people seem to have the values to be productive members of American society, why would we question their concern for "recognition" of their own ethnic identity?

Another study, published in 1990 by Wallace E. Lambert and Donald M. Taylor, *Coping with Cultural and Racial Diversity in Urban America*, dealt with people in Pontiac and Hamtramck, Michigan, the latter a minicity within the inner city of Detroit. The four largest ethnic groups in Hamtramck are Polish, Arab, Albanian, and African-American. In Pontiac, Puerto Ricans and Mexican-Americans, African-Americans, working-class white Americans, and middle-class white Americans were interviewed. This Lambert and Taylor study dovetails with the study of Portes: both find that it is quite possible to be an American without being

Americanized to the degree that one loses one's ethnic, cultural, and linguistic differentiations.

All the ethnic groups studied by Lambert and Taylor, including middle-class whites, favored multiculturalism. Working-class whites in the study were overall neutral. (Schlesinger's attitude would apparently play well among low-income nativists.) Perhaps immigrant groups that now have moved into the suburban middle class and more rural people (neither are included in the study) are the major upholders of assimilation today. The rise of militia groups and survivalists would be extreme examples of desperation assimilationism. The Lambert and Taylor study carefully reveals that for many Americans there no longer is the compulsory choice between their particular ethnic culture and assimilation. In fact, many Americans now believe they are co-shapers of their biculturality, i.e., a person can add on an ethnic identity to being an American. Ethnicity is an option and an increasingly favorable one at that. This version of multiculturalism would be soft and not separatist.

Where different ethnic groups disagreed was whether ethnicity (culture and language) should be carried from the home, church, and neighborhood into the public schools. Mexicans and Puerto Ricans, Arabs and Albanians, and Polish (third generation) were more disposed to going public with their ethnic heritages and languages. Middle-class whites found this unacceptable. So there is a boundary problem here between the ethnic haves and have-nots regarding where to draw the line. The same ethnic groups favorable to multiculturalism believed that this extension of ethnicity into the public schools was the best basis for interethnic relations. To deny ethnic groups the opportunity to maintain their own cultural identity would, it was believed, create hostility and rob these groups of their personal identities.

The Polish-Americans, being more socialized as third-generation Americans, expressed no "ethnic chauvinism," as if their own group had a monopoly of rightness. Mexicans, Puerto Ricans, Arabs, and Albanians were less tolerant of other ethnic groups. A sense of place, security, and self-confidence among Polish-Americans may be the decisive difference between them and other ethnic groups, who tend to see themselves as standing apart from all other ethnic groups. Yet, at the same time these ethnic groups affirmed their belief in being American in order to succeed in an American world, especially concerning their children's education.

The only group that responded to multiculturalism in a negative fashion is the white, lower income, working-class group. According to

Lambert and Taylor, they are a "suspicious, unfriendly, and potentially threatened enemy of cultural and racial diversity." As for black Americans surveyed in Hamtramck and Pontiac, they compare well to Polish-Americans and middle-class whites in favoring multiculturalism over assimilation. But they are closer to Arabs, Albanians, Mexicans and Puerto Ricans in favoring courses on ethnic cultures in the public schools.

We need a social movement (similar to the way the labor union movement once operated) to rally the rainbow ethnic spectrum to work in common to provide better life opportunities for all. Such a movement cannot afford to ignore ethnicity, class, and gender. Once there is a greater sense of place and security for the more alienated ethnic groups, heated conflict among ethnic groups will diminish. Multiculturalism offers the recognition and dignity that brings such acceptance and respect.

UNITARIAN: Americans indeed are groping for something substantive to give them meaning and identity in a world fragmented by the pursuit of individual self-interests and pleasures. However, we do not think Americans will find what they are seeking in particularistic ethnic and religious communities. The recent research done by Richard Alba and Mary Waters concludes that ethnic identity is tenuous and an option, not a hardened, fierce identity. An ersatz appeal that does have all the pretenses of uniting Americans (especially younger Americans) is popular, mass media culture. There is considerable ethnic posturing and crossing over in popular culture. But there is nothing long-lasting and serious there. Popular culture has all the characteristics of shock appeal, flirtation with the offbeat, and iconoclastic diversion to fill in the hole that exists in our leisure time.

We need to investigate and analyze within American political culture the civic or public philosophy that has united Americans in the past and can reunite us again today. Before doing so, we can learn from Plato's attempt to found a city, a *kalliopolis*, in his dialogue, *The Republic*. There has to be some basis for people to come together and stay together. Plato chooses to tell a myth or "noble lie." A "noble lie" is only a lie in words, not a lie in the soul, which would be vicious and self-destructive. A lie in words remains true to the soul's telos. Thus eventuates Plato's "Myth of the Earthborn," a noble lie in pagan religious language. We are all equally brothers and sisters of the earth except that as we exercise the potentialities of our soul, differences among us appear. In the best educational environment, *politeia*, individual souls truly reveal themselves, and differences in our various natures are discerned. Some of us are gold, others silver, and the rest bronze. The point of this anthropological myth is to portray what justice means: equals for equals and unequals for unequals. Persons within a just polity will understand why they are both equal and unequal to each other. This myth both unites and differentiates according to peoples' natures as revealed by exercising their potential and discovering whatever their educational achievements are. Nature means potentiality, not a hard, fixed substance. Remember, stories about metals are not to be taken literally because in words alone this myth is a lie. This "noble lie" is neither exculpatory nor compensatory, assuming (and this is the big crux) that a just polity can be so constituted.

The Myth of the Earthborn unites people in a common humanity since we all descend from a common source, the Earth Mother. Within our unity or wholeness are differences or partialities, but our differences serve to variegate and glorify our wholeness insofar as everyone receives his or her just due. The resort to such a myth may appear (or stimulate the) utopian. However, utopianism is the modern, fallacious literalization and concretization of the mythical (which by definition is supposed to remain nonliteral and nonconcrete). What, then, is the point of "the mythical" if it is not but another manipulative construction project? Myth represents human aspiration, responsive norms, and profound transrational experiences (the open society). All premodern myths characterize cultural variations while at the same time pointing to transcultural, common truths. Certainly myths, as opposed to abstract principles, relate to the everyday lives of a people (the closed society) and offer nourishment. We are no longer entirely within a mythopoeic society, so we know that not all myths are equal. In the case of Plato's myths there is a mixture of Greek traditional sources and philosophic teaching. Myth is a synoptic effort to comprehend the whole, psychologically drawing individuals, in spite of their self-interestedness, toward an understanding of how we all participate in a common wholeness. Myth bespeaks a kind of patience with the imperfections of particularistic reality that we do not find in the will-to-power urges of constructive and deconstructive modernists.

DIVERSITARIAN: The unitarian logically has to believe that there is some vantage point, objective and transcendent, outside the historical flow of human affairs, that offers a place to reconcile, overcome, and pass judgment on the diversity of affiliations and interests that people have.

Such a unity and conformity would be stifling of natural human diversity, and therefore would have to be a forced imposition on people. We logically believe that all identities are constructions, and that there is no more than this. We support the free play of such constructions with very few limits beyond respect for others, an egalitarian attitude, and no violence. On our grounds of constructing reality, the unitarian cannot avoid supporting some individual or group perspective. It is simply falsification to deny such relativity and particularity. What is the big deal? Why cannot there be many truths rather than just one big grand truth? Consequently, any construction of an overall American civic or public philosophy is bound to be skewed and biased, favoring those who have the greater power, in our case WASPs.

Plato's Myth of the Earthborn is very manipulative because its objective is to find a basis for justifying the inequality of many who will never become rulers. A contrived unity which fixes people in certain classes (metals) enables rulers to get compliance in terms of the so-called "justice" of this regime. Contrariwise, we have an entirely different sense of justice not based on the fictions of some oppressive "human nature." There is only the human condition, which means that fortune rather than independent talent predominately determines who we are. Even our inborn nature, or natural endowments, are a matter of fortune. All of this encourages us to want to lift up the disadvantaged and to equalize life's fortunes or conditions. Plato's authoritarian pyramid needs to be countered with a pluralism of interlocking circles of people. Everyone finds his/her nourishment in one or more circles. It is not clear at all how these particular interests and pursuits can ever be transcended. If everyone would just leave everyone else in peace, why then would there be a need for some overarching community and rule?

UNITARIAN: We have irreconcilable understandings of human beings. Your aggregations of people never attain an overriding community. The constant pursuit of particular interests invites conflict, not reconciliation. It is difficult on your terms to see how a people will form any national community to achieve greatness.

DIVERSITARIAN: Too much "greatness" in history has always been at the expense of others. We are better off finding guarantees and immunities for our individual and group identities.

UNITARIAN: The only way to limit such injustice and exploitation of others is to find common beliefs and commitments. A distinction has to be made between "assimilation," which you rightly fear to be coercive and the loss of cultural identity as opposed to "integration," which is respectful of diversity while bringing people together for the sake of unity.

The critique of American liberal individualism now being developed within the communitarian movement (see Amitai Etzioni's journal, *Responsive Community*) may provide the best basis for an American self-critique and an American reconstruction of unity. The unity achieved by Americans in the past no longer serves us adequately, and quite possibly we have forsaken many of the inner resources upholding that unity. However, we certainly find no succor in some radical, revolutionary wiping of the slate (our traditions) clean. Not only has the dominant WASP culture failed to integrate at least three minority ethnic groups (African-Americans, Hispanic-Americans, and Native Americans), but also the philosophy of liberal individualism fails to nourish the souls of many Americans irrespective of their ethnicity. Integration by definition requires a sense of community beyond the economically acquisitive individual and the persistent demands of individual and group rights (or are they interests?).

Examples of individualism today that stand in the way of integrating ethnic minorities are found in the following statements: "I made it without any government handouts!" "I can take care of myself, why can't you?" "There are enough opportunities for anyone to get ahead." "You get yours; I have mine." "Everyone has rights and freedoms. What more do they want, privileges and preferences?" "I am not prejudiced; prejudice and racism are a thing of the past." The usual counters to these statements are charges of "institutional racism," the formation of ethnic group politics, and the passage of massive governmental social programs as solutions. In addition, ever-increasing government entitlements will supposedly pacify those who find themselves in need.

Public opinion polls reveal the tremendous loss of trust and confidence in our national government institutions. "Ross the Boss" Perot becomes a hero figure, a billionaire populist, even though in interview situations he is unable extemporaneously to answer specific policy questions put to him. Politics used to be our national pastime; now entertainment and mass media popular culture dominate the American psyche. Politicians cravenly go to the talk shows, MTV, and sporting events to chase after the fleeting attention of many Americans.

What would a rejuvenated politics be in-between statism (Big Brother) and individual self-indulgence (Social Darwinism)? Real communities are not groups; they are not the sum of individual interests; and they are not statist or governmental bodies. Of course, there are individuals, groups, and governments corresponding to vibrant communities and characterizing to a degree such communities.

Can we find substantive, mediating associations between isolated, alienated individuals and the decision-making center of governmental power? Communities (not interest groups, which are an inevitable, factional, and ideological by-product of liberal, pluralistic individualism critiqued long ago by Madison) are associations of diverse people dedicated to the kind of substantive purposes and goals that eventuate solidarity, fellowship, and togetherness. There is a logical and natural connection between the advocacy of individual rights and the advocacy of group rights. Groups right are no more than the collective rights of individuals who take seriously the basic right of association. Somehow we have to find a way of getting beyond "rights" as masks for interests (see Mary Ann Glendon's *Rights Talk*).

What is it that promotes the bonds of friendship? It is certainly not customary to have to bring up one's rights among friends. Adversarial clamoring about rights and interests is decidedly antifriendly. Yet we have an adversarial character to our popular culture, legal culture, media culture, and political culture. Liberal, individualistic pluralism, the hallmark of liberty and rights, worthy in and of itself, has no answers for friendship and community unless we point liberty in the direction of community (order) as the contextual basis for liberties and rights. Not just a formal, constitutional framework that tends to be taken for granted by a free people. A vibrant and meaningful community will advance from procedural freedom to substantive freedom. Thus, we have to ask, what is it that constitutes culturally and ethnically a community in the best of terms?

The American community is constituted overall by a distinctive political culture—the habits, traditions, and customs that define our American identity. No easy task is it to pin down and generalize what is fundamentally pluralistic and multifarious (un-neat). Nevertheless, the following prominent characteristics of American political culture can be discerned:

(1) The American Dream and the work ethic: work hard and you will succeed, thereby having all the conveniences and comforts in life that

you so desire.

(2) Change, opportunity, progress, and upward mobility: energetic and businesslike people can make themselves and the world better through the unleashing of their self-interests; an optimistic unlimited potential movement.

(3) Pragmatism and capitalism: the test of anything is material, trial-and-error experimentation as to whether it works or not; risk-taking pioneers determine whether the marks of success, sales and profits, will occur.

(4) Middle-class society of the common person: certain bourgeois virtues of sobriety, duty, frugality, and honesty will dissolve the inegalitarian hostility between the rich and poor so that a middle class (i.e., no class) of relatively prospering equals will eventuate.

(5) Fighting, antiauthoritarian spirit: people are likely to contend that "I have my rights; no one can tell me what to do," bespeaking a nondeferential populism on both the political left and right, rooting for the underdog against some big, established powers.

(6) Adversary culture: we bang heads in our law courts and in the mass media and may the better person or product win out in this competitive battle.

(7) Participation in public-spirited, moral crusades: be it the environment, civil rights, cigarette smoking, drunk driving, we have crusading, join-up movements as a counterpoise to the free-wheeling liberty and individualism of Americans.

(8) Diversity and tolerance: after letting it all hang out, a diversity of individual interests and desires occurs and logically requires tolerance in the laissez-faire free market of gratifications, hence our model of popular culture to the world.

There may be conflicts within this American political culture between traditionalist streams and individualistic/libertarian streams, between different roles for government, and between positive and negative moods about politics. Social reformers may be at a loss to find solidarity in the pursuit of social justice and equality, and they may resort to more and more governmental, legalistic policy mandates, creating quite a division between them and less-government, individualistic (do-it-on-my-own), libertarian (I-do-it-myself) dispositions. At the root of our divided government of Republicans and Democrats in Congress we have this conflict of ideologies about the "more" or "less" role for government and the relative emphasis on liberty and equality.

Yet a functioning political culture frequently has antinomies. (See the excellent account, free of academic presumptions, by Kai Erikson, *The Buffalo Creek Disaster* for a grass-roots study of political culture in a West Virginia community.) In this sense, we can go beyond tolerance of different interests, including different ethnicities, to *respect* otherness and welcome its inclusion to whatever degree and in whatever form we can make compatible. The compatibility is not logical, but practical and therefore flexible.

Remember, our political culture is based on change and adaptation and not on a fixed, rooted ancestry. Thus FDR's statement is on target: "The principle on which this country was founded and by which it has always been governed is that Americanism is a matter of the mind and heart; Americanism is not, and never was, a matter of race and ancestry." We do not want hardened categories of race and ancestry that foreclose what human ingenuity can achieve.

DIVERSITARIAN: You truly have bitten off more than you can chew and digest to achieve some sort of American unity. First of all, your eight attributes of American political culture are fundamentally WASPish. Cultures that are highly individualistic, inward, and work-oriented (e.g., Jewish-American and Asian-American) do quite well in this WASPish milieu. WASP culture is so sober, reserved, frugal (Puritanical), legalistic (contractual), and competitive (adversarial). Asian and Jewish cultures (also black Caribbean peoples who were Anglicized) seem quite adaptive to these cultural characteristics, and judging by most measures of entrepreneurial success they have succeeded in America. On the other hand, African-American, Hispanic-American, and Native-American cultures are similar to each other in being the antithesis of the characteristics of WASP culture. They are communalistic (tribal), slow-paced (the beautiful rhythm of Spanish life and mañana), gregarious and expressive, and cooperative (soul brothers and sisters). A slower pace of life is actually more healthy than the rat-race, career-climbing, ulcer-ridden, stressed-out life of WASPs. Anglo philosophy and religion are so literal, fundamental, and univocal. But African, Hispanic, and Indian cultures are so playful, rhetorical, metaphorical, and polyphonic.

Is not it true that the hotter, looser, Latin and African cultures have a different sense of work and leisure (play) compared to the colder, severer Anglo, Asian, and Jewish cultures? Another difference is the denial of the public/private separation. African-American, Hispanic-

American, Native-American and Arab-American cultures are inclusive cultural/ethnic groups that naturally infuse their private values into their public actions. The fact/value dichotomy is alien to them, and a rigid wall of separation between religion and secular activity would be impossible. Too often, deracinated intellectuals do not understand these ties and pulls of religion and ethnicity.

We need to learn about each other's cultures and ethnicities rather than demanding that one or the other give way. There is a place for all this cultural/ethnic variation without having to decide that one is superior to the other. Today in the United States and in the mind of the unitarian, an Anglo culture does the dictating. The alternative is to realize that we can benefit from the richness of our diversity not just because of the aesthetic beauty of such diversity, but also because we then can have more proportion and balance in our lives. Different ethnic communities and cultures have a lot of positive, concrete contributions to bring to the table. Has not our Yankee, entrepreneurial culture degenerated into a rat race producing ulcers and burnout? Have we Anglo-Americans found the proper balance between work and play? Do not both environments of work and play need to be upgraded? There is a time for individualistic competition and another time for teamwork cooperation. Does family law, political conversation, and public policy issues have to be always so adversarial? Can not we begin to solve some of our problems without the heavy bureaucratic, standardizing hand of government?

A point-by-point critique of your eight attributes of American political culture can be made from a multicultural perspective. First of all, the American Dream would be fine if there were enough decent jobs (jobs with a future for advancement) available to all. So energy and desire do not automatically lead to upward advancement. The American Dream is a fiction because it assumes equal opportunity educationally, but the great inequality of funding for school districts and the nonlearning environment in so many of our inner city schools obliterate this avenue of upward mobility. Secondly, pragmatism, capitalism, and the middle class are so materialistic and spiritually hollow that even most of those who succeed on these terms are unhappy with themselves.

Thirdly, the character of antiauthoritarianism in our adversary culture is fundamentally negative and offers no promising alternative to what is wrong in our civil society. Fourthly, Americans do get caught up in crusades and movements, but they tend to fade and burn out rather quickly. And lastly, while there is greater tolerance of diversity in the

United States today, there is not the respectful recognition of differences. Racism and sexism quickly are revived when matters come to a head (e.g., the O.J. Simpson trial, the role of Hillary Clinton). There is very little that is auspicious concerning our traditional political culture. Primarily, we believe that reversion to and acquiescence in some American political culture is meant to take the wind from our sails in our fight against racism, sexism, and classism.

UNITARIAN: Racism, sexism, and classism are best fought on an individual, case-by-case basis. It is a kind of lunacy to see O.J. Simpson used as the universal image of male wife-abuser as one women's group has done, irrespective of the details of his trial that led to his acquittal. The kind of "justice" that some people seek (both on the right and the left, among nativists and multiculturalists) would unravel all the liberal protections in our criminal justice system (e.g., a defendant's right not to testify, the beyond a reasonable doubt norm to convict, rules for admitting evidence, etc.)

DIVERSITARIAN: But racism, sexism, and classism are systemic, and only systematic (not piecemeal) change can get the justice we have long sought.

UNITARIAN: All institutions are imperfect, and the revolutionary attempt to get justice through total system transformation leads to gross excesses because no one is infallible. What is the point of dialoguing if you already have the total answer? It is by discussion and worked-out compromises that we gradually make amends.

DIVERSITARIAN: Too many of us who are organizing on a multicultural basis are not willing to put up with some acceptance of the status quo, a kind of quietism and passivity. You seem to forget that racism, sexism, and classism are totally unjust and that there can be no compromise here.

UNITARIAN: In principle yes, but in practice it is ofttimes unclear whether racism, sexism, and classism has occurred. For example, there are some, maybe many, racist, sexist, and classist outcomes (e.g., job hirings, student body composition in a university) without any racist, sexist, or classist intentions or plans. Of course, we both agree that changes need to take place to correct racist, sexist, and classist outcomes, but this requires considerable negotiations, and there will be variations—a diversity of responses.

DIVERSITARIAN: We do have in common the belief that there needs to be more coming together in communities (you would say community). Only when people within their diverse communities are strong and viable enough can negotiations leading to greater community occur. We are more aesthetically impressed by the kaleidoscopic array of diverse communities and the richness of such different, particular bodies of people. This is freedom at its most magnificent. On the other hand, unity means for us mass conformity, coercion, loss, and abstraction from the vibrant diversity of concrete, everyday life. Once people (e.g., women and African-Americans) find their personal identity in their own communities, then they will have the strength and backing to interrelate with other communities.

UNITARIAN: Our position is quite different. We see many Americans longing for common ties and bonds. Note the great success of William Bennett's books on common stories and virtues. At a time of breakdown and secession, when our Union was greatly endangered, Abraham Lincoln addressed the soul politic: "We are not enemies, but friends. We must not be enemies. . . . The mystic chords of memory, stretching from every battlefield, and patriotic grave, to every living heart and hearthstone, all over this broad land, again touched, as surely they will be, by the better angels of our nature." Unity offers the experience of wholeness, order, and harmony, and there is great aesthetic delight in oneness. On the other side, diversity leads to fragmentation, conflict, anarchy, and loss. The Judaic-Christian symbolism of one body and many members expresses our belief that there is no meaningful identity or difference without incorporation into one body. We need to explore how all our differences participate in one community by way of citizenship and a common humanity. Too often the differences espoused by minorities and disadvantaged groups are based on negatives not positives. Negatives drive us apart, while positives bring us together.

256   *Epilogue*

BIBLIOGRAPHY

Alba, Richard. *Ethnic Identity*. New Haven: Yale University Press, 1990.

Anderson, Bernard. *Imagined Communities*. London: Verso, 1992.

Asante, Molefi Kete. *Afrocentricity*. Trenton: Africa World Press, 1988.

Beer, Samuel. *To Make a Nation*. Cambridge: Harvard University Press, 1993.

Bernstein, Richard. *Dictatorship of Virtue*. New York: Knopf, 1994.

Blum, Laurence. "Philosophy and the Values of a Multicultural Community." *Teaching Philosophy* 14.2 (June 1991):127-134.

Dionne, E.J. *Why Americans Hate Politics*. New York: Simon and Schuster, 1991.

Elshtain, Jean Bethke. *Democracy on Trial*. New York: Basic, 1995.

Erikson, Kai. *Everything in Its Path*. New York: Simon and Schuster, 1976.

Etzioni, Amitai. *New Communitarian Thinking*. Charlottesville: University of Virginia Press, 1995.

Euyang, Eugene Chen. *Coat of Many Colors*. New York: Norton, 1995.

Fuchs, Lawrence. *American Kaleidoscope*. Hanover: University Press of New England, 1990.

Gates, Henry Louis. *Loose Canons*. New York: Oxford University Press, 1992.

Glendon, Mary Ann. *Rights Talk*. New York: Free Press, 1991.

Graff, Gerald. *Beyond the Culture Wars*. New York: Norton, 1992.

hooks, bell. *Yearning*. Boston: South End Press, 1990.

Kallen, Horace. "Democracy versus the Melting Pot." *Nation* (February 18, 24, 1915): 190-194, 209-212.

Kymlicka, Will. *Multicultural Citizenship*. New York: Oxford University Press, 1995.

Lambert, Wallace and Taylor, Donald. *Coping with Cultural and Racial Diversity in Urban America*. New York: Praeger, 1990.

Lind, Michael. *The New American Nation*. New York: Free Press, 1995.

O'Sullivan, John. " America's Identity Crisis." *National Review* (November 21, 1994): 36-43.

Ravitch, Diane. "Multiculturalism: E Pluribus Plures." In Berman, Paul. *Debating P.C.* New York: Dell, 1992.

Schlesinger, Arthur. *The Disuniting of America*. New York: Norton, 1992.

Takaki, Ronald. *A Different Mirror: A History of Multicultural America.* Boston: Little, Brown, 1993.

Taylor, Charles. *Multiculturalism and the Politics of Recognition.* Princeton: Princeton University Press, 1992.

Waters, Mary. *Ethnic Options.* Berkeley: University of California Press, 1990.

West, Cornell. *Beyond Eurocentrism and Multiculturalism.* Monroe, Maine: Common Courage Press, 1993.

Wiestelier, Leon. "Against Identity." *New Republic* (November 28, 1994): 24-29.

INDEX

MAJOR CONCEPTS IN POLITICS AND POLITICAL THEORY

This series invites book manuscripts and proposals on major concepts in politics and political theory—justice, equality, virtue, rights, citizenship, power, sovereignty, property, liberty, etc.—in prominent traditions, periods, and thinkers.

Send manuscripts or proposals, with author's vitae to:

Garrett Ward Sheldon
General Editor
College Avenue
Clinch Valley College
University Virginia
Wise, VA 24293

DATE DUE

GAYLORD			PRINTED IN U.S.A.